ACTION!

ESTABLISHING YOUR CAREER
IN FILM & TELEVISION
PRODUCTION

by
sandra r. gordon

Action! Establishing Your Career in Film & Television Production
by Sandra R. Gordon

Copyright © 2002 by Sandra R. Gordon
All rights reserved

Book Design by Two of Cups Design Studio, Inc.

Library of Congress Cataloguing-in-Publication Data:

Gordon, Sandra R.
  Action!: Establishing your career in film & television production /
by Sandra R. Gordon.
    p. cm.
  ISBN 1-55783-584-5
  1. Motion pictures—Production and direction—Vocational
guidance—United States. 2. Television—Production and
direction—Vocational guidance—United States. I. Title.
  PN1995.9.P75 G64 2002
  791.43'0232'023—dc21

                              2002008096

British Library Cataloguing-in-Publication Data
    A catalogue record for this book is available from the British Library

APPLAUSE THEATRE & CINEMA BOOKS
151 West 46th Street, 8th Floor
New York, NY 10036
Phone: (212) 575-9265
Fax: (646) 562-5852
Email: info@applausepub.com
Internet: www.applausepub.com

SALES & DISTRIBUTION

North America:
HAL LEONARD CORP.
7777 West Bluemound Road
P. O. Box 13819
Milwaukee, WI 53213
Phone: (414) 774-3630
Fax: (414) 774-3259
Email: halinfo@halleonard.com
Internet: www.halleonard.com

UK:
COMBINED BOOK SERVICES LTD.
Units I/K, Paddock Wood Distribution Centre
Paddock Wood, Tonbridge, Kent TN12 6UU
United Kingdom
Phone: (44) 01892 837171
Fax: (44) 01892 837272

ACKNOWLEDGEMENTS

I can't possibly fit onto one page all of the people who were so vital in shaping my life and getting me to where I am now, but I'll come as close as I can.

thanks:

➤ To Mom and Dad, and Paul, who are always supportive, and who continue to be more proud of my achievements than I am. Thank you for being my local publicists, for teaching me that I can do anything I put my mind to, and for being supportive of my nomadic life and career choice even when you thought I was crazy. I love you. (*And okay, I admit it, I was wrong— Dad, thank you for bringing your camera to the Emmys.*)

➤ To my other family: Allison, Eden, Francesca, James, and Tory, who have stuck with me all of these years through the long hours, intense stress, my moving all over the place (special thanks to the two of you who are always unloading the boxes), and for putting up with me and my undying need to always be doing something and never sitting still. You are all so special to me and I treasure your friendships. To each of you—I love you man!

➤ To Kathy and Doug (my other agent) for being so ultra supportive of this endeavor from the beginning. Your words of encouragement mean more to me than you will ever know.

➤ To Jennifer Gustafson and Melissa Thornley for being constant supporters from the get-go, and for giving my career a new start. Every day you inspire me to be a better person. To you and to everyone at The Whitehouse for being so understanding of this undertaking and supporting my ambition to see it through. And to Mike Berning for not only being supportive, but also for your enthusiasm and honesty. You were a huge help in so many ways.

➤ To Scott Mendel, Jane Jordan Browne, and the group at MPD, Inc. for all of your efforts and for taking a chance on me, and to Rob Sullivan for your introductions and advice. To Mark Glubke, Jenna Bagnini, Michelle Thompson, and everyone at Applause Theatre & Cinema Books, thank you all for working so hard to make this a reality.

➤ To Christine Coates, Karen Lopez, Deb Munies, Georgene Smith, Fred Fouquet, and George Doty IV, who, even though you are far away, have been so encouraging and offering of your support—and who are always there to supply me with a good laugh when I need it.

➤ To Adam Wodon for having patience and generously building www.sandrasite.com.

➤ Most importantly, a very sincere thank you to the people in the television and film industry who took time out of their crazy schedules to help me with the facts. Thank you for sharing your stories with me. This book would not be worthy of reading if it weren't for your wisdom and insight into the business. It has been so great to go through this incredible life's journey with you all (in addition to those mentioned above): Kim & Bart Blaise, Matt Blitz, Tom Bohn, Kevin Boyd, Karen Carter, Amy Cham, Jimmy Chin, Dan & Kim Clancy, T. Coe, Gabrielle Cohen, Hal Eisner, Eric Fersten, Marcie Friedman, Dave Goetz, Karen Goodwin, Eloise Greene, Eddie Guttierez, Allen Hall, Brook Holston, Bob Hudgins, Eric Jewett, Suzy Kellett, Peter Kenan, Peter Kuttner, Teddy Larkowski, Marjorie Leder, Jennifer Lung, Paul Marks, Lisa Masseur, Meridith McGlon, Jeff Melvoin, Moira Michiels, Jill Neibert Garnhart, Hugh O'Brian, Hugh Aodh O'Brien (yes—two different people), Jeremy Oswald, Terry Quinlan, D. Richtor, Ilka Rivard, Hal Sparks, Adrienne Swan, Ken Topolsky, Juan Vela, Dave Weinman, and Rob Yale.

TABLE OF CONTENTS

FOREWORD

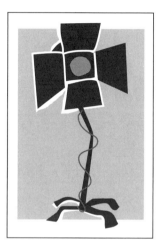

When it came time to check off that box on my college applications—"What is your major of choice?"—I was stumped. Is this what it all comes down to? When I check off this box my destiny will be laid out before me.

Then I did it.

I checked off "communications." I mean, I watch T.V., right? How much fun would it be to make T.V. shows? Once I checked off that box, the seas parted and the sky cleared. I was on my way to the perfect career.

As we enter the new millennium, so many people are checking off that box. But what is next? We check it off but where do we go from there?

For our parents and their parents, jobs were necessary means for earning money. Careers developed from these jobs. Women were not necessarily expected to have a job at all. But for college graduates in this generation, the career comes first, then the job. We need to find a way to create the full picture that will make us happy and fulfilled in addition to paying those bills. Those of us who checked that box for a creative career path know that we need challenge and excitement along with the salary.

Whether it is to be a television producer, a film director, or a camera operator, we have a goal, but how do we accomplish it?

That is what this book is for: to help people find their way. I was like the thousands of college freshmen that chose a creative major, yet I had to fumble through it alone. Now that I've cleared my path, I can lead others through some of the hurdles.

There are many stages to go through, from school through the first year out in the "real world." On top of that, there are all of the creative people and personalities you will encounter along the way. This is a unique field and a unique way of life. It is best to know what you're headed for before you make the move.

I find that most of the recent graduates I speak to are seeking guidance as to how to get started in this business. Many are beginning their search without knowing what is out there to be found. I hope to answer the questions that are out there and to dispel the fear of getting that foot in the door and taking it to the next level.

For some people, working in a television or radio station, or on a feature film, is merely a stepping stone to another career. For others, it is their destiny. You don't really know until you get there. This guide is to give newcomers the ability to find themselves and to help them trudge through a tough industry.

And for you eager readers who are flipping ahead to the middle of the book to get to the part where I tell you how to find a job as a film director, please go back to chapter 1 and read the book straight through. Remember, I've been where you are; I'm only trying to help. The early stuff is just as important as the end goal when you are trying to find your niche.

There are many "how to write a resume" books, but not many books like this one. Structured in a simple, straightforward manner, beginning with college and internships, it continues through choosing a field, where to send the resume, how to keep the job, and how to move up. *Action! Establishing Your Career in Film & Television Production* gives an overview of this process and sheds light on how the people in this industry think, and how you can join them in their thinking. It leaves some of the specifics up to you, the job hunter. This is a creative industry, and most people trying to break in have their own style. As the author, I am not looking to pass on my style, but rather to give you suggestions on how to best apply yours in order to make headway in the production business.

Many readers will be college students, but this book does not intend to discount or turn away others. It is not limited to young people or people with degrees in creative fields. This book is for you, the person who is interested enough in "the biz" to take that first step in reading a little about it, in order to see where you may go from here.

This book will be an easy, yet informative read. My hope is to pass on the knowledge I've gained so that you may do the same after your career has skyrocketed you to the top.

Good luck!

SECTION I:

BEING AHEAD OF

THE GAME

CHAPTER 1

The Biz—An Insider Look

There is a flash, then another, and suddenly the fans in front of the theater explode with excitement. The guests of honor traipse along the red carpet, donning their fashionable sunglasses. They stop and wave at the crowd. To them this is all part of the package, a mere formality. To the screaming fans it is part of their handsome appeal, a brush with fame. Yet to the cameraman it is annoying. "Why can't they just keep it moving? I need to get a shot of the next guy!" The security guard feels the whole ordeal is a nuisance as he looks through the crowd hoping that none of the crazy stalker-types will do anything harmful this time. All this and the show has not even begun.

We see the glamorous people on the E! Channel in luxurious gowns, modeling for the cameras. As spectators we all think we know what it would be like to work in the film and entertainment business. Maybe you have friends or family in the business who will likely tell you otherwise. It is easy to disregard what others tell you when you have made up your mind. However, it is important to have an understanding of the film and television business before you get involved. The next few chapters emphasize the beginning. By this I mean the beginning stages of creating and achieving your career goals. Maybe you are a student, or perhaps an experienced businessperson making a mid-career change. In any event, you are here to accomplish a goal: To find work in film or television production and to turn it into a lasting career. To do this it's best to start with the early stages of the hunt and to move forward together to reach the ultimate goal that you will create.

The Low-Down

Entertainment is a ruthless industry, whether it is behind the scenes or in front of the spotlight. There are so many people vying for one job. The human resources department at Sony Pictures Entertainment receives twenty thousand unsolicited resumes per year.[1] And that is only one of many studios receiving production resumes. For every fifty (entry-level) production assistant resumes that come to a production coordinator of a feature film, only 1–3 people are hired for the position. It is very easy for department heads to weed through the masses of people breaking in to find the type of person they need. You can be that person by staying one step ahead of the game. Know where you're headed. Know your short and long-term goals. We are going to work together to figure out those goals.

Celebrities and entertainment gossip have changed the way we view the world. The United States is the world's hub for providing entertainment in film and television. With the invention of cable and digital television, film and video are more prevalent and have become more glamorous as workplaces in the eyes of the general population. People worldwide look to the media to take their mind off of their problems, to give them new ideas, and to provide role models in their lives. It is no wonder that the same media outlets have become so compelling as career choices. The thought of being able to shape the minds and opinions of the general public gives some people a tremendous sense of power. For others, the idea of being connected in some way to the glitz and glamour of celebrities in Hollywood offers even greater appeal. It is important to have a full understanding of the realities behind these ideas before choosing this career. This is not to say that power and celebrity do not exist or cannot be exciting and fun. However, you need to understand what comes with these notions in order to understand how to obtain them.

Glamour—The #1 Myth

The glamour people associate with stardom isn't really there. That is, unless you're a multi-million-dollar-earning celebrity. I may be wrong, but I don't think there is a tremendous amount of glamour in that scenario either. Glamour is an image we find on television and in magazines. Celebrities indulge our fantasies in return for a paycheck and an opportunity to get ahead in their field. Of course there is money to be made, as there are also luxuries to enjoy. But like everything else in life, glamour comes with its own price to pay.

Dirty Laundry

Having the title of "director" sounds glamorous, doesn't it? John,* the office pro-

---

1 Statistic provided by Sony Pictures Entertainment Human Resources Department, 2001.
* Not actual name

duction assistant on a weekly television series for CBS, thought so too. That is, until he met the director of one week's episode. This director walked in with a duffel bag full of laundry. No, not to use for a prop, this was his dirty laundry. Unusual? Even more so when you consider that this director flew into Chicago from Los Angeles. Yep, he brought his dirty laundry two thousand miles. He was too busy to get to it himself so he brought it to work, plopped it down in front of John, and said he'd pick it up when it was ready. After questioning his co-workers, John learned that this particular director never seemed to have time to do his laundry and always brought it with him from Los Angeles to have the office assistants tend to it. The moral of the story is that this business keeps you so busy that you don't have time to wash your clothes. Or is the moral of the story that you may just find yourself doing an extra load or two in an entry-level position?

Getting Down and Dirty

Film, television, and radio are very rigorous, tiring, and sometimes strenuous work-places. No, not rigorous like a military soldier or a lumberjack, but in their own relentless way. Production people do not wear tuxedos or ball gowns, power suits, or even sports jackets to work on a set. Such clothing would just get very dirty during the 12–15+ hour workday. Production jobs do often require running around, climbing ladders, carrying equipment, and so on, depending upon the position. It is not all red carpets and paparazzi. The images of celebrities shown on award shows or "behind-the-scenes" documentaries may only be the good footage that didn't end up on the cutting room floor, or the tape recycle bin for that matter. Working in production can be a lot of fun and can earn you a nice living; just remember that no job is all fun all of the time.

Steel-toed Boots

By the nature of their existence, steel mills are not clean workplaces. The steel mills that we used on *Rudy* were open to the elements (wind, snow, and rain) and full of dust, dirt, and all sorts of materials I had never seen before. As a location assistant, it was my job to supply the entire cast and crew with hard hats and safety masks so that no one was injured or breathing toxins. You can imagine what our clothes looked like after a day in that environment. Not to mention that the water from the snow leaked into my boots and every hour I was changing into new toe warmers to replace the ones that had frozen to my socks.

Working in production takes people to places and situations in which they had never dreamed they would be. From rooftops to mountaintops, submarines to airplanes, film and television crews live an exciting lifestyle of exploration and variety. Some crew positions provide the opportunity for travel, and some provide unique chances to view a hometown in a new way. There is glamour in some of the opportunities that can be easily taken for granted. One former camera assistant tells of his job in sports broadcasting, which took him to the Olympics, Monday Night Football, and the Indy 500 trials—where he was not a mere spectator in the stands. He had the best seats in the house—on the track as the cars whizzed by.

Video assist operator Kevin Boyd also enjoys his unique experiences. For *We Were Soldiers*, he described how the crew worked in extreme heat with dust, dirt, and snakes everywhere: "Stunt guys running out on fire. . . you don't get that in an office." Carrying heavy equipment up rickety ladders to an attic or climbing a mountain with cables in hand—working in film production is definitely exciting.

Rudy! Rudy! Rudy!

Barricades, cranes, space heaters, you name it and it is encountered by crew people on production sets. It was snowing so heavily that you couldn't see the full stadium, but that didn't stop the crew from heading up the ladder of Notre Dame Stadium to plant Camera 3 on the roof over the announcer's booth. It was University of Notre Dame versus Boston College and the stadium, as always for a Notre Dame game, was sold out. People were crying for tickets on the sidewalk, hoping that there would be a student looking to make an extra buck. But tickets are hard to come by for any Fighting Irish game and these people were out of luck. We should have felt lucky to be there, and I suppose we did. But we also felt cold and wet! Holding on to whatever we could find just to keep from falling off the roof was challenging enough. (The challenge of accomplishing the shoot made this football game much more exciting.) Our outfits were soaked through. My eyelashes were frozen. Thick snow gear, boots, hats, gloves—messy clothes were the key to survival on this one.

Inquiring Minds. . .

Do you read *People*? Are you up-to-date on what Hollywood hunk Gwenyth Paltrow is dating? Do you know how many times Matt Damon has been to the gym this week? Have you ever asked someone for an autograph? If you can answer any of these questions with a "yes," there is something important you need to know before you work in the entertainment industry. Celebrities are people like you and me. They have jobs. They sent a resume in at one point in time and got hired. Hopefully it was from doing their job well that they were successful, and for no other reason. The problem is that Americans (among others) are obsessed with television and film actor familiarity. People in our society feel that we can somehow relate to these fictitious characters we see in our living rooms. They put familiar faces up on pedestals and promote the idea of celebrity and stardom. Get it out of your system and remind yourself that actors are just people. You are not going to get any respect by being star-struck on your first day at work. Besides, if we keep feeding celebrities' egos, they are only going to get more and more stuffy, which just makes everyone's job a little harder. When you work in production, you will need people to be as cooperative as possible. So cancel your subscription to the tabloids and sign up for business trades. Trust me.

Working in entertainment is exactly that. . . it is work, although there positively are perks to take advantage of in this work atmosphere. A non-corporate setting, the adrenaline rush from working feverishly to accomplish a task, the camaraderie of a crew family, and working outdoors and in new territory are some of these perks. All of these advantages can make this industry a thrilling place in which to work. But of course it is not all sunshine and roses every day. Long hours, high stress levels, an extremely fast pace, and many deadlines are traded for the glamour of working in production. By knowing what you're in for there will be no surprises, and it will be easier for you to adjust to your first job in the industry.

CHAPTER 2

The Goal—Paving a Path

to the Future

A part from a select few, most people are not in grammar school when they realize "I want to be a doctor." So when is it that we know what we want to do with our lives? Should it be obvious when we are taking an algebra class just how algebra will come in handy for our first job out of school? Of course not. How is it that people are able to define their dream jobs early enough in life to have the opportunity to work their way to the top?

Planning Ahead

It's hard to imagine your life ten or twenty years from now. It's hard enough to imagine what tomorrow will be like. And quite honestly, who wants to worry that far into the future? But something that most people do not do until it is too late is to put their priorities in order before pursuing a career in film production. It is tough ten years down the road when you've etched out your path only to remember that you wanted to have three kids and a dog before you were forty. It's not to say you can't have these things later, or that your goals won't change. Just have a little talk with yourself about what your true goals are. Write them down and put them away. Keep them in the back of your mind so that you can help yourself through some tough decisions later on down the road.

Questions To Ask Yourself:

• Where do you see yourself five years from now?
• Where do you see yourself twenty-five years from now?
• Will you have a family?
• Will you have a big house or a small house, or will you be living on a boat?
• Will you be famous, or will you be very successful but in a quieter way?
• Are you living in a big city or a rural area?
• What is your immediate goal right now?
• Are you trying to get any job, or do you have a specific job in mind?
• Are you just trying to learn about the field, not necessarily to get a job within it?
• What activities do you like to do? Sports? Hobbies? Do you plan to continue with them later?
• Will you be using these hobbies or sports twenty-five years from now?
• Are you interested in incorporating them into your career down the road?
• What type of income are you earning?
• What type of income do you expect to be earning in the future?

Remember to put these written goals away where you can find them later to update them. These are your goals now—when you have yet to plunge headfirst into your career. You will find that some of these goals change later as you progress. People who are working with no plan, not even a temporary one, will often lose the race to the better job. A wishy-washy, uncertain attitude about where to aim your energy will allow others with clear direction to pass you by. You may reach your goals, and you will then need to set new ones for a new challenge. Having something to aim for is important as you are first looking to make a name for yourself in your career.

Now that you have a few ideas sketched out, take a look at some of the opportunities that are available in the business. Research is important for establishing a base from which to begin your pursuit. Having a basic knowledge of the jobs available in your field will help you to begin to tackle your goals.

Assessing Your Interests

There are a tremendous number of opportunities to be explored in the entertainment industry. Chapters 6–16 will take you inside each crew position for an idea of its day-to-day responsibilities. While you are preparing for the jump into this field, think about what you enjoy doing and what you will look forward to on a daily basis. Evaluate your favorite areas of study and make a list of your hobbies. The idea here is to begin to identify your likes and dislikes and to match them to an area of study. Eventually you will encounter a job description that suits you.

SCHOOL SUBJECTS

Accounting/Business/Math

Did you think that moviemaking was limited to creative people? Don't forget the people who run the studios and put together and maintain the budgets. If you enjoy using math or business skills, keep pursuing those subjects. There are plenty of entertainment jobs out there for you.

Art and Design

There are many people in production who use their artistic skills to make the story you are seeing more believable. From concept to physically creating the art and interior decoration, there are many opportunities to use your creative energy in film and television production.

Cooking and Service Industry

Are you a gourmet chef? Do you enjoy watching people eat your delicacies? Chefs also have a home in the production industry.

Technology-related

From cameras and sound recording devices to lights and computer graphics, electronic technology plays an important role in production. If you are a hands-on person who enjoys working with electronics, specialized gear, or even just a standard sure-shot camera, there are places for you on a production crew.

Fashion

From wardrobe to cosmetic and hair design, the fashion world plays an important role in accurately portraying a character in a film or television program. If you like working with clothing or giving makeovers, don't discount your passion as a job asset.

I will go into more detail about the opportunities available to you in chapter 5. For now, keep up with the subjects and hobbies that you enjoy. Try to master your crafts so that you can continue to pursue the things that you enjoy the most and turn them into a successful career.

CHAPTER 3

The Undergraduate—Making Your

College Experience Work for You

"It's a wrap everyone!" Well now, that's not something you might expect to hear in high school. Welcome to the new millennium. More and more high schools are now incorporating radio and broadcast television courses into their curriculums. Many students are involved with film clubs in their high schools as well.

Similarly, many colleges and universities have increased the size of their communications departments, with more and more schools awarding degrees in film, television, and radio. The opportunities for education in the entertainment field are endless, although it is entirely possible to achieve success in production without having studied the subject in a classroom.

In order to make it in the entertainment field, it's best to start as early as possible. Now, this is by no means required. However, there are many benefits to gearing up early if you're ready.

"In high school, take the opportunity to risk and fail. Don't be afraid to screw up."

—Hal Sparks, actor

High School

Television and radio stations within high schools are places to help students develop their interests and enhance their skills as they are learning. They also provide a safe social environment that involves teamwork and cooperation. As high schools are preparing teenagers for college, offering a professional curriculum such as communications is becoming more popular. By starting in high school, students have the opportunity to try out their interest in filmmaking early on to see if it is a direction they might want to take during college. It also provides a chance to learn the equipment and to be a step ahead of classmates as a college freshman. If you are currently in high school and are able to participate in this way, it will definitely give you a head start. But to those of you who didn't realize an interest in entertainment that early on, or didn't have the opportunity before, there is still hope for you!

Rage in Harlem

Kevin is an accomplished video assist operator who often travels from movie to movie for his work. He got his first job from a skill set that he learned in high school and maintained through college. Yearning to test the waters in film production, he went after any position he could get when *Rage in Harlem* came to film in his hometown. Based on his high school experience as a movie projectionist, he made himself useful to this production by setting up their projector for **dailies**. While doing this, he networked with the people around him and later landed a job as a camera production assistant (P.A.), where he learned the skills that drive his career today. You just never know which extracurricular activity will pay off after high school.

University

Obviously, college is an institution that serves many purposes. Along with providing further education in basic courses and an advanced degree, it serves as a learning tool for life in general. In college, students learn to live away from home for the first time and to function independently. They learn to cook, to clean, and to socialize, to name a few lessons. Many take for granted the broad range of areas that college actually covers in educating them for the future. Just as it is necessary to learn about your interests and the subject that may one day become your major, it is also important that you don't lose sight of the other subjects that actually play large roles in those fields.

Universities both large and small often offer a wide variety of classes, from Ancient Indian Traditions to Advanced Chemistry. For the future producer, writer, or even prop master, it is beneficial to take time in a curriculum to learn about a new subject. Having a broad knowledge in other areas of study will not only impress a future employer, it will also provide background for writing, knowledge about a filming location, and the like. A director who isn't familiar with other cultures and "real life people" won't be able to coach actors on how to play everyday characters.

In addition, classes in mathematics, accounting, computers, and writing all provide skills that will be needed on any job in production. To have at least an understanding of these subjects is important as you attempt to work your way up the production ladder. Many students do not look ahead into the future and thus put off taking these subjects. That can be a big mistake. It is easier to incorporate diverse subjects into a course load while you are in college than to have to brush up on them later.

There are all types of colleges and universities. Some are stronger in one area of education than others. Schools that focus on film or arts and entertainment may sound right for you if you are certain of your future career. Be careful if you do choose a school that focuses on film and television. There are some schools that will teach you to be a director or a producer, which is wonderful. However, they may not be giving you a realistic perspective of the industry and the job market as a whole, and they may not be giving you straightforward and realistic job-hunting advice—just be open-minded. By reading a book like this one, you are already one step ahead.

> **"The last thing you should take in school is television. . . You have to learn about the world to get into this business."**
> **—Allen Hall, consulting producer and director, WGN-TV**

Choosing a Major

Deciding on a major can be very stressful and nerve-wracking when a person is not certain of his or her future role in the working world. As I mentioned in chapter 1, there can be pressure to check a box on a form asking for a declaration of major without really knowing why or how you came to pick that particular major. Some schools have programs for undecided people to explore the options that are out there before they need to make a binding decision. This allows you to experiment with different areas of study until the right path becomes clear. Other institutions require the decision to be made up front. It is important to remember that this is only school. People change, needs change, ideals and goals change too. You can always change your mind later. Do not let marking that box cause you undue stress.

Options

Something that many people who are entering into production do not realize is that you can have a strong and active interest in television, film, or radio and still find a job in these fields even if it was not your declared major. In fact, this is one of the most well kept secrets and is only evident after graduation. Unless you are going into a technically specific field like engineering or camera work, you can choose practically any major and still find opportunities to work in the entertainment industry after college. There are many people I work with in the film business who have history, business, or even law degrees. They eventually became producers, directors, prop masters, set decorators, and so on.

How does a person major in a liberal arts subject and still pursue a creative field? It's simple—by taking advantage of the college environment. By reading books because they are interesting and pertinent to your goals, not just because they are required for a class. So before you jump into hours of television production classes, think about other subjects in which you may be interested. Decide on whether or not you can fit these other subjects into your class schedule if you choose to major in television or film. Perhaps it would be easier to incorporate a few television or film classes into your curriculum as a liberal arts or business major. Or you might choose a creative major and consider a minor in a different subject. There are many ways to achieve a well-rounded education that will benefit your career.

For example, in junior high school I was required to take a language course. Most of my friends took French because it was such a romantic language. I was always the practical one. I took Spanish. I liked it enough to get by. (Having a teacher who found creative ways to incorporate Ricky Martin and Menudo into my education was a big help when I was a teenager.) I stuck with Spanish throughout high school and then decided that I might as well continue in college since I'd made it this far. It was tough. I was over-extending myself with numerous activities but I sensed that knowing Spanish might really come in handy somewhere. I was right. Speaking Spanish gave me one of my first job opportunities in film, and it undoubtedly helped me through many others.

Se Habla Español

During my summer internship on *Mo' Money* I worked in the locations department. We were filming a chase scene in a mall. I worked with storeowners to ask them to keep their lights on at night, and to have their doors open so that we could make the mall look like any other daytime shopping center. After making my rounds at the shops, I headed to the set to offer my help to the crew. I was new and unsure of myself, but willing to do just about anything they needed. I was standing behind the director and actor Damon Wayans when the sound mixer came over the radio. Apparently there was a noise in the background that was faint but yet disrupting the scene. We all looked around and realized it was a jackhammer. Doing my part to help, I was sent four blocks away to the source of the noise to ask them to kindly stop jackhammering on the street while we were rolling film. Sounds easy enough, right?

What I didn't expect was that the man doing the jackhammering would not understand me. Once he stopped and could hear me, I realized that he didn't speak English, only Spanish. Luckily for me, the chapter in my textbook on transportation that dealt with parking and towing was covered in my most recent semester. I remembered balking at how pointless it was to have to learn street repair and automobile terminology during class, and had tried to keep a straight face when we acted out a skit about an upset student who got a parking ticket. But I wasn't balking this time as I stood in the middle of LaSalle Street at midnight grasping for the words to explain to the construction worker that we needed him to stop jackhammering on the street whenever I raised my hand. It worked, and I stopped the noise that was disrupting the shoot.

My boss remembered that day and others like it. When it came time for his next feature film, he ran into trouble. He had a building that he was trying to use as a location, but the manager of the building didn't understand English, only Spanish. I had a job next day where I used my Spanish language knowledge continually. It was a long job on a good film. I'm so glad for the classes that I took that were not related to my major—and for my professor insisting on teaching me the "useless" vocabulary that I had found so amusing.

Extracurricular Activities

Sports, parties, dance clubs, concerts, Jell-O wrestling. . . the best part of college for many people is the fun stuff that happens outside of the classroom. For students interested in arts and entertainment, there are many activities available on campus. If there are no related activities available, the ambitious student will create them.

So often I hear people say "I should have paid attention" or "I should have taken that class." "Should haves" are unfortunately very common as we grow older. However, they are preventable. There is no room for regrets in your life today. You simply need to focus on the here and now, and to make the most of what you have. With this philosophy, the eager person pursuing production needs to be proactive, and to establish a lifestyle and agenda that will not lead to regrets.

Each day take a look at your activities in a positive light. Use them to enrich your life. Whether it is a simple errand or a complicated project, all of these actions contribute to your personality and your attitude, which embody your spirit and essentially drive your career. In a nutshell, appreciate even the small things. Each experience we have in every minute of our day shapes us. It shapes our personality, our interactions with others, our environment, and essentially our world. Keeping this theory in mind, we need to work it into our careers as well. Classes we take, books we read, lectures we attend, games we play, and hobbies we enjoy all contribute to our education and our strengths and weaknesses. They shape our opinions, our goals, and our desires.

Everyone should choose some sort of activity to participate in during college. Whether it is working in the dining hall, performing in an open mic night at the local theater, or making a video of friends on campus, you should choose an activity to occupy your free time that provides hands-on experience to add to your textbook learning.

So where do you find the activities that are right for you? Well, if you are studying film, radio, or video, there are probably plenty of groups to join at your campus. Look for listings in the department. Does your school have its own student-run television station or is there a public access station in town? Does the school have a radio station? Are there students majoring in film or television that need an extra pair of hands on a class project? You bet they do. The more motivated people there are to help out on a project, the smoother the project will go. Be a part of the film community. Also, there may be casting calls for the local play, or perhaps the soccer team has tryouts. Get your feet wet in different areas. You don't have to do something film-related to grow from it and to draw from it for your career. However, it is a good idea to participate in at least one project in your school that is related to your major or your future career. For a person interested in film, the answer is, of course, to work on a film. Find film majors that need help on their class projects; find film classes that need volunteers. If you are interested in television or video, see if there is a station or local group that is making videos and is in need of assistance. There are essentially three reasons for choosing an extracurricular project that is related to your future career.

Reason number one: education

Whatever group you join or position you take will undoubtedly teach you something more about your trade that perhaps you never would have learned in class.

Reason number two: testing the waters

This is your first experience in your career. Perhaps you have your hopes set on being a cameraperson. You sign up to be a cameraperson on the school's in-house talk show. By signing up you will be better trained at this craft and you will also have the opportunity to try it before committing all four years to it. Who knows? You may learn that it wasn't what you thought it would be and decide to go in a different direction with your next step already planned. Or you might learn that it is more difficult or even easier than you had anticipated. With this knowledge you can alter your future curriculum accordingly.

Semesters

Fred and George and I created a soap opera at Ithaca College. We held a contest to find its title, *Semesters*. We labored over our brainchild and treated it as if it were on ABC following *General Hospital*. George was majoring in film and was interested in being a writer. He had been writing on the side and participating in filmmaking by helping with student films. George decided to take on the role of head writer for our soap.

Fred also was majoring in film. He had an interest in editing music videos and had been learning the craft of editing in his classes. They both spent time on campus over the summer, when classes were not in session, to learn to operate the newly upgraded equipment. By being one step ahead of the other students, they were proficient with the equipment before the semester began and had made friends in high places who gave us access to what we needed to make our production run smoothly.

I wanted to be a producer. The three of us were all acting producers, but my role was more visible within the station, as I attended meetings and worked on scheduling and equipment "rental." That was how we got our start in this business while we were in college. Since then, George has become a successful writer in Hollywood. He has worked on several TV series and recently sold a screenplay. Fred is also successful as an editor of music videos and commercials. I am a producer. By testing the waters in an extra-curricular activity, we found our niches. George confided to me recently, "Working on *Semesters* was a better education than any class I ever took."

Reason number three: networking

When you join a group, the people that join with you are in the same position as you are. They too are testing the waters. Now is your first opportunity for networking. This is where it all begins. These people—the anchors, the TelePrompTer, the camera operator, the makeup artist—are the future of the business. Four years from now they are the people that you will be competing with for opportunities, or working with on projects in the real world. These people are your chance for a start. These are important people and contacts that you can have forever. Now is the time to put your plan into action. Some of them will become your best friends in the world. Some of them you may not mix well with, but you all need to find a comfort zone because you will inevitably run into them later on down the road and you may need to work together or possibly help each other. They may open many doors for you, and you likewise for them.

On Broadway

We were crazed; it was certainly a fast-paced office that day when we realized we needed more visuals for the documentary that was going to air that weekend on the local affiliate. We needed something to go along with the Broadway Shows theme that had been discussed in the third segment. I remembered hearing that Suzanne was working at a company related to Broadway shows in New York and I looked her up. I hadn't talked to her more than once since college even though I had been keeping up with her through the stories I was hearing, but we picked up where we had left off and caught up with each other's lives. She was able to help me out of my jam by sending me programs from the latest and greatest shows, which we were able to use as visuals in the segment. I was very grateful, and I owe her one—our documentary won an Emmy!

My friends laugh that I keep in touch with too many people, or that I am too busy flying to weddings all the time. What they don't realize is that what started as having co-workers in school budded into having co-workers in life. Many of my college friends that I began my career with in the bowels of a college building while working on my first "TV show" turned out to be great friends and confidants. They also have been able to help me in many areas of my professional life and I have returned the favor as often as possible. The people that I used to work with on my larger-than-life college projects (my "cut and paste" classes, as we used to call them) have gone on to succeed professionally in various careers, including as news writers, engineers at ESPN and CNN, sitcom producers, production coordinators on major television dramas, film editors, news reporters, and so on. Had I burned any bridges with these people in college, I might not have been able to ask for help or advice from them later, and they would not have been able to ask for my help either. We share in our climb to the top. In many cases we have chosen complimentary fields and are able to bring business to each other. The moral of the story is to think of all your classmates as your future co-workers. Try to treat them all with respect and to lend them a hand. The favor will be returned when you need it and may be the step you need to finding your first job.

So find your student film or local cable access station. Volunteer to be the lighting person for your neighbor's class project. Look to your advisor or department head to guide you if you are lost in your search. And don't be afraid to ask professors or other students. They will teach you what you need to know, and they will greatly appreciate the interest and the extra hand you are lending. They may even treat you to chicken wings and a beer.

Just be careful that you don't over-commit your time to extracurricular activities. You need to save time for the classroom and for the sleep you'll need before the next party, track meet, football game, or whatever else you choose.

CHAPTER 4

The Internship—Spending Your

Free Time Wisely

I n this day and age it is almost necessary that a person have an internship to gain experience before obtaining a position in production. It is not mandatory to have an internship on your resume. However, there are so many college students beginning their experience as interns that they create competition for people with no previous experience who are trying to break into the business. If you are out of school and can afford to live without a paycheck for a while, it is beneficial to find someone willing to put you to work for peanuts.

What is an Internship?

An internship is a period of employment where a person is hired in exchange for school credit or a stipend rather than a regular salary. That person is generally used for secretarial work or as a runner depending on the company's needs. For instance, one television station may use an intern to answer viewer phone calls, whereas another may decide to have the intern assist in the talent green room or run errands for the producer. In smaller companies it is likely that an intern will do hands-on production work that only a paid staff member would be able to perform in a larger company.

For the company, the intern is free labor, an extra body to help out with mundane work that is necessary but perhaps too time consuming for the busy staff. In some cases it is an opportunity to first test out a job candidate without making too many sacrifices in paychecks, benefits, and training. For the intern, it is a first look at the industry and a chance to learn about production first-hand. It is also an opportunity to network. The term **networking** is thrown around the entertainment industry on a regular basis. It is used to describe the art of meeting people and using them and their contacts to your benefit. An internship may lead to a future job. It is an important stepping-stone and an invaluable experience if used properly. The film business is often based on relationships. Internships afford you the opportunity to form connections with people and to gain a trial run in a work environment. Having had an internship tells the employer that you have some knowledge of what to expect in the workplace, and that you are not totally green.

Volunteer

If you are not in school and can afford a post-college internship, you can use this opportunity to work your way onto a company's payroll. Similar to temping, an internship program (or offering to work for free at a company for a specified period of time) will allow you and the employer to get to know each other. You can learn the business and prove your worth before the employer is prepared to begin outside job interviews. Many camera operators get their start by offering to help at camera rental houses, just as grips may begin by working at lighting rental houses. By working to prepare the gear for a production company who will rent it for a shoot, you learn the equipment and get to know the people who use it. Having worked in a rental house will give you the edge because you are able to familiarize yourself with the equipment. Similar situations can be found for many other departments such as makeup, props, or catering, to name a few. Use your imagination and whatever resources you have available to find the plan that will work best for you to get your foot in the door and to seize every opportunity.

Factors

Again, let's go back to the basics. Where do you find an internship? First it is important to think about your goal. You are, of course, looking for work experience. Other factors to consider are:

1)   Where do you physically want to be looking (in your hometown, in a bigger city, or elsewhere)? Working in your hometown will allow you to be near friends and family, which may be financially important to you. Small towns and big cities each have their advantages and disadvantages.

A small town will often provide internships that allow the intern to perform more tasks, which will prove to be useful later on jobs in larger markets. For instance, a small town radio station will possibly allow an intern to work audio controls, make producer-type phone calls, and the like. A bigger city may only allow an intern to observe rather than participate in much of the activity. On the other hand, having a better-known company in a larger market on your resume may make it easier to be taken seriously in future interviews.

2) What is your cost of living? Do you have to relocate to find your target internship? Relocating is expensive and stressful. If you only have a short period of time for this internship and don't plan on making the relocation permanent, is moving practical?

3) Do you have friends or family in the city you are choosing? Without them, it may be a lonely place for you.

☞ Note—Some companies may hesitate to take a person in as an intern or employee if he or she is not a resident of the area. If you are relocating for the position, be sure to have confirmation of the internship before you pack your bags.

4) During what time frame do you want this internship to take place? (Is it a college semester or summer break? Are you flexible?) Different types of work have different "busy seasons." A feature film can film at any time of the year, depending on the story in the film (and local weather conditions), whereas an established episodic television drama will most likely film during the fall, winter, and spring, and take a hiatus for the summer months.

5) Availability. Do you have all day to devote to your internship, or are you taking an additional evening job? That will affect a production job such as a feature, which may require a twelve-hour day. A person with daytime-only availability is more apt to find an internship in a studio, post-production facility, or similar company that has more of a regular 9–5 day. Production people tend to work all hours, and expect that of everyone involved, unless prior arrangements have been made. It will no doubt be more difficult to turn your internship into a paying job if you plan to work shorter hours than the rest of the staff when you are an intern in a busy production office.

How to Find an Internship

What is your area of interest? Is there an area of the business that is important to your career goal although it may not be your favorite subject?

Obviously if you are interested in being a makeup artist, then an internship in a makeup studio will be appealing. Don't forget the other avenues that can lead to your area of interest. Perhaps you are interested in eventually being a camera operator on a sitcom. Working as an intern on a sitcom is a promising start. Another option would be to work at a company that rents camera equipment—a place to learn about the camera itself. Or say you'd like to be a producer for commercials; you might think the ideal internship would be with an ad agency or a film company. However, working at a broadcast television station may also give you insight into the advertising world if you're in the right department. It never hurts to see things from other perspectives. Using your internship to its fullest potential is a key to success.

What resources are available to you for obtaining your internship, and does your school have any restrictions or guidelines pertaining to your course credit?

Many schools have some sort of career counseling department that will often help students find internships. They offer anything from guidance to helping a student to find his or her areas of interest to finding the appropriate company for those interests. There are a large number of companies that will send their intern requests for posting at local colleges, and many have internship programs worked out with schools on a year-round basis. Some career counselors or school advisors may go as far as overseeing the internship. Many will require the student to complete schoolwork, such as essays related to the internship. Always check the guidelines of your school before taking an internship.

Each school also houses an alumni-relations department. This department houses information on all alumni, and many schools will have frequent contact with alumni in your field. Perhaps they will let you look at the alumni list from your hometown or from your field to see if there is anyone you can contact regarding possibilities at their places of employment. Alumni are great job resources. They know what types of skills you might have because they have the same educational background. By seeing your internships and/or college experiences on your resume they can instantly assess your work ethic or capabilities to some extent. Often, alumni prefer to hire from their alma mater simply because of this comfort level.

Be sure to research the company from which you would like an internship. It is important to learn the company's internship guidelines. Many companies will not allow for even an *unpaid* internship, depending on whether your college or university can meet their criteria.

Once you have narrowed your interest area and have an idea of where you physically want the internship to take place, the rest is simply research. Look in the classifieds section of the local newspaper, Yellow Pages, and Internet job sites to find companies hiring in your field. They most likely will not advertise internships, but you can search for places to call to inquire about possible internship programs that may be available in the industry.

Another source of information for finding internships is the local Film Office or Film Commission. Every state has some sort of office, related to the mayor or governor's office, that is the primary contact for all film work in that state (see appendix). The film industry, including commercials and student films, brings in a large source of revenue for the state. In addition, the local film community benefits from having a department solely dedicated to bringing films to town. They are usually in contact with producers many months before a given production even sets up an office in town, and can often prove to be a great source of information for the local filmmaker. Some film commissions have a "job hotline" for local crewmembers to call for any production openings. The commissions themselves may have internship programs as well. Call your state or city's film commission to inquire about internship possibilities. (See appendix, p. 193.)

Local unions can provide a tremendous wealth of information. If you are inquiring about a position that falls under a particular union, call the local chapter and let the union know your interests. They may be able to guide you toward productions they are currently working on that may need a P.A.

Put the word out. This is where you begin your networking training. Tell your family members and have them tell their friends. . . Let the town know that you are looking for an internship. Chances are that a friend of a friend of a friend of your mother's will help get the word out and the word may actually spread to a television station or film company that takes interns. Don't be shy. The worst thing that can happen is that your whole town knows about your job status. They probably think that filmmaking is "cool" so they will only be impressed.

Roommate Connection

During my semester abroad in London, I met Michelle. She was not studying film or television, and helped me to focus on other topics for a change. At the end of the semester we realized that by the time we came back to the states, it would be very difficult to find a summer job. The other college kids would have a jump start since they were in town and could start job-hunting sooner than we could. The previous summer Michelle had worked at a bank. There would probably not be any place for her there during the short seven weeks that would remain of the summer by the time we returned.

I was surprised to hear from her after only our first week back in the states and was even more surprised to hear what she had to say. She had found an internship for me on a movie! Michelle had called her old bank to inquire about job openings and to network in her field. What she found was that there were unfortunately no openings for her there. During the rest of her conversation, she learned that the feature film *Mo' Money* would be shooting a scene at the bank. Her contact gave her the name of the location manager who was coordinating the shoot for the bank, and the rest is history. Michelle thought of me, her movie friend, when she heard about the film. She didn't know if they were hiring but she went out of her way to get the contact information for me, and I found myself a summer internship on the film, which led to paid work after college. You never know who will find you the opportunity or what that opportunity will be.

Dressing for the Role

Once you have found an internship and are ready to begin, you must prepare. Buy yourself appropriate clothes to dress the part. In most instances, as a production intern, you will not be expected to wear more than jeans and a T-shirt. Being a creative field where people are working long hours, production crews tend to dress for comfort in extremely casual attire that can take the rigors of the job. If your internship is with a broadcast television station, you likely will be expected to dress for a corporate environment. As an intern you are representing the company, you will need to dress the part. Be sure to ask your internship coordinator what is expected of you, so that you are prepared on Day One. It is always wiser to dress a little bit nicer than to be slightly underdressed at your workplace. It has been said that you should dress for the role that you want to obtain. The way you dress will certainly make an impression on your co-workers. It will tell them what you are capable of and will show them that you mean business. If you work in an environment where everyone is wearing shorts and T-shirts this doesn't mean you need to wear a suit. But you do not necessarily need to dress at that same grungy level. Consider the environment and your goals, and make your wardrobe decision accordingly.

Intern Tips

As I mentioned before, internships tend to offer mundane work such as filing and handling phones. You must use your internship to its greatest potential, which means learning the business via these chores. For instance, when you are asked to file something, glance over it before you file it unless it is confidential or personal. Think about what it is that you are filing and also where and why it was sent in the first place. Being nosy is a great way to learn about what is going on in your office, and how information is processed in your company. Just use your discretion on what is meant for your eyes and what is personal. For example, I used to tell our interns at *Party of Five* to pass out sixteen copies of the daily production report to a list of people that included the producers, studio executives, myself, my boss, and others. Then I recommended that they not only read the report, but also ask questions about it and try to understand why all sixteen people needed to have this particular piece of paper. I explained that a production report is a valuable piece of paper that basically sums up all of the costs for the day, including actor and crew hours, equipment rental, film, lunches, problems that occurred, you name it. Afterward, the interns were able to deduce that the producer and accountants would need the report to know the costs and to maintain the budget, the studio executive would want to ensure that the production company was not spending loosely, and so on. This exercise taught the interns to appreciate the paperwork and also enabled them to learn a little more about other people and their positions.

The bottom line here is to pay attention and to question everything, even if you are only questioning it to yourself. You need to seize every opportunity to learn from your internship and/or your first job so it may lead you to your next one.

Company Representative

As mentioned previously, you are a representative of the company. So when you are speaking to a client (whether it be Robert Redford or the studio's groundskeeper) you need to speak in a professional manner. Often, employers will assign the intern to act as a receptionist. In this case you are the link between the company and the vendors or clients. You are the first impression these people will get of the company you are working for. Therefore, speaking clearly and politely will go a long way. On many occasions, calls come from arrogant producer-types who are short with receptionists over the telephone. Try not to be intimidated by these people and always act courteously. Remember that "the client is always right," whether or not you agree. You are there to satisfy that person's needs. Arguing with a client over the telephone will misrepresent the company and will cause your employer a loss of business, which does you no good.

It is worth noting that it is not unheard of to have an important executive notice your good phone manners. This kind of notice can be rewarded down the line.

We Interrupt this Broadcast. . .

As an intern in the creative services department at an ABC affiliate, my part-time job was mostly centered around answering viewer phone calls. The questions that viewers asked never ceased to amaze me. One morning I was finding out where a viewer could purchase a couch like the Quartermaine's on *General Hospital*, the next day I'd be talking to an obsessed *Jeopardy!* fan who missed the answer to the final question and desperately needed to know what it was. The most hectic days of call answering were when the President of the United State would interrupt a soap opera to talk about a special event of national importance. The President never was very sensitive to the plight of the daytime viewers who needed to see their soaps. One day in particular I found myself on a touchy call. A viewer was incensed by the popular show *Twin Peaks* and called to demand that it be taken off the air. She was raving mad and would not give up the fight, claiming that her dogs would bark whenever the show came on. Being a representative of the company in my position as an intern, I had to forgo my gut reaction to say, "Just turn the show off and your dogs will stop barking." Instead I calmly discussed the situation with her and let her know that her message was important to us and would be passed on to the proper people. That call, and others like it, lasted for an hour. By remaining calm and maintaining my composure, I made an impression on my employers. (And now when I watch *Jeopardy!* I always find myself listening for the final question.)

Never Complain

You can ask a thousand different questions if you have to, just make sure you understand the task. Use a pen and paper so that you don't have to repeat the same question. Watch your tone; even the slightest hint of complaint in your voice will be a slash against you in the mental record that your employers are keeping. There are plenty of people looking for jobs in this industry, any of whom will happily replace you. There is no room for negative attitudes or laziness. As an intern you are the lowest on the totem pole and at the beck and call of everyone else. You will be asked to do some ridiculous things in this business, and the mere fact that you were asked to do them is likely derived from someone having done that (or something similarly ridiculous) himself as an intern. In an intern position you will most likely survive the assigned duration of time, but a bad attitude on your record will scar your chances of being hired on salary at a later date. It can hinder your chances of employment elsewhere when your future employer calls your internship supervisor for recommendations. What sounds ridiculous to you is obviously helpful to someone else, or he or she wouldn't ask you to do it. It may help to place yourself in the other person's shoes for a moment. Maybe the production coordinator has been on the phone all day and she can't make it to her car to pay the meter in time. The point is . . . there may be a good reason for why you are being asked to do this chore. Helping to do a personal or out-of-the-ordinary task may be a life-saver for your boss. Your personality and a positive attitude will carry you far. Doing this deed and the others that follow will help to propel you to a higher level. Doing a silly task and doing it to the best of your ability can go a long way.

McGyver to the Rescue

My friend was an assistant to a producer for a cable station in Los Angeles and she was constantly being asked to perform personal tasks for him. One night she was asked to take his car in to have the remote-lock fixed and the alarm checked. After several trips to the mechanic, it seemed that all wires were in place and the alarm was running well. It caught everyone in the office by surprise when one day the alarm started sounding full volume in the parking garage. Her boss was out and the entire studio was complaining as they were trying to get their work done but the alarm would not stop screeching. Her solution was to use a brad fastener that was holding that week's script together and she went to work on the car. (Can you hear the *Mission Impossible* theme music ringing in your ears?) She dismantled the dashboard and pulled the right wire (no, this is not a made-for-TV-movie; this is a true story!), saving the day, saving her co-workers' ears, and sealing her reputation for being a Jack-of-all-Trades. She made herself invaluable once again.

Keeping Busy

Never sit around doing nothing. (Chatting with the boss, talking to friends on the telephone, surfing the Internet, reading a book. . . these are all considered "doing nothing.") Looking bored tells your co-workers many things about you. It tells them that you are not resourceful enough to come up with things to do to help the office. It also tells them that perhaps you are not necessary to the department and that maybe they don't need to hire an intern in the future. They may infer that you are lazy or unambitious, which would lead them to conclude that they would not benefit from hiring you for a paid or full-time position.

Stay busy. File things, clean the copy machine, clean out the refrigerator, or offer to run an errand. When you absolutely cannot think of a darned thing to occupy your time, walk around the office and offer your help to others. You would be surprised at how many people have a million things to do and can find a way to utilize your time. Again, since you are paying attention to what you copy or fax, you will learn about their positions and their workload. Offering your help tells people how great you are, since you thought about them in their time of need. They will think of you later when wanting assistance in the future. Don't ever twiddle your thumbs as an intern, or at any job for that matter. When you can't do anything to help, use your time to learn. An internship is a course for learning. By being an intern, you may have the freedom to sit in an edit suite and watch the editor at work. Or you may have the opportunity to sit on the set near the director. In this situation, sitting on the job is okay since you are observing to learn, not just slacking off. Use your time wisely to learn about the areas that appeal to you as you are developing your interests and goals.

Joey the Intern

On *Party of Five* we had an intern who set the perfect example for "what not to do." We'll call him Joey.* Joey was from the East Coast, with an accent to prove it. Joey was so full of himself and the fact that he was working on *Party of Five* that I imagined him looking at himself in the mirror before he came in every morning, telling himself how great he was.

One day I went to the set and found Joey reading a book. Not a production manual, but a fictional novel. Now, it's pretty bad to be an intern reading a book on the job. It's really bad to be an intern reading a book and to let other people see you reading a book. It's extremely bad to be doing it where I saw Joey doing it. He was sitting on the set. No, not next to the director, he was physically on the set. Joey was sitting on what is called a **hot set**. This is a set that is **camera ready** and should not be touched. He was sitting on a bed on which the actors were about to perform an intimate scene. He was sitting on the bed while people around him were working. In that single moment the entire crew had made their decision about Joey. He lost the respect of all his co-workers, and any hope that he could ever have for being hired onto this long-running show in the future.

Needless to say, I did not give raving reviews about Joey to his internship coordinator. As a matter of fact, I felt compelled to tell the truth that he so badly needed to hear. He was rather upset at his mediocre review and at the prospect of not having any responsibilities given to him for the rest of the run of the show. But I spoke with him and opened his eyes to the fact that, yes, it is a great opportunity to work on a well-known and popular show, but it is not to be taken for granted. You need to earn your place as a crewmember as well as a landmark intern. The bottom line is never show your boredom and always make yourself useful. Let Joey's attitude teach you a lesson before you learn it the hard way.

---

* Not actual name

Networking

An internship, like all of the other social situations we have discussed up to this point, is yet another opportunity to network. You are working with experienced production people. Once you feel comfortable in your position, it is time to practice your networking skills. This is your golden opportunity to mingle and to get to know your co-workers. Leave them with a good and lasting impression of you and your contributions so you can call on them later for a favor or two.

Remember, even the inexperienced or unfriendly co-workers can be important to you down the line. Making friends and getting to know everyone involved in your project will help you as you begin your connections to the future. Today's mailroom attendant is tomorrow's studio executive. Get to know everyone and use your internship to propel yourself to a paying job the next time around.

At the end of each week at your internship it will benefit you to keep a log of what you have done and what you have learned. You should be able to fill a few pages of a notebook. Every night jot down what you learned or did that day. Put it into a spiral notebook or journal of some sort. Stretch your imagination; find one item to prove that you did something significant each day. For instance, you brought the scripts to the mailroom—did you learn any other tidbits of information during conversations with co-workers along the way? Did you meet anyone new? Did you learn a new route to the mailroom via a golf cart? Your internship log is a key part to your "job." This may sound tedious but consider it work that is necessary to your position. If you are not able to find anything to write about at the end of the day, you are not seizing enough opportunities. You need to piece together all aspects of your job, your department, your co-workers and their jobs, and how you are treated and guided through the job. All of these pieces will blend to give you a well-rounded knowledge of the business. To succeed you will need to understand your field inside and out.

An internship is basically your first job experience in your profession. By learning the ropes and having an opportunity to absorb what is going on around you, you will be one step ahead for that first paid job. Interning is the chance to get to know what positions interest you, and an opportunity to network in the industry. Once you have been an intern, you can interview for a job with the confidence that you know what you're in for and that you know you can handle whatever is coming your way.

SECTION II:
THE REAL
WORLD

CHAPTER 5

The Crew—Getting To Know

Your Job Options

The dream begins with you in your cap and gown, walking onto a stage. You are shaking hands and receiving that diploma that you worked so hard for. How did you get here? Where do you go now? The second question is the one you are probably thinking about as you finish your undergraduate education.

You've had your classes and your video, film, or radio projects. You've listened to advice from your parents (well, maybe "listen" is a strong word), but you've heard some whisperings about what you should do when you graduate. This is a stressful time for many. It is difficult to remember to relax. It is also difficult to not feel as if the first job is the most important job of your life. In some ways it is. Your first job, and every job thereafter, will provide insight into your interests, your talents, your likes and dislikes. It is a stepping-stone for your career.

However, the first job you take does not need to be permanent. It is a study tool from which you will grow. Finding any job at all in the field that piques your interest will be a great learning step for you. Therefore, finding the supreme job is not necessary, which is good because the likelihood of finding the perfect job right after college is pretty slim.

You may have been a star in college. Your professors may have called you "brilliant" or assured you that you will be the next Steven Spielberg. Try to be realistic. There are very few people who beat the system and get their dream jobs straight out of school or right after they decide to switch careers. For the majority of film and television graduates, the only choice is to start at the bottom and work up. Producer Lisa Masseur once used this analogy during a conversation we had about the business: "A film major thinking that he will get a job as a director right out of college is like a business major thinking he will get a job as a CEO of a company as soon as he graduates."

Job Options

It is difficult to carve out your niche if you don't really know what the options are. The following chapters give brief descriptions of some of the production jobs and the function of their departments in film, television, and often in special event planning.

The goal of this book for you is to find an entry-level position in entertainment production. In most cases, that position is an assistant, whether an office, set, or personal assistant. This section will give you a basic overview of what opportunities are available in production. As an assistant you will have the opportunity to see first-hand what is out there and to figure out where it is that you want to go next.

☛Note—There are other areas to work in such as development and various positions within a studio, broadcast station, or network, but this overview will give you an idea of where to direct your energy. You will be able to use some of these positions to boost yourself into other areas or perhaps even other fields later on.

The positions described in this section reflect an average crew for a feature film or television drama series. Depending on the budget and size of the production, some of these jobs listed here may not exist, or crewmembers may take on dual roles.

CHAPTER 6

The Hierarchy—"Above the Line" and "Below the Line"

Cast and crew positions are separated into "Above the Line" and "Below the Line" items in the production's salary budget. These categories basically differentiate between the talent and producers or select crew who are paid per contract or on salary and the rest of the hired crew who are paid via time sheets with regular daily, weekly, or bi-weekly paychecks.

Executive Producer

Generally speaking, the responsibilities of the executive producer can vary on a television production, feature film, or special event. In most cases, the executive producer deals with the bigger picture. In some cases this person may solely fund the project and have nothing further to do with its evolution. In other situations, this person deals with the big-name talent, the studio, and the financial backers to the project. Executive producers may have the ultimate responsibility for the project and its financial success.

☞Note—On a television series, the title of executive producer or producer will often be given to the creator of the story's concept, or to the top writers of the series. In these cases, the producer will likely deal with the story and creative aspects of the production rather than taking a monetary or managerial role.

Producer

On a feature film or television production, this person oversees the actual production as opposed to strictly dealing with the talent and finances. Again, the position's responsibilities may vary depending on the production. On a television series, the producer will meet with the unit production manager (UPM) regarding costs and will act as the go-between for the executive producer and the filming company. In this scenario, the producer is responsible for making certain the crew stays on target in terms of schedule and monetary budget. He or she will speak to the director to discuss the schedule during the day, keep tabs on the crew's hours, and stop any foreseeable problems that may possibly keep the crew late, leading to overtime charges. The producer is involved with the development of the project, bringing all of the larger elements together.

Unit Production Manager (UPM)

Sometimes also doubling as the producer (or titled as line producer), the UPM is directly involved with overseeing and managing the budget. This person is the leader of the crew and is the ultimate decision-maker on expenses for each department. As this person oversees the day-to-day operations of the production process, he or she generally aims to become a producer. A good UPM is very knowledgeable about each crew position and knows the filmmaking process inside and out.

Director

The director is the creative head for the entire production unit. He or she provides the artistic vision of the production and translates the screenplay or teleplay into the movie or television show. From directing rehearsals during the course of production all the way through the editorial process, the director is responsible for bringing the script to life. This person regularly meets with the producers and various department heads to give them direction to lead them into his or her vision of what the final product should look like. During the shoot, the director is not only responsible for the visual content of the scene, but also for keeping the crew motivated and happy.

Other "Above the Line" positions include the director of photography in the camera department and the production designer in the art department. Search for these department descriptions in the rest of the section to read about their roles in production.

CHAPTER 7

The Production Department—

The Heart of the Production

The production department is the heart of the production company, which runs the entire shoot. It encompasses several areas, which are broken down loosely as follows:

The Assistant Directors (A.D.s)

The assistant directors, along with their assistants (set P.A.s), act basically as the management team for the shooting crew. The focal point for the direction of the project, they are the go-to people for any problems, questions, or concerns regarding the shoot, and are responsible for making sure that everything happens as planned (or if something needs to be changed, they implement the change and form a new plan of attack). Working with the cast and each department of the shooting crew, the A.D.s make certain that the production is kept moving according to schedule. As soon as the production falls behind schedule it will begin to go over budget, so maintaining a tight time schedule is essential. Also, the A.D.s are on-set problem solvers who ensure safety and keep the cast and crew happy so that production continues to run smoothly. The following are the positions of the A.D. department and their general responsibilities:

1) 1st Assistant Director (1st A.D.)

Just as it sounds, this person assists the director. It is not to be confused with the director's assistant, which is an entirely different job. This job requires on-set experience, pays much more than a position as a director's assistant, and is a union position in the Director's Guild of America (DGA), as are all of the A.D. positions on a union project.

The 1st A.D. is in charge of the entire set and "runs" it during the shoot. He or she gives the verbal command to roll or stop rolling the cameras, and maintains order and safety on the set. Working very closely with the director, UPM, and producers, the 1st A.D. creates the **shooting schedule** and ensures that each day's shoot is moving along according to plan, changing future schedules to compensate for problems or creative changes that inevitably occur along the way. For instance, if Day 6 on the schedule was set to take place at the beach but the weather report called for thundershowers, the A.D. would work with the director to have a **cover set** or rain plan for the day. They might decide to shoot indoor scenes instead, thus changing the shooting schedule to move the beach scene to another day. Working with the rest of the production team on set, the 1st A.D. organizes the movement of the cast and extras and plans how to get them to the set promptly when the camera is ready. This job involves a lot of schedule juggling and patience with actors. Being a 1st A.D. is a job for a person who has the ability to listen to two things at once, who is good with people, attentive to detail, and assertive enough to be strict with the cast and crew about timing issues. A team player who can take it all in and still handle the stress, a 1st A.D. who wants to move up the ladder generally moves into either a director or UPM role (although being a 1st A.D. can be a lifelong career in itself).

2) 2nd Assistant Director (2nd A.D.)

Yep, next in line to the 1st assistant director. This person carries through the directions given from the 1st assistant director, which often include overseeing and placing the extras. (Imagine doing this with a crowd of hundreds as in a film like *Braveheart*.) The 2nd assistant director is officially responsible for creating the daily **call sheet** and **production report**, gathering information from the 1st A.D. and all department heads to prepare for the next day's work and to recap the present day's activities. The 2nd A.D. also ultimately follows through on crisis management (there are plenty of crises) on the set, and assists the 1st A.D. with time management during the shooting day.

The Sky is Falling

The crew to the pilot *Silent Witness* is standing quietly outside of a prominent hotel along the Chicago River as the lead actress is saying her lines. This is the real thing and since it's being recorded, not a noise is being made other than her quiet line. Suddenly the cameraman feels a bump on his head. The crew looks up, wondering what is falling down from the sky. It's springtime, surely it isn't snow? Nope, in fact it is a guest at the hotel who has decided to throw ice cubes from his 8th floor freezer down onto the set. Now it is up to the 2nd assistant director to work with the locations department to send someone to the 8th floor to stop the bombardment, and there are still four more hours of filming to go . . .

3) 2nd 2nd Assistant Director (2nd 2nd A.D.)

Need I say more? This person does the dirty work for the first two assistant directors—paperwork. This person assists the 2nd A.D. with creating the **call sheet** as directed by the 1st A.D. He or she also checks and verifies the crew's time cards, and relays that information to the production report to be turned in to the production coordinator. (From there it is distributed to the studio executives, producers, and other departments as necessary.) The 2nd 2nd A.D. regularly checks in with the production office to relay shooting status and other relevant information from the set. This person is an expert on all union regulations regarding time cards and is responsible for collecting all time cards on a daily or weekly basis. Accordingly, he or she is to make sure that all payroll paperwork is filled out properly to turn in to the accounting department. The 2nd 2nd A.D. is also an expert on regulations dealing with the actors' hours and their contractual needs, as well as the regulations pertaining to minors or animals involved in the shoot. As for interacting with the cast, the 2nd 2nd A.D. will often be responsible for leading the **first team** (lead cast members) through their hair, makeup, and wardrobe routine, making certain that they are following the time schedule so as to not delay the shoot. On a bigger show with a large number of extras, the 2nd 2nd A.D. may be pulled away from typical duties to assist on set with extras placement and management with the other A.D.s, P.A.s, and extras coordinators.

Script Supervisor

As the continuity person, the script supervisor watches every frame as it is shot. He or she makes notes of line changes, costume flaws, the actors' physical positions, how long it took to say the line—anything that will have to be matched later on when the camera is looking at the same scene from another angle or the continuing scene.

Wearing a stopwatch to time the duration of each scene throughout the shoot, this person sits beside the director at all times. He or she also meets with the camera loader to mark on the **camera logs** which takes are to be developed according to the director's instructions. As this is a specialized position, classes are available (in some larger markets) to learn how to be a script supervisor. Most people learn by watching and befriending a script supervisor who will mentor them and teach them the trade. Script supervisors have their own type of shorthand that is universal only to the film world. This person is usually a script supervisor for life, or until he or she leaves the business. It is a tough job because it requires much focus and concentration for the full twelve or more hours of filming daily.

Production Office Coordinator (POC)

Production office coordinator is a thankless job, yet it is the crux of the production. The POC runs the production office and is the key source for all information on the show. He or she is ultimately responsible for getting all information pertaining to the production, including schedules, contracts, and scripts, to the cast and crew from the beginning to the end of the project.

As one of the first people hired onto the crew, the POC sets up the office as the pre-production process begins. From finding office space to ordering office equipment and hiring the office staff, the POC gets the production office organized, remaining in charge through to the show's wrap. The POC also coordinates all of the travel and hotel arrangements for cast and crew, sometimes working with real estate agents to find accommodations with special requirements for long-term stays. For example, when the D.P. needs a four-month lease for a two-bedroom apartment that will allow two large dogs, or when an actress requires a garden behind her apartment plus sky-lights in her bedroom as part of her contract (yes, these things have actually happened).

The POC also works with the camera, grip, and electric departments to schedule, order, and monitor all of their equipment rentals throughout the duration of the project. He or she will work with those departments along with the transportation department to see that the equipment is picked up and returned in a timely fashion so as not to incur overage costs or late fees.

Additionally, the POC speaks regularly with studio executives and talent managers to take care of their needs throughout the project, for example, talking with the star's manager who is calling to work out publicity shoots or to request a day off for the actor to take care of another commitment. Every day the phone consistently rings with new information to dispense and new fires to put out. At the end of the day the POC has accomplished it all, until the morning when it starts all over again.

An archetypal day for a POC on a feature film or television series will be twelve or more hours, sometimes up to eighteen hours per day, 5–7 days per week with little (if any) lunch break, definitely no true lunch hour. For smaller productions the job description may change. A smaller budget may leave the coordinator without support staff and therefore more work, or he or she may actually have more flexible workdays. In addition, a network or studio POC job may possibly be more routine and therefore not as manic or fast-paced. In any case, it is a big job.

POC is a good position for a super-organized, fast-thinking, resourceful, level-headed person. This person is the go-to person for *all* of the crew and reports to the UPM with just about everything. Since the coordinator will be dealing with all crewmembers, along with studio executives, agents, managers, and vendors, on some level, it is extremely helpful to be a sociable or friendly people-person when working in this position. The job is filled with responsibility yet has limited oppor-tunity to grow into another, higher position within big-budget film productions.

The production coordinator is responsible for many aspects of the production, but usually must discuss key decisions with a department head, UPM, or producer before enforcing them.

The production coordinator must be a perfectionist and a person who can handle multiple tasks while talking on the telephone and/or to live people simultaneously *all day*. I mean *all day*—how POCs find time to go to the bathroom is sometimes a feat in itself. The POC has the one job that truly touches each and every department, cast, and crew member. The string that ties the production to the post-production and studio side of the project, it is an all-encompassing position. If you are an organized workaholic who enjoys stress, then this job is for you!

Assistant Production Office Coordinator (APOC)

Being an APOC is a tough job. This person has to report directly to the overworked production coordinator to take on the production office overflow. Responsibilities are largely office/managerial for the APOC. Focusing on information distribution, the APOC works with the POC and A.D. department to ensure that all pieces of production are ready for the next day, and that any information about upcoming days is passed onto all who will be affected. Distribution of scripts, script changes, and shooting schedules to cast and crew; typing, filing, and distribution of insurance and actor contracts are only a part of the daily work the APOC manages. Typing and computer skills are key. Although there will be no tests on these skills and you are not expected to type 65 wpm, they will come in handy.

Being able to oversee the production secretary and production assistants in the department while maintaining a level of sanity in a fast-paced environment over a 12–15 hour day (again with no lunch hour) is vital. The glamour in this and in the POC position is in knowing absolutely everything there is to know about the program or film and its production and getting to know the entire crew. This position generally leads to the POC position unless the APOC decides against continuing on to another film and chooses to take his or her skills elsewhere at the end of the project.

Production Secretary

The assistant to the APOC, this job is purely secretarial in most cases. On smaller or lower-budget productions it may not even exist. Duties include filing, typing, and computer work, as well as handling incessant phone calls simultaneously. The production secretary relieves the APOC of much of the filing and distribution chores in the office. Being a production secretary is difficult because it involves multi-tasking and dealing with the crazed APOC and POC at the same time. On the plus side, it is a good stepping-stone to learn about many departments and about pre-production. Also, being a production secretary is a good place to learn to multi-task, which is crucial to many production positions, including those that lead to producing or directing. This position generally leads either to the APOC position or to post-production coordinating, if the production secretary doesn't decide to move into a different department after learning about the other available opportunities on the crew.

Office Production Assistant (Office P.A.)

Once known as gofers, now called runners, P.A.s are the entry-level position on any production. The office P.A.s go for just about anything the production office needs. Picking up film, delivering a table, shopping for the office refrigerator, delivering scripts to actors, picking up doggie biscuits for the producer's pooch—you name it. All of this running around makes owning a car imperative. If you want this job and have no car, rent one or run out and buy one. It is virtually impossible to be taken seriously for an entry-level position on a production when you have no car, although there may be exceptions to this rule in cities like New York or London, where subway transportation is known to be quicker than driving.

P.A. Stories

It was rumored on *Return to Me* that the production coordinator sent the office P.A. out to buy her tampons. I know that the coordinator has no free time, but one can never be prepared enough for a request like that unless he or she is either married or working as a P.A. In this case, the office P.A. supposedly went out for the tampons and upon his return found himself being hollered at in front of his co-workers because he bought tampons with cardboard applicators, not plastic. Ah, the life of a runner.

Being an office P.A. is the place to start if you are interested in moving into production coordinating, learning about producing, or just getting your foot in the door for any position. At the end of the day, after answering the phones in the production office and running to the set for whatever crazy task you are given, you can learn about where you'd like to work in your next position. Various runs give the office P.A. the opportunity to interact with many other departments on the crew. There is a lot to learn in this position. It sounds easy, but you have to play your cards right to advance to the position you really want. Remember, all of these jobs require long hours, offering no lunch hour and often no designated dinnertime either. Office P.A. is the most abusive of them all, but it provides an excellent training ground.

Fido

On *Party of Five*, our office P.A. was sent to an actress's house to bring the next episode's script to her. When the P.A. rang the doorbell, a rather ferocious-looking dog greeted her. With no mailbox to leave it in, she decided to slide it through the gate. Not only did the dog jump for her arm, he made the script his dinner. After several employees in the production office had to listen to lectures from the actress's agent on how important the script was and how it needed to be delivered as soon as possible, the P.A. had to make another forty-five minute trek later that evening to again be confronted with an empty house and a ferocious dog.

Set Production Assistant (Set P.A.)

Just as it sounds, these are the assistants for the shooting crew on the set. However, they do not leave the shooting location for their runs as the office P.A.s do. They are almost always found on-set or by **base camp**, situated there to carry out tasks for the 1st, 2nd, and 2nd 2nd A.D.s. Generally, the set P.A. maintains crowd control of people passing by on the street, informs the crew of changes or new activity in the schedule, takes care of actors' needs while on-set, and runs back and forth across the set to accomplish anything needed by the A.D.s.

There is a hierarchy among set P.A.s. The most senior set P.A. is referred to as the key set P.A. His or her main responsibilities are finding people (mostly actors) when the director needs them and **locking up** the set (closing the perimeter around the set to onlookers and noisemakers to keep people quiet and out of the camera's view). This person will often assist the 2nd A.D. with paperwork and tracking the cast's whereabouts throughout the day. (The entire department must be keeping an eye out for the cast throughout the day. This way when actors are needed for a scene they are located quickly and do not delay the shoot by causing people to stop what they are doing to hunt them down.)

Set P.A. is the entry-level position for someone who wants to learn about the set and the other crew positions. A person in this position generally strives to move into the 2nd 2nd A.D. position in hopes of becoming a director or producer someday, unless he or she finds another area of interest to pursue along the way.

Lock up the Whores

Kelly* was working as a set P.A. off of the New Jersey Turnpike. On one particular night they were filming at a truck stop. As filming got underway, so did the truckers' nightlife. While the cameras were rolling, the noise of cab doors being opened and shut continued. That was, until the 2nd A.D. radioed to Kelly to "lock up the whores." By asking her to "lock up," he was telling Kelly to keep the truckers and their lady friends quiet throughout the night as the camera rolled. Kelly was mortified at the thought of knocking on the cabs of the semis to ask the prostitutes to stay inside until it was safe (in terms of the filming) for them to come out. With her walkie-talkie headphones on, the hookers thought she was a cop and began to panic. Relieved not to be arrested, they complied with Kelly's request.

Assistant to the Director

Different from the assistant director positions, this is a non-union, entry-level position. As a director's personal assistant, this person can be asked to take on many responsibilities. Depending on the director, the assistant might help him or her to get organized for the day's meetings or shoots, or he or she may be asked to return

---

* Not actual name

important phone calls or pick up dry cleaning. One never knows. The more the assistant gets to know his or her director, and to make a good impression, the more responsibility he or she will likely have. On a positive note, this position will probably be privy to information that is confidential or at least unknown to most of the other crewmembers. The assistant to the director will likely interact with every department, and will have access to the set at all times. It is a wonderful introduction to the business. It is also great for networking, as this person will not only get to know the director, but will also have the opportunity to interact with other influential people just by answering important telephone calls and taking detailed messages.

Making Reservations

Allison had wonderful communication skills. She was very outgoing and very social. She quickly made friends on the crew and was enjoying her job as assistant to the director. What she hadn't expected was the love affair in which she would be required to meddle. By the end of the production, what had started as a few phone calls had turned into an organizational challenge. The director was cheating on his wife and Allison was in charge of lying to her, and of course making the hotel and/or dinner arrangements. Along with learning about storyboards, production design, and shooting schedules, she learned how to creatively arrange her director's schedule, including his itinerary for his wife, and how to plan ahead for last-minute changes to the plan (due to surprise visits from the women in his life!). At least she got to know a lot of key restaurant owners and hoteliers, which came in handy for her days off when she needed to get away.

Parking Production Assistant (Parking P.A.)

In New York City, there are parking P.A.s. These are P.A.s who covet parking spaces and spend the night (or day, depending on the shooting schedule) keeping people from taking the spaces before the production company's trucks arrive. Using orange cones, sawhorses, or just their own bodies, parking P.A.s mark off and guard their spaces. In good neighborhoods or bad, in rain or sunshine, their job is to protect the spaces for the crew to use. This job can be quite challenging when angry neighbors want to park their cars by their apartments at night, or when rowdy drunkards feel like stealing the cones. It is a job for a resilient and strong person who can defend his or her spaces.

Assistant to the Producer

Again, this assistant position is an entry-level job with endless opportunities. The producer's assistant will also be expected to answer telephone calls, take detailed messages, and complete other important tasks to help the very busy producer throughout the day. In this position, an assistant will likely be expected to have computer knowledge to work with budgetary spreadsheets and to type correspondence. Once again, this type of assistant position is a prime networking opportunity, as it deals with the producer's clients as well as each department of the crew.

CHAPTER 8

The Accounting Department—

Tracking the Money

Yes, accounting. Remember, someone has to watch the money being spent on these projects. Often, people in creative fields run away from math and business subjects. But like any workplace, production is a business. Once you work on these projects in any capacity, you will find that a few math and economic classes wouldn't hurt. If you are interested in producing, understanding accounting or budgeting is critical. However, many production accountants do not have a degree in accounting. It is a trade learned through exposure and experience on a production. The producer works very closely with the accountants to plan and maintain the budgets, both low and high.

The accounting department on a feature film or one-hour television drama generally has these five members:

1) Production Accountant

This head of the department oversees all accounting matters related to the project. The production accountant maintains the budgets of the entire production and works closely with the producers to see that each department is keeping within the perspective budget. Working with the others in the department, the production accountant generates **cost reports** and works closely with department heads, the UPM, and the producer to make certain that each cost is accounted for and provided for within the budget.

2) 1st Assistant Accountant

The production accountant's right-hand person deals with all current expenditures from each department to ensure the checking accounts are balanced and to track spending in each area as it pertains to the budget. By tracking **purchase orders** from each department, the 1st assistant accountant also provides projected expense information to the production accountant. He or she makes sure that all of the expenses (either real or estimated) from each department are constantly updated for the production accountant to use in the cost reports.

3) 2nd Assistant Accountant

The 1st assistant's right-hand person, the 2nd assistant accountant performs the department's data entry and filing duties, coding and entering all expense information from each department, as well as receiving and entering all of the accounts payable as they roll in. The 2nd assistant matches invoices to the purchase orders filled out by each department and tracks their accounting codes to the proper budgets. This person also talks to vendors and sets up accounts for every person or place that provides services or items to any department. From grocery stores for the craft service department to department stores for the wardrobe department to lumberyards for the construction department, the 2nd assistant accountant oversees and interacts with all of the crewmembers' purchases for the production.

4) Payroll

Just as it sounds, this is the person who gets the paychecks to the cast and crew by working with the studio and payroll company and processing the paperwork for the sometimes two hundred or more employees of a given project.

5) Accounting Clerk/Accounting Production Assistant

Depending on the size of the production, the accounting department may or may not have this position available. Accounting clerk is an entry-level position and is generally a good way to get an understanding of accounting and the production office functions on a film or television program. This person assists with all clerical duties, such as typing, answering phones, and running errands as they pertain to this department. Since the accounting department interacts with each department on the crew, the person in this position interacts with department heads and the job can be a way to learn about accounting or different departments within a production crew.

The accounting department is quite possibly the only department that may be fortunate enough to work only 9 AM–6 PM Monday–Friday. However, in many situations they too work on weekends or late into the weekday evenings.

☛Note—broadcast and cable networks and major studios have positions in business affairs that provide financial services to their companies as well as their in-house productions. These services may include preparing budgets, analyzing costs, and general accounting and tax services. The possibilities for using business and/or mathematics while working in a creative field such as entertainment production are endless, yet they are often overlooked.

Where is the glamour in an accounting job? Well, only the payroll person gets to handle everyone's money. Only the accounting department is able to see where the millions of dollars are actually being spent on any given show. Also, the accounting department has an overview of all of the other departments and what they are doing with their time and money on any given day. It is a wonderful opportunity to explore the other departments from the business side. As the payroll person you will often talk with the actors or their agents on how they'd like their hefty paychecks to be sent to them—not a bad perk! Besides, where else can you be an accountant and not have to wear a suit? These accountants often wear T-shirts, listen to rock music, and bring their pets to work. No pocket-protectors here!

CHAPTER 9

The Look of the Scene—The Art,

Property, & Construction Departments

ART DEPARTMENT

Broken down into various positions, the members of the art department (I.A.T.S.E. members on a union film) are:

1) Production Designer

As the head of the department, this person is responsible for the total visual design of the project. The production designer works with the director and other department heads to create the overall look of the show, including color schemes and designs for each set. This is usually a person who has studied art and has architectural drawing skills. Being accountable for the department's activities and ultimately responsible for the department's budget, the production designer relies on a strong art department to help achieve the vision of the director.

2) Art Director

It is the art director's job to make sure that the production designer's dreams for the look of the film become a reality. To achieve this, he or she breaks the script down into each location or set to budget for construction and paint labor, working closely with the production designer, UPM, and production accountant. It is the responsibility of the art director to direct the construction department, paint department, and any other trades involved (i.e. welders, special effects, etc.) to create the look that the production designer and director are envisioning. He or she also works very closely with the set decorator to keep these visions on track. Wearing many hats in this department, the art director must be able to adapt to the many responsibilities thrown in his or her direction.

3) Set Designer

A highly artistic position, set designers have drafting skills and art or architectural backgrounds. The set designer takes measurements at each location and creates the blueprints for the production designer's vision, which the construction and paint departments use for their set-building. The set designer works with other department heads to coordinate all aspects of production as they affect the set design. For instance, he or she teams with the D.P. to adjust the set design to meet lighting requirements and with the wardrobe department to use costumes to enhance the production's design. The set designer reports to the art director, who ultimately makes these decisions final.

4) Set Decorator

The set decorator also works closely (and under) the production designer on a conceptual basis to decorate each set with the appropriate furnishings in order to make it look like it should for the scene. This person breaks down each scene into what needs to be purchased or constructed for decor, creates and oversees its budget, supervises the set dressers, and works with the construction and location departments to schedule the dressing of the sets. Often this person works with local vendors to research furnishings, negotiate special discounts and rental rates, and solicit donated items. This is a very business-savvy position, as the decorator must work with many vendors to find good deals. It is also a creative position that requires an artistic and creative eye for design and detail, along with research and organizational skills. Having knowledge of furniture, art, and their history is important for the set decorator to be able to transform each set into a room or rooms from the proper era for the production's time frame. Being a set decorator also requires the ability to maintain budgets and to handle responsibility for numerous valuable pieces of furniture and appliances under fast-paced, stressful conditions.

5) Lead Man

The lead man is the set decorator's right-hand man (or woman). He or she directs the members of the swing gang (the set dressers), creating and administering their schedules, to dress the set with the decorative pieces that have been purchased by the buyer. Managing the department's budget and the daily process of prepping and striking all set dressing elements of each set, the lead man is the hands-on operational person for the department. Handling the huge job of overseeing the plan the set decorator has put into motion for each scene, the lead man plays a key role in the department.

6) Buyer

Depending on the budget, there may be no buyer or there may be several buyers. These people shop for the decorations in question. The buyer must be resourceful and creative in hunting down the items needed for set decor, keeping the budgetary constraints and color schemes or other criteria in mind. Being a buyer is a good position for people who enjoy shopping for clothes, furniture, and knickknacks—anything you could ever possibly want to buy.

7) Swing Gang (Set Dressers)

These small groups of people are the furniture movers for the show. They drive around in a van or truck and physically pick up and deliver the furniture and knickknacks that are purchased for the set. Then they deliver them to their final destination on the set. At this point they become a group of interior decorators. From table lamps to desks to Christmas trees, this branch of the art department actually "dresses" the set under the supervision of the lead man and/or set decorator to give it the final look you see in the project.

8) On-Set Dresser

The on-set dresser is on the set with the shooting crew at all times. He or she sits within earshot of the director or assistant director in case an additional piece of set dressing is needed, or an existing piece needs to be moved for any reason. (For example, if a piece of furniture is blocking a camera angle, or if an actor needs more space to move for a shot.) The on-set dresser maintains the continuity of the set during and between breaks in shooting. This person has an eye for detail and knowledge of how the set should look to fit the set designer and set decorator's plans. He or she is patiently waiting for anything that needs to be done to the set decor during the shoot.

Old Fashioned?

On a feature staged during the Depression Era, the streets were magically changed into that era. Well. . . no, it wasn't magic. It was the art department. As the camera was sixty seconds away from rolling, one art department person noticed an air conditioning unit that certainly didn't look right for the year. Instantly, the on-set dresser and swing gang were rushed to tear down the unit. The longer they took to take it down, the more the production lost from waiting with so much time and money at stake. The air conditioning unit was glued onto the building and had obviously been attached there a long time. With the help of the location manager to work out the situation with the building owners, they went to work. Carefully removing the bird's nest from the top of the air conditioner, they were able to save the scene, save the birds, and continue filming.

9) Art Department Coordinator

Much like a production secretary or APOC, this person coordinates all aspects of the art department. The art department coordinator sets up and maintains the department's offices, hires and oversees its assistants and interns, and sees to the department's daily needs. In many cases, the person in this position also deals with the copyright and clearance issues for objects and background pieces used in the decor of the sets. (In a major studio's production, the studio may have a similar position in their office to take care of these legalities.) The art department coordinator tracks the budget of the department with the art director and set decorator, distributes purchase orders, and tracks these purchases as they are delineated in the budget. A resourceful coordinator with a limited budget will have to be clever in assisting the department heads to find good deals for creating art decor to use on sets.

Another aspect of this position is often **product placement**. Dealing with major corporations, this part of the job coordinates using specific products as set decor and props in exchange for advertising by having their product brand names and/or logos prominently displayed within the scene.

This position is essential to the department but it also has its moments of grunt work, from getting the department's lunches to running all over town for a specific paint. Research and deal making, budgeting, organization, and management are the primary responsibilities of the art department coordinator. In the art department, the coordinator position is the highest level for a management or organizer type of person. This position allows you to get to know the inner workings of the art department. It is a good place to be if you like to get out to go shopping once in a while, and if you have any interest in interior design or architecture. It is also a position for people who like to work with others as a team as this person also acts as a liaison with the production office, the accounting department, and other departments while the crew works together to create the scene for the day's shoot.

Being an art department coordinator is a wonderful way to get to know the other departments and their roles. Being incredibly organized and having computer and telephone skills are necessary, but having an interest or background in art and design is not. Although having either interest or experience in art will be beneficial, you can learn about art while you are on the job; it is not a prerequisite for the position. Often the art department coordinator will make the transition from the art department to the production department, to later work as an assistant production coordinator.

Magazines

Mandy didn't know what she was getting into when she had to get clearance for magazines that would be prominently displayed in a scene of the feature film she was working on. She never imagined that one day she would be getting paid to flip through porn magazines, but there she was, looking closely at each page. She needed to research the photographs on the covers to get copyright and contact information that she could use to get permission to show the photos in the film. It really gave new meaning to researching periodicals. It was a little strange to be making the purchase. No doubt the cashier believed her story when she said she really needed these magazines for her job.

10) Art Department Production Assistant (Art Department P.A.)

Very similar to the office P.A., this person is the runner for the art department. The main difference between the two is that the art department P.A. will often find him or herself running to art-supply stores and shopping for decorating materials, which obviously the production office would not need. The rest of the job description is the same, ordering coffee, filing, managing heavy phones, copying, you get the gist. . .

PROPERTY DEPARTMENT

Consisting of the prop master and his or her assistants, this department is in charge of the set property or props. The prop master creates and oversees the budget for all props and is ultimately responsible for this department. He or she will initially read the script and meet with the director to discuss ideas for the more prominent props, and for the overall look of the props for the project. Working with the art department, the prop master must buy, rent, or create props that fit into the decorative look of the scene and the film, taking into consideration the time period, environment, and the characters' personalities. Then, he or she will formulate a budget and schedule for obtaining the props, sometimes creating them rather than purchasing or renting them from a store. Often falling under the umbrella of the art department, the property department may utilize the art department coordinator to assist with such needs as purchase orders and clearance issues. Depending on the situation, the prop department may also need to work with outside companies for product placement, in which case contracts are signed to have specific brands used for prominently displayed props in a given scene. For example, the Wilson volleyball used in *Cast Away* played a major role throughout the film.

In addition to providing the props, this department also works on them to give them the look they require for the scene. Some props are weathered to give them an antiquated or worn look; others may be painted to change their "just purchased" look or broken to fit the action taking place in the scene. In a period film or show, a prop may have to be old-style but not antiqued. In this case, an old dresser from 1942 may need to be re-stained or painted to look new for 1942, or an old book with aged binding may need to be glued and/or painted to look unused from that era. When a production takes place over an extended time period, or when a prop goes through changes during the story, the prop department must also maintain continuity, having many props adjusted to fit the aging process. Using the Wilson volleyball example, the prop department had several volleyballs to work with for various stages of its look during the film. It started out brand new in its package but took on different faces and grew different weeds in its head as the story unfolded. A film is not shot sequentially, so the prop department would have to have several volleyballs to work with, maintaining continuity by working with the script supervisor and shooting schedule to call on the appropriate volleyball look according to which scene was being shot. This is one of the many organizational tasks involved in managing the props.

In this department, "props" covers anything from a doctor's thermometer to a janitor's broom. You name it—they supply it. This is the department that had to supply and to keep track of hundreds of swords and shields for *Braveheart*, or had to keep count of the light sabers and laser guns for *Star Wars*. Speaking of guns, members of the prop department also watch to make sure that their props are used properly and safely. Members of this department must ensure proper use of guns and other weapons and work with the A.D.s to maintain safety with props on the set at all times. For action films that are very heavy on guns or knives, a special prop unit will be working on just the weapons, while another prop department works on the props for the rest of the project.

These people have all sorts of odds and ends in their trucks (or office) and are similar to the locations department because everyone comes to them for miscellaneous needs. The prop department is a place for organized people who enjoy shopping and being creative.

Happy Birthday

It was James' birthday while he was working on *While You Were Sleeping*, and we were completely unprepared to celebrate, although we had all the right intentions. So we ran to the craft service table hoping for a cake (you never know what you might find on one of those tables) but the only thing left to eat was a box of Pop Tarts. The ever-reliable prop master was able to supply us with a candle (although this candle, meant for a chandelier, was a bit large for a strawberry-frosted pastry), and we were able to gather a part of the crew to sing. It was definitely a memorable birthday party for us all. It's a good thing we could rely on the prop master, who was organized enough to come up with a candle and matches on the spot.

GREENS

Another department that falls under the art department umbrella is greens. This department provides and maintains the plants & gardens for each scene as necessary. Depending on the size of the production, greens may be just a category within the property department or it may be a large department by itself.

The greensman works with the art department to place scenic plants and flowers, grass, and trees on or in a set. In many cases this job entails using an existing garden or yard to make it fit the look needed. This may entail trampling the garden to make it a mess or enhancing and beautifying it. This job can mean re-laying sod or taking out bushes to replace them with flowerbeds. Or, it can mean providing the fern that is always in the family's kitchen on a sitcom. This job sounds simple, but remember that this fern needs to look fresh and alive for next week's taping. Like the propmaster, the greensman is responsible for managing inventory of the plants, continuity of greenery in each scene, and managing the budget for the plants and their upkeep.

Throughout the shoot, members of this department work with the production department to keep up with the schedule and to plan ahead for the various greenery needs for the production. The greensman also must work closely with the camera, grip, and electric departments to move or relocate plants as needed to make room for the camera and lighting equipment for each shot. A job for a person with a green thumb, it takes a great understanding of landscaping, plants, and their needs. This position also calls for an eye for beauty as well as the organizational skills to formulate a schedule for planting, watering, and feeding the plants.

ANIMAL DEPARTMENT

On some shows there is this pseudo-department for animals. The prop department often is responsible for finding and hiring the people for this department. Actually it's usually just the one person, the animal wrangler. This person is not necessarily a production person. This person tends to be more of an animal trainer who learns about production by the nature of the job. The animal wrangler may only train dogs, or perhaps has a wide variety of pets for the director to choose from. Animals can range from bees or insects to snakes, dogs, or monkeys. You name the animal, there is a person who has one and who makes it possible for that animal to appear in movies safely and healthily for the animal, the cast, and the crew.

CONSTRUCTION DEPARTMENT

This department consists of the carpenters, painters, and plasterers who build the set and large prop pieces for the production.

Construction Coordinator

This department head creates and manages the construction budget, schedules, and agendas for the department while overseeing what can be very large crews. The construction coordinator is one of the first crew people hired and reports to the art director on a regular basis to discuss set construction plans. After setting up accounts with vendors for materials and supplies, the construction coordinator works very closely with the art department to physically create the look envisioned by the director and production designer. For each set, he or she plans a building schedule for the duration of the production, while overseeing the construction crew and managing their time along with the money that is being spent.

A job for an organized person with a producer mentality, the construction coordinator can handle high stress and balance budgets, understands construction, and has the managerial skills to lead a large group of people. Under the construction coordinator are four key players to the department who manage its main branches.

1) The Carpenters

Leading the carpenters' crew is the general foreman. Also titled "propmakers," these people physically build the framework and walls for sets that are built on soundstages. Using blueprints from the art department, this is where the basework is formed for the drawings to come to life.

2) Painters

Headed by the lead scenic, the painters do more than apply paint to walls created by the carpenters. They have mastered the art of painting to create a specific look on these walls. Whether a wall needs to look like it is old and dirty or a floor needs to look like a marble mansion foyer, the painters work their magic to make a plain wooden set wall or floor into a painted, wallpapered, marbleized, stucco, or other decorated design.

Also in this department (if budget allows) is the scenic artist. Just as there is an on-set dresser for the art department, this person is the on-set representative for the construction department. A very highly skilled person, the scenic artist needs to have the artistic eye and know-how to be able to handle the immediate needs of the director during the shoot as they pertain to the set construction. From plastering to painting, this person wears many hats and performs each duty with precision and skill at a very fast pace. A demanding job, the scenic artist is an incredible talent. This position is hard to fill but provides a busy career for those who find success in this area.

3) Plaster Group

Led by the plaster foreman, this group of people builds the sets and large prop pieces that are made of plaster, such as rocks and stones. For example, the polar bear exhibit at a faux zoo may consist of mountains of rocks in a pool of water. These rocks are created by the plasterers and painted by the painters, all working together within the construction department.

4) Laborers

Overseen by the labor foreman, these people assist the entire department. They clean and organize the constructed sets and studio stages during construction and once the basework is complete.

These jobs are all physically demanding and necessitate art or construction skills. However, a higher education in these crafts is not necessary. Although it will undoubtedly be an asset to have a background in construction, plaster, or painting, working in this department on productions can be learned through experience. From working in the field you are able to gain knowledge and to make the contacts necessary to become part of a crew family. Often, the construction crews will find a group that works well together and will do their best to help each other to stay in this tight-knit group from project to project.

Freddy Goes to Church

It was just another ordinary day for Dave when the director of *Nightmare on Elm Street IV* came to him with his request. This director had had a dream the previous night (no, not about Freddy). He dreamed that the church [being used for the next morning's shoot] was upside down. He asked Dave, "Can we do that?"

Without delay, Dave and his crew quickly went to work. In just one night (having worked all day), they scrambled to hang the completed church set from the ceiling, although it was originally made for the floor. As the shooting crew arrived to the set at six in the morning, the paint was drying and the laborers were sweeping up the last of the sawdust. Whew, another day begins and the crew has a set on which to shoot.

Construction Auditor

Like the art department coordinator, this person oversees and coordinates elements of the construction department. Acting as an estimator, purchaser, and payroll person, this position takes on many characteristics of an accountant within the department. The construction auditor is often an excellent way for a person to break into production, although his or her interaction with the rest of the crew is minimal. It is also a way to break into production accounting. Of course, it can be a long-term career choice as well. Otherwise, the construction auditor can use knowledge learned on the job to later grow into a higher management position overseeing the department. In this case, it will be good to have knowledge and understanding of construction, materials, tools, and labor. However, as an entry-level position, these skills can be learned on the job.

CHAPTER 10

The Talent—Casting, Extras, & Stunts

CASTING DEPARTMENT

The casting department is almost always a private company or casting person hired by the production company. To get into casting you will want to also read a book specifically about casting. These people are in a different world from the filming crew. They generally have a pool of talent to pull from or a list of agents to contact to find people to match their needs. In this department you have to be able to work with actors, which is a feat in itself.

Extras Casting

Entirely separate from the casting department, extras casting is very different. Usually performed by an outside company, extras casting hires the thousands of extras (**background artists**) that fill the background in the filmed scenes. It is a very challenging department as it deals with a wide variety of personalities and egos during a frenzied workday. Along with hiring the extras, this department coordinates and oversees their scheduling, wardrobe, pay, and management of their time while they are at the location. Whether there is only one extra or five hundred extras, this department is responsible for casting all of them and managing them through the filmmaking process.

Extras Coordinator

For every ten or more extras on a feature, there is generally a coordinator hired along with the crew to manage them during the shoot. If there are less than ten, the producer may decide to forgo the cost of a coordinator, and make handling the extras another responsibility of the 2nd A.D.

Should there be hundreds of extras, there will generally be one coordinator for every hundred. In any case, the extras coordinator is on set with the shooting crew. This person is one of the first to arrive to the set (along with the locations assistant and the caterers) to check in the extras. At check-in, the coordinator makes certain that each extra has filled out paperwork and has the appropriate wardrobe (or coordinates hair, makeup, and wardrobe with those respective departments as necessary). The extras coordinator manages the needs and the flow of extras throughout the day and checks them out at **wrap**, ensuring their skins (payroll vouchers) are completed properly.

Extras casting is a department for people-friendly, ultra-organized go-getters. By interacting with other crewmembers, the production office, and the set, the position of extras coordinator provides a wonderful way to learn production and to get a foot in the door.

Inmates

Moira was interested in working in film, but had no contacts and no ideas for where to start looking. Her friend was cast as an extra and got Moira a position as an extra on a feature in town. Being resourceful and observant, Moira watched the extras coordinator on set and realized it was a position that offered the opportunity to explore film production first-hand.

After her scene was done for the day, she decided to stay to observe the rest of the shoot. One week later, Moira was calling every extras casting company in town in pursuit of a job and a new career path. Because she was persistent, she met the right people and quickly landed a job in an extras casting office, where she worked seventeen hours on her first day. Her second day of work was not your typical introduction to a job. Her second day led her to prison.

Moira was sent to Statesville Prison where Oliver Stone's crew was shooting *Natural Born Killers*. Her office? A prison cell. The extras were inmates and she was there bright and early to check them in.

Not knowing about walkie-talkies or proper set protocol, she learned her job by trial and error and by paying attention to her co-workers. Just when she thought a second day of work couldn't be scarier, the power went out and she found herself sitting in a dark prison cell full of hardened criminals. Eventually, power was restored and she only had to go through similar blackout situations two more times during the shoot. Moira made it through her second day, and the many that followed. She was able to use her first job as a catapult into a strong career in film. Now, years later, she has moved on from her prison experience and is a producer in Los Angeles.

STUNT DEPARTMENT

Stunt performers are actors who perform the physically challenging roles in the story. As stunt coordinator and performer Hugh Aodh O'Brien says of his trade, a stunt person is "like a human insurance policy for the actor." Whereas an actor cannot risk getting hurt without damaging the movie's schedule, a stunt person is specially trained for the action and takes the necessary precautions to minimize the health risks involved. But this job involves more than jumping off a building or riding in a fast car. Stunt work takes focus, passion, and learned experience.

Stunt Coordinator

If a scene requires a stunt, there will likely be a stunt coordinator to create and execute it. This person works with the director and producer to find out what image is needed and goes about telling the story in the best way—keeping the director's style and vision in mind. The stunt coordinator also works with the producer, UPM, and transportation captain (when vehicles are involved in the stunt) to make this magic happen within the allotted budget. He or she makes the plan, hires the stunt performers, and directs their actions. A stunt coordinator is well-trained in performing stunts, but is also a person with strong communication and problem-solving skills who must devise and articulate the plan for a given stunt. Being a stunt coordinator involves much planning, from assessing the purpose of the stunt to working within the budget to complete a process that (with special effects and/or creative editing) will make a scene believable.

In a few rare opportunities, stunt coordinators may also find themselves with the opportunity to direct. When **pick-up shots** are needed with a **second unit**, the stunt coordinator may be asked to direct the stunt people in order to recreate stunt scenes. For example, the editor and director may decide that a scene as it was shot isn't working well without a close-up of a gun struggle. The stunt coordinator may possibly direct a smaller unit of crew to shoot that missing piece of the scene while the main crew continues on the regular shooting schedule. In this scenario, the stunt coordinator may also be a member of the DGA and add direction of that scene to his or her directing resume. This is rare, but on occasion it does happen. More often, the stunt coordinator will work with a 2nd unit director to shoot the scene with the 2nd unit crew.

At press time, approximately 3500 people calling themselves stunt people are looking for work in L.A. Out of these, only 200–300 people are actually employed as stunt performers at a given time. It is a competitive field with few opportunities. But for adventurous people, it can be a great career. One minute you're falling out of a helicopter, the next you're flying a car 180 feet off of a bridge. If you like adventure, high-risk activities, and being in front of a camera, this could be the job for you.

CHAPTER 11

The Food—Catering &
Craft Service

CATERING DEPARTMENT

gain, the catering department is a private company hired to work with the crew. Caterers travel around the world and get to meet every member of the shooting crew and the actors. A good caterer will gain many friends on a production—he or she will learn about different likes and dislikes among the crew and work favorite foods into the meal plan. Inevitably, someone on the cast or crew will have a weird diet and will ask the caterers to add specific food items to the menu. The caterers work over fourteen hours a day. Having to be ready with breakfast when the crew arrives, the caterers are often on the set at 2:30 or 3 AM and don't leave until around 3 PM (when they first begin grocery shopping or preparing for the next day's meals). Budgeting and organizational skills also apply to this department, as the caterers must budget for their food and supplies that vary day to day depending on the size of the cast, crew, and extras for each day's shoot. Catering is a job for someone who is friendly, enjoys people, and truly loves food and cooking.

CRAFT SERVICE

This at times can be the most difficult, messy, pain-in-the-ass job on the film. Craft services started off in the early days of filming as a laborer that cleaned up around others and provided the occasional cup of coffee. It has evolved into a function that can best be described as a caterer or personal butler to the entire cast and crew, not to mention the often-hungry extras. The craft service person works within a given budget to provide a constant spread of snacks and beverages during the shoot. Most importantly, his or her role is to ensure that a constant supply of water is available to the crew at all times, and that the set area is clean of all garbage. Usually, there are many more refreshments provided than water and coffee. Craft service often sets up an over-excessive display. The crew is working long hours, in many cases under horrendous weather or staging conditions that in any other profession are probably considered illegal. As the craft service person, you want to keep the crew happy, so you provide munchies and nourishment throughout the day. Also, there are the non-union crew members who are so busy that they may never make it to lunch and rely on the craft service spread to feed them during the day (whereas union crew members have lunch stipulations in their contracts). It is a difficult budget to work with, especially when trying to be creative with food over a long period of time.

The craft service department provides coffee in the morning with an assortment of snacky breakfast foods. In order to do this job, the craft service person is one of the first people to arrive on the set. The coffee is brewed and snacks are set out just as the caterers' breakfast is being cleared, in case someone is already hungry for a bagel even though he or she just ate a full helping of pancakes and a bowl of cereal with a glass of carrot juice. But I digress.

After a few hours (coffee constantly brewing all day), the donuts turn into finger foods. On a lower-budget project, one may find an assortment of candy bars, bags of chips, and the ever-so-popular licorice sticks. With more money comes more food. Higher-budget shows may go so far as to have the craft service person setting up a grill and making spicy chicken wings or guacamole dip from scratch. Once the food and beverages are displayed, the craft service person's role shifts to cleaning as he or she must pick up after the slobs who leave their coffee cups and gum wrappers lying around the set.

Don't be surprised if the craft service person has a cappuccino maker, two coffee pots fit for an army, three coolers filled with soda cans, a blender, toaster, frying pan, mixer, and an assortment of knives—all of which are personally owned and rented with a fee charged to the filming company. The snacks continue all day, with the 30–60 minute exception for lunch. Six hours after lunch, union regulations demand that the crew wrap up for the day or else have a **second meal** (also known as dinner). If the shoot is still continuing, the producer may decide to spend the money on this meal. In this situation, the craft service person has to arrange for a last-minute dinner for up to 185 people (possibly even more) to be delivered and served at the location. If the problem is foreseen ahead of time, the caterers may return to cook it rather than have the craft service person order more food (thus creating an even longer day for the caterers).

Coffee Stories

During the remake of *Miracle on 34th Street*, we filmed the Chicago Thanksgiving Day Parade. Of course, in this case a crew would need to be willing to work on Thanksgiving. There were no craft service union members (or non-union crew members for that matter) willing to work on Thanksgiving Day, so by direction of my boss I was offered to the UPM to be the craft service person for that shoot. Have I mentioned that I don't drink coffee and before this point had only made coffee *once* in my life, failing miserably? Nonetheless, I was instructed to pick up the equipment and the food early in the morning and to be prepared to make coffee for three hundred extras and approximately thirty crewmembers. The night before the shoot was my high school reunion. Sadly, I had to leave the reunion early to run to a craft service person's house to borrow his van filled with tables and equipment for the job. I parked it (against building regulations) in front of my building since I had no alternative with no budget and no notice. By the time I reached my bed it was 2 AM, since I also stopped at a grocery store for fruit and of course. . . coffee.

At 4 AM I headed out to the opposite end of the city where our generator was stored at a National Guard Armory. I attempted to lift the generator out of its area only to find a thick padlock and chain around it. After a guard helped me cut the bolt and load the machine into the van, I ran to Dunkin' Donuts for the rest of the breakfast treats and headed to the set. Upon arrival at a corner in downtown Chicago, we quickly realized the generator was broken and I had to run back to the South Side to pick up another. Same routine and again the new generator was not working. By the time I returned with a properly functioning generator, the crew had stormed off to start their work with coffee from a local vendor and I was left alone to conquer the masses of extras. My boss had allowed my worthless assistant to hop onto a golf cart to accompany a camera crew, leaving me alone with the tasks ahead. I lugged the heavy pot down Michigan Avenue, spilling stale coffee water all over my legs while it was 40 degrees outside. To make a long story short, the three hundred extras hated the coffee and complained about it all day. Meanwhile I couldn't be both in the hotel with the extras *and* down on the street with the crew to fulfill their food needs. You can never please everybody. In my short-lived experience as craft service, I found that you can barely please anybody! That is unless you're a really great craft service person.

Oh, and by the way, I never re-hired the guy that was supposed to be my assistant that day. He disregarded his hired duties to jump onto a golf cart with the cameraman. Not a good way to impress your boss, although who knows. . . maybe he impressed the cameraman. We'll cover on-the-job etiquette in later chapters.

CHAPTER 12

The Art of Technology—

The Camera, Grip, Electric,

Sound, & Video Assist Operators

CAMERA DEPARTMENT

This is a creative, yet highly technical, department. Camera-related positions on feature films or television series are generally I.A.T.S.E. Cinematographer's Guild positions. (If we're talking about a union film, all crew members must be affiliated with a union for their trade, where applicable, in order to be employed on the film.) The camera crew members are highly trained on specialized film camera equipment. For broadcast television or corporate videos, the camera department is trained differently and takes on a different form. The following description is based on a feature film or television series camera crew. The department is comprised of:

1) Director of Photography (D.P./Cinematographer)

The D.P. works with the director, production designer, and **gaffer** (for lighting) on the look of the film. It can be said that the D.P. is the eyes of the director. He or she is in charge of all camera operations and technical aspects of lighting and photographing the project. It is the D.P.'s job to assist the director in choosing camera angles and **setups**, as well as setting the mood via lighting. This person works with the camera operator and 1st assistant camera to select camera gear. Ultimately, the D.P. instructs the camera and grip departments on where the camera is placed, how it moves, what type of film to use, and how to light the set to properly tone and color the film.

On smaller productions (depending on the budget and scope of the project) the director may also take on the role of director of photography and/or camera operator.

2) Camera Operator

This person actually operates the camera, taking direction from the D.P. Watching the scene through the viewfinder (eyepiece) of the camera, the operator is responsible for providing the shots, placing the actors and set design in the appropriate place within the frame to achieve the best look possible. To achieve this, the camera operator may work with the director, D.P., and 1st A.D. on actor blocking and the on-set dresser or propmaster for placement of décor and props in relation to the camera.

Depending on the personalities and relationship between the D.P. and the camera operator, the D.P. may concentrate his or her attention on lighting and leave blocking and setup to the operator. Or, the D.P. may prefer to oversee every detail of the operator's work. Members of each camera crew operate together differently. A cohesive crew that has been together for a while will stick together and bring each other work, finding a good system that works for them.

3) 1st Assistant Camera (1st A.C.)

The focus-puller of the camera, the 1st A.C. is the person responsible for the technical operation of the camera and lens, and the person that oversees the rest of the department once the D.P. makes the plan clear.

Responsible for having the camera in focus, the 1st A.C. plays a crucial role for the production crew. The 1st A.C. will often be seen with a tape measure, measuring the distance from the actor's marks to the camera in order to have the appropriate focus for the lens on the camera. The 1st A.C. works with the grips to ensure smooth camera placement and to make sure the lights are placed appropriately so as not to result in glare on the camera lens. As the camera is moving during the shoot, he or she is adjusting the focus on the lens accordingly.

The 1st A.C. is also an extra pair of eyes and hands for the camera operator and director of photography. He or she makes certain that the department has all of its proper gear for each shot on each shooting day. Working with A.D.s and the POC on the shooting schedule, the 1st A.C. acts as a department head in overseeing the paperwork and equipment rental for the department. The 1st A.C. also oversees the rest of the department, and is responsible for making sure all of the equipment necessary to film for the day is provided.

4) 2nd Assistant Camera (2nd A.C.)

The right-hand person to the 1st A.C., the 2nd A.C. wears many hats. This person works with the script supervisor and sound mixer to label the slate, ensuring proper scene numbers are used whenever they are referenced on film. They also work together to note which scenes are good enough to be used in the final edit, and which are to be scrapped. By being in charge of "clapping" the **sticks** at the **heads** or **tails** of every scene (the behind-the-scenes movement that is most seen in watching "making of" documentaries or shows like *Entertainment Tonight*), the 2nd A.C. is marking the point on the film and the sound reels where the picture and audio can be linked together in post production. It is a synchronization marker that is crucial in order to ensure the sound and picture will be tied together at the perfect point.

This person also works with the camera loader (when budget allows for a loader) to maintain a running total of the film bought and used on a daily basis. The 2nd A.C. turns in these **camera reports** to the APOC each night.

One of the primary functions of this position requires a lot of physical exertion. The 2nd A.C. is constantly running back and forth between the camera truck and the set with various pieces of equipment (lenses, matte boxes, etc.) as they are needed. Along with supplying the equipment to the 1st A.C. and operator, the 2nd A.C. documents the equipment and lenses used in each shot in order to keep continuity in the scenes' looks throughout the production. The 2nd A.C. gets a good workout and takes a great deal of physical abuse from the camera department on a daily basis.

5) Camera Loader

On a production with a larger budget, the 2nd A.C. has this assistant, the camera loader. This person loads and unloads the film for the camera. He or she may also be asked to manage the paperwork for the 2nd A.C., although the 2nd A.C. will still be held accountable for any mishaps. This is the entry-level position for the camera department, unless the department has an intern or production assistant. Many camera loaders and A.C.s begin by working for a camera equipment rental house in order to learn each piece of equipment.

Not a position to be taken lightly, this person is responsible for the film being shot. He or she actually handles the physical film, loading it into the camera magazines for the 1st A.C. to load onto the camera. The loader keeps records of all unexposed and exposed film, reporting daily to the production office in order to track the expenses that are being spent on this negative. It is a grunt job for this department, but a crucial one. If the film is scratched, broken, or lost, it will cost a lot of money to re-shoot, and the camera loader must not allow for these mistakes.

Lights Out

On a feature film shoot in New York, the loader was in the darkroom on the **camera truck** where, of course, it was dark. What he didn't know was that he hadn't actually entered a darkroom where the lights had been turned out. Rather, the power to the truck, which had been running on a generator, had been turned off. The generator operator is an expensive person to pay, and once the shoot was wrapped he was done for the night. He had turned off the power supply to the truck. When the power was turned back on, the lights came on in the dark room, thus exposing any film that was not yet stored away. It just goes to show how every detail matters when you're making a movie. Always check the light switch.

6) Camera Production Assistant (Camera P.A.)

Similar to a set or office P.A., this is the equivalent entry-level position in the camera department. Not every camera department has the budget to hire a production assistant. This person moves equipment back and forth from the truck for the 2nd A.C. and assists the loader in organizing the paperwork for the camera logs. It is the perfect job for getting to know the department and a place to start to one day become the camera operator or director of photography. It will help to have knowledge of camera equipment for this position.

For the camera department, sitcoms are slightly different from drama series or feature films. On a stage with three or four cameras operating simultaneously, each cameraperson needs to know his or her mark and movements for filming an entire episode in one night. On a film or drama series, there is usually only one camera operating (unless there is a stunt or special effect that needs to have several cameras aiming at once to get it all in one take).

In live broadcast television (news programs, talk shows, etc.), a camera operator will shoot with video equipment either using a tripod, dolly, or pedestal on a studio stage, or using a hand-held camera on-location. In this case the camera operator will need to move, focus, and control the camera for him or herself as opposed to having the assistants to each control separate movements of the one camera. The gear may be different but the job still requires a person with a visual eye and the ability to handle and maintain the equipment.

In any situation, the camera department is one of the few departments on the shooting crew that is constantly moving and working. Many departments have to wait for their position to be needed, whereas the camera department is always either setting up or actually filming. It is a tough and very physically demanding department.

Women in the Camera Department

More and more women are getting into the technical positions on films. Women are now often found in the camera department, although they are still in the minority and are often treated that way. Many women work as either loaders or 2nd A.C.s. In response to the men around them, these women tend to be thick-skinned and very capable. They are out to prove that women are equal. Very strong both physically and mentally, they can take it all.

By doing your job well and becoming close to your co-workers in the camera department, you can find yourself a place on a camera team. Being a part of a well-oiled machine, you ensure yourself future work as your friends and teammates will want to bring you along to their next job.

ELECTRIC DEPARTMENT

The electricians are the people who plug in the lights. Obviously there is much more to the job than that, but that is the primary function of the department. It's a hands-on, down-in-the-dirt job for people who know their way around electricity. They deal with lighting, actually manipulating the lights and making sure the correct power is supplied to the correct areas for lighting and any other type of electrical needs that may arise (air conditioning unit, fans, heaters, you name it).

Gaffer

You've seen the name in the credits and always wondered what it was; a gaffer is a head electrician. The gaffer oversees the lighting needs and works with the D.P. to create the proper lighting tone for the scene. A gaffer has knowledge of the various film stocks and how they relate to light, enabling him or her to collaborate with the D.P. on how the lighting should be set for a scene. He or she arranges for the lighting equipment package to be used through the entire shoot, and determines the manpower that will be needed in each scene according to the shooting schedule and meetings with the director, D.P., and camera department. A gaffer is often a career-long job; however, there are many gaffers who work their way up to becoming directors of photography as a next step in the chain of command.

Best Boy

The best boy electric in this department refers to the 2nd in command. This person is the lighting technician who oversees the crew of electricians each day. On a production, extra electricians will be hired on a day-to-day basis or as needed since sets and tasks change each day. The best boy also orders and keeps inventory of the lighting equipment and related supplies throughout the shoot. Making relationships and dealing with the vendors, the best boy makes certain that the proper equipment (working within the budget for the department) is available, functioning, and ready for every scene throughout the day. The best boy works with the A.D.s and the gaffer to keep on top of the schedule, watching to ensure the proper lights and gels are standing by as needed.

The gaffer and the best boy are full-time positions for the duration of the project, as they are in charge of the department. The length of time for a regular electrician to be on a production varies depending on the electrical demands of the shoot. Being an electrician on a production is a difficult position in that each location has different electrical situations and different obstacles to work around. With all that juice it's a dangerous job.

Rain Shower

It started to rain as Danny stood atop a **condor** overlooking the conservatory in the park during a shoot for *Sable*. Working with the electric department on his first day on a movie set, he found himself holding onto a gigantic light, trying to keep it steady while the steady rain turned into a pouring thundershower. Productions generally do not seek shelter from rain unless lightning is spotted, and although the sky looked menacing, the only electricity around was the current pulsing through the production equipment. Making matters worse, the powerful wind was relentless. The director was getting more restless with each minute, and screamed out for someone to steady the light. All eyes focused on Danny (well, as many eyes as could see him through the downpour), pleading with him silently to hold the light down. The problem was that he was holding the light perfectly steady, despite the heavy gusts of cold wind. It was the condor that was waving back and forth! Danny shouted out to them that he was in fact holding the light down, along with a few words I must censor. Eventually, the lightning did force the production crew to run for shelter, but not until Danny was thoroughly soaked. Fortunately, he made it through the shoot in the rain, as did the light. Once he was down on stable (muddy) ground, Danny was reminded that he had been using a radio frequency that the whole crew was listening to when he had shouted vulgarities to his boss about holding the electrical equipment steady. Oops.

GRIP DEPARTMENT

This is the other mystery title people wonder about when watching film credits. Working with the director of photography and the electricians, the grips rig the light and camera supporting equipment. They place the lights, the light stands, and the different pieces used for shading, masking, and diffusing the lights (such as fabric to tape over windows for hiding sunlight). Basically, they move any lighting equipment that isn't plugged into an outlet. They also rig camera equipment to various pieces other than the standard tripod, such as a moving **dolly** or the side of a car. Although the grips do not deal with actual electricity, many often work on other projects as electricians, and vice versa (more often the case on smaller projects in smaller markets). They are often knowledgeable about both positions. Grips and electricians alike are added on to crews for bigger locations on an as-needed basis.

Like in the electric department, there is a key grip (head grip) and a best boy grip (2nd in command). Again, the best boy works with vendors to coordinate the various pieces of equipment needed to rig lighting or camera equipment for each shooting day. The people in these positions work with the director of photography, camera, and electric departments to expedite camera placement and lighting.

The Mirror

During *Freedom Blues*, Kim was a jack-of-all-trades. She scheduled, ran errands, and coordinated the shoots. It was a low-budget independent film and many departments' responsibilities overlapped. One of hers was to act as a grip by holding a mirror. It sounds easy but this was not your ordinary mirror, and it wasn't hanging in an ordinary place. Kim had to hold a large mirror over a bed so that the camera could get the proper angle for the love scene being portrayed. Not only was she holding a mirror next to a love scene, she was hovering over it. She had to precariously perch over the couple while standing on the very edges of the bed frame with the mirror in hand. Trying not to shake or move while the camera was focused on the object in her hand, Kim thought about her life and what a strange series of events it has been for her thus far. If her friends could see her now.

The dolly grip specifically deals with the dolly used for moving camera shots. Working with the camera operator on timing and positioning, the dolly grip pushes the dolly while the camera is rolling on a scene.

The title of rigging grip applies to the grips who rig the equipment before the shooting crew arrives. For very large-scale sets the rigging grips may arrive a full day ahead of the shooting crew to set up lighting grids on the ceiling or any number of devices to prepare for the shoot.

The number of grip positions on a project, like electricians, can vary day-to-day. In either department, these are job positions meant for the true freelancer.

Hanging by a Rope

The rigging grips did not realize what they were in for when they came to work at the National Guard Armory for *Baby's Day Out*. An old building used to store military vehicles and to act as a training ground for the National Guard, it was not usually used for filming a set of this magnitude. As a matter of fact, at the time this set was considered to be the largest indoor set ever created. The scene called for a construction site, and the production company brought in steel welders to create the first five stories of a steel-framed building. It was up to the riggers to hang from ropes and ceiling rafters to rig the lighting equipment and backdrops from the high ceiling. In order to do so we brought in cranes and lifts to bring them up and down throughout the day. As the armory was not equipped for exhaust fumes, our production materials created quite a mess. At the end of every day, the grips would come down from their perches covered with dirt. Their faces looked like those of cartoon characters after a bomb has exploded—entirely black except for the whites of their eyes. Our locations department did everything we could to find and situate large fans in the building, but the armory was so gigantic that they barely made a dent in the fumes. Ah, but the show must go on. Aside from most of us being tested for carbon monoxide poisoning, we carried on as if this was normal. Such is the life of a rigging grip.

SOUND DEPARTMENT

This department consists of the following positions:

1) Sound Mixer

As the head of this department, the sound mixer is ultimately in charge and responsible for all of the production sound being recorded. This is a technical position that requires knowledge of all the equipment necessary to accurately record the sound dialogue and effects. In rain, snow, high winds, or near heavy traffic (airports are hell), this person needs to be able to record the actors' lines clearly with no interference. He or she is also responsible for maintaining continuity with background sound, which can be difficult under extreme weather conditions. The sound mixer does everything in his or her power to get the audio for each scene as perfect as possible so that extra work does not have to be done in post production to hide audio problems. Aside from the dialogue being spoken in a scene, the mixer will often record ambient sound or wild track. In many cases, special sounds such as a school bell or a special clinking noise used in a scene (sounds that may be difficult to reproduce later) will be recorded separately. These sounds are for the editors to use during the post-production process.

Considered to be both a creative and technical job, the sound mixer must also be an organized person. The mixer needs to take copious notes of what was recorded to refer back to when a sound or piece of dialogue is needed by the director or editor at a moment's notice. With a keen eye for detail and an understanding of the entire production process, the sound mixer is always one step ahead of the director, recording the sounds and dialogue that are needed to make the scene complete.

2) Boom Operator

The boom operator is the tall, strong-armed person who holds the **boom microphone** in front of the actors while dialogue is occurring in a scene. This job takes not only sturdy arms, but also patience and incredible resilience to stay alert during a long day of shooting. The boom operator has to know the scene and the actors' cues, lines, and personalities. Moving the microphone back and forth between bodies on cue with actors who improvise or a director who changes his mind on staging or dialogue can be very challenging. As the sound department's on-set eyes and ears, the boom operator helps to inform the mixer about any additional sounds that will be needed as well as any potential audio problems within a scene. A good boom operator can stay on top of these variables to assist the mixer in pulling off clean dialogue recording with no glitches.

Another aspect to being a boom operator is working with the camera, grip, electric, and art departments to be able to accurately hold the mic out of the camera frame without tripping over light stands (or without being burned or scraped by lights), cables, or pieces of set decoration. Knowing camera movements, lenses, and actors or extras movements is all a part of this challenging job.

3) Utility Sound and Cable Person

This person works with the sound mixer and boom operator to properly hook up all equipment and to make sure cables are not seen on camera, in the way of others, or pulling on the microphones if the action is moving. The third person of the sound crew, the utility sound must have a working knowledge of all of the sound gear and must be able to take over the mixing board or boom mic if assistance should be needed. Often an additional boom mic will be necessary for the scene, in which case the utility sound will step in to man it. This person also maintains the equipment and needs to know how to fix it under pressure when it breaks down during a shoot. The first person from the department on the set in the morning, the utility sound preps the equipment for the day and, of course, breaks it down and packs it at wrap. This cableperson usually moves up to boom operator and aims to become a sound mixer in the future.

Video Assist

On a shoot that has any money, you will likely find a video assist operator (or two) set up next to the camera. This highly technical position provides the equipment and service to allow the director to see the results of the shoot as it is happening.

What began as a simple hook-up of a video camera to a monitor adjacent to the film camera has evolved over the years into a computerized mini movie station on the set. The video assist provides the equipment and expertise to shoot the scene as the cinematographer sees it through the camera. With the technology available today, they cannot only play back onto a monitor what was shot, but can also quickly edit it together with previously shot scenes. The director is then able to test the scene to see if the footage will work as planned once the film is processed and edited together. This saves money in unnecessary re-shoots and gives the director the opportunity to add any angles that may have been overlooked. The equipment may also allow the operator to store all of the shots for future reference, which comes in handy for continuity debates and during post production, when the editor and director may want to develop a scene chosen during the shooting process.

The director works very closely with the video assist operator. It can be a very demanding job, dealing with a very stressful environment. Having an agreeable personality will be helpful in this position. Having a good relationship with the director will often be a deciding factor in getting the job on a production.

The video assist operator will either rent his or her personal equipment to the production company or will work for another company that is hired as a package by the producer. The best way to learn this position is by being an assistant and learning it on the job.

CHAPTER 13

The Characters' Looks—Hair,

Makeup, & Wardrobe Departments

HAIR AND MAKEUP DEPARTMENT

Just as it sounds, these are the people who take care of the actor's hairstyling and makeup needs for the shoot. On a union production there is generally a department head for hair and a department head for makeup, and each has an assistant. Often the department head will want to be responsible for the star's hair or makeup, while the assistant will do some of the secondary actors, although that is up to the department (and in some cases, the actor) to decide. For a non-union production (and union productions that make special arrangements), the makeup and hairstyles are often combined into one person's duties. On many occasions, actors have hair or makeup artists they prefer to work with, which will determine staffing in this department. Additional people are brought on for scenes with more actors if necessary. A body makeup artist will be on hand for scenes involving full or partial nudity. Hair and makeup people have to deal with people up close (which is always interesting when encountering an actor who just ate an onion bagel or garlic bread). During cold and flu season when noses are running, the makeup artisst are there to make that red nose look its normal tone, and during the summer they are there to take away that T-shirt tan line. Not a job for a germophobe who doesn't like to touch or be touched, the hair and makeup artists are very hands-on.

Lickable Art

On the game show *Big Deal*, contestants were chosen from the audience to do out-rageous things for money and prizes. Among other things, one favorite was to cover people in honey and put them in a wind machine with dollar bills. They would win whatever money stuck to their bodies. Every day was different, and you never knew what the writers were going to come up with next. One day Gabrielle, the makeup artist, was wondering if maybe she should have taken some culinary classes in college. They had chosen a couple out of the audience to play an unusual game. The male contestant stripped down to his shorts, and Gabrielle's department covered him with temporary tattoos. Similar to the children's game "Memory," this man's wife was given ten seconds to see his body tattoos and to try to remember as many as she could. They then took him backstage and went to work on phase two. Now Gabrielle was cover-ing each tattoo with circles made of cake frosting, white with a cherry-flavored frosting on top as if it were a sundae. Once all of the tattoos were covered in the frost-ing, Gabrielle was charged with the job of painting the rest of his body in chocolate frosting. Covered in protective clothing and latex gloves, she went to work with a spatula and her Betty Crocker's container, creating a sticky mess. The wife's job was to lick the white circles off to reveal the tattoos, hoping to match alike symbols to win the prize. At least the wife was in charge of clean up this time, not Gabrielle!

Makeup can also include special effects makeup such as adding a scar to a cheek-bone, making an actor age before your eyes, or turning a teenager into a zombie. For special effects makeup, an artist will put in very long hours and play an even more integral role in the shoot. Usually for very big special effects work like in horror movies, or makeup to age a character, a special effects makeup artist will be brought in to work only on this makeup and not the regular everyday makeup that is used on other characters. It is a specialized position.

The makeup artist will work with the camera and electric departments to ensure a realistic on-camera look for the actor. Familiar with the various looks that different types of film will give to an image, the makeup artist will need to have conversations with the director and the D.P. to plan the actors' looks for the project. On-camera an actor's makeup will look a lot different than it does under natural or fluorescent lights backstage. A good makeup artist will know how this makeup will look on-camera, and will do his or her best to keep the actor calm in the chair beforehand. Sometimes having a mirror handy before the shoot will not help a situation, as actors will panic and fear that they will look horrible on-screen. It is the hair and makeup artists' job to maintain calm and understanding, and to make the actors look as wonderful as pos-sible on-screen, even when off-screen they look like they haven't slept all night.

Being the first department to start up in the morning, this group can put in long hours and is sometimes among the last to leave for the day. Although doing this work would seem to be a quick job (depending on the number of actors and the type of hairdo or makeup needed), these people are required to be there for all of the shooting hours for scene changes, touch-ups, and any look-based problems that come up during the day. For special effects makeup, the artist will usually need to stay after wrap to assist the actor in taking off the makeup, which can take just as long as putting it on, sometimes hours.

It helps to get along well with high-maintenance actors when you work in production, especially in the field of hair and makeup. Having patience and ultimately befriending an actor can lead to many future jobs down the road. Actors rely on hair and makeup artists to make them look good to the masses. When they find an artist they like, they often stay loyal to that artist and bring him or her onto productions as a part of their negotiations with the production company.

Although some hair and makeup artists are licensed cosmetologists, trained in hair salons, or trained in industry makeup application classes, there are many who learn by training with artists on sets. Just as a director may begin as a production assistant who worked his way up, a makeup artist may begin as an intern or assistant who learns from a mentor and from hands-on training.

WARDROBE (COSTUME) DEPARTMENT

Exactly what it sounds like, this department plans and provides for all costumes on the production. This includes every single actor on the screen in a given scene. The department head will read the script and discuss the wardrobe for each key character with the director early on in the planning. He or she will then hire assistants and most likely seamstresses to help carry out the plan.

On a show that is taking place in the current time period, a lot of effort is made to keep in fashion and also to be consistent with the characters and the story in the script. First, the actors' measurements are taken in an initial fitting. With this information, a buyer will head to the malls to go on a shopping spree that would make any shop-a-holic jealous with envy. For instance, a network television series spends hundreds, if not thousands, of dollars per week at high-end department stores like Bloomingdale's to make sure that even the small characters who only appear in one scene are keeping with the show's image of trendy yet simple outfits. This department will also have clothes on hand for extras unless there is a crowd scene, in which case the extras will be asked beforehand to come with a few options of a certain type of dress. In that case the wardrobe department will inspect the extras and make minor changes to their appearance when necessary. The seamstress comes in handy here and also in fitting the wardrobe for the cast.

Once the outfits are purchased, the wardrobe department will go to work to adjust their sizes to fit the actors. They will also treat the outfits to make them appropriate for the scene. For instance, they may wash and rewash jeans to make them look worn, put stains onto a shirt for a slob character, or dye shoes to match a dress. The scenarios are endless. A lot of work goes into creating a character's look and keeping it realistic to the time period, plot, and personalities within the story being told.

The wardrobe department will likely have a larger staff of people, including more seamstresses, if the production takes place in a different time period. For instance, in a period film such as *Shakespeare in Love*, the wardrobe department will have to re-create clothing from that time period, which obviously requires more staff and materials, not to mention money and a lot of planning.

As in any department, this one may also have P.A.s or runners. A wardrobe P.A. will undoubtedly run to fabric and clothing stores as well as the usual lunch and coffee runs or stray errands that come with the title. The wardrobe P.A. will also help with keeping inventory of clothing, washing, ironing, and hanging the pieces on racks as necessary. Knowledge of clothing (and how to do laundry) will come in handy in this position. This department is good for people interested in fashion and in the clothing business. It is a plus if you enjoy shopping and can get along with high-maintenance actors.

CHAPTER 14

The Where—Location &

Transportation Departments

LOCATIONS DEPARTMENT

This group generally consists of the most tired and stressed-out people on the crew when the project is mostly shot on-location. It is a very unique department in that the staff's day-to-day activities are constantly changing and they have a sort of freedom in coming and going on their own schedule. They interact with the neighborhoods and everyday people, which can be nicer than reporting to an office cubicle every day, and they have an opportunity to discover unique and fun places in a given city.

These people are responsible for the actual locations where filming is taking place. The process begins several months before the shoot, sometimes even up to a year prior. The department is made up of a location manager, location assistants, and scouts, depending on the size of the project. The location manager will budget for each location that will be needed for filming according to the script, having discussed what they are to look like with the director. He or she will "scout" each location for the director to see, adding on additional scouts to assist on bigger productions. To find these locations, the scout will simply drive around looking. An experienced scout will have an idea of where to start hunting before getting into the car. Once a location is found, the scout takes pictures of it in a specific way that allows the picture to look almost panoramic upon development. Actually, it is comprised of several pictures, which are later pasted together like a jigsaw puzzle onto a folder for the director to flip through. Several options are given, and often the scout will have to continue searching over and over again until the director is happy. While taking pictures the scout will contact the owner of the property to ask permission to film there, which is often more difficult than it should be. (Think about how you would react if a stranger approached you and asked if you would allow a hundred other strangers into your house to film a movie. You'd probably want to call the police.)

For each location chosen, arrangements for locations adjacent or nearby to the shooting site will need to be made for **crew lunch** and **extras holding** areas. Therefore, scouting continues as the locations department searches the area and signs contracts for these important places. In addition, the locations department works with the neighbors living and working near each shooting location to let them know about the shoot and how it will affect them. The department also works with these neighbors to change the outward appearance of their property if necessary for wide camera angles where their property is also seen even though they are not the camera's primary focus. For instance, if a scene is filming outside of a restaurant, the dry cleaners next door to that restaurant will be seen in the shot. Therefore, the dry cleaner may be asked to keep his store lights on and to have the door ajar, as if the shop was in fact open.

Once the locations are chosen and contracts with the owners are signed, the locations department is responsible for:

1) Managing the budget for each location being used throughout the entire shoot.
2) Ensuring that parking lots or allotted spaces are clear for the crew vehicles and production trucks before they arrive for the day.
3) Hiring and managing security for the location and/or parking and stage areas (in some cities).
4) Making the maps to direct the crewmembers to the locations.
5) Hanging signs (directional arrows) on the street for those crew members who inevitably can't read maps and will get lost even though they've lived in this city their whole lives.
6) Making certain that the crewmembers do not trash the location and that it is left cleaner than it was found when the crew arrived.
7) Following up with the location owner on any bills for damage and to make sure it was a pleasant experience for them for future filming possibilities.
8) Obtaining permits from the city as necessary for parking on city streets, using city police officers or other workers from other departments, blocking off streets, and so on.
9) Coordinating with the city for any re-routing of traffic, turning on and off street lamps, or taking care of other issues involving public property.

Don't forget that the location manager and/or assistant will want to use these neighborhoods and these locations on future films, so they need to make sure that local people are happy and willing to do this again. Often the locations department works closely with the city's film commission to ensure that the city and its residents are treated properly, and that the proper city permits are acquired. Since members of this department coordinate all of the parking and logistical set-ups on-site, they need to be there before the caterers to make sure the catering truck is parked in the right place. Therefore, someone from the locations department is on the set sometimes as early as 2 AM.

Now remember, the locations department oversees the location throughout the shoot and locations people have to be there to make sure it's left nice and neat at the end of the day. That means staying an hour after wrap while the crew puts their equipment away. Sometimes it can mean working for more than eighteen hours a day. Locations people don't sleep much. While one person is running the set (being the point-person on the set for questions or problems that deal with the physical location), other people in the department are either preparing for tomorrow's location or continuing to scout for locations being used later on in the schedule. Often this preparation work and scouting continues on the weekends or during what is a day off for the rest of the crew. Good locations people who take their jobs seriously will not take most of their weekends off, and many will not get paid at all for their overtime.

Sleepless in Chicago

We're filming on Lincoln Avenue, a busy street. It's a night shoot, therefore there are rigging grips who set up in the non-shooting hours to have the lighting ready for the evening. They arrive at 8 AM with me there to work with them as a location assistant. They are putting color gels over the street lamps and hanging equipment on rooftops that will affect the lighting. Meanwhile, the set dressers are decorating the street to look like winter, with Christmas décor, banners, and so on.

I am there to interact with storeowners and city workers, to make sure the process happens smoothly, and to take care of any number of situations that may arise at the location. The shooting crew arrives at 2 PM to start their day, which means they'll be here until at least 2 AM, but the way this shoot has been going it's more likely going to be 4 or 5 in the morning before anyone leaves.

My "shift" is supposed to end at 8 PM but there are just not enough people to help with all of the issues that have come up and I stay. Next thing I know, it is 2 AM and I've been here seventeen hours. I leave for my home in the suburbs and turn around at 7 AM to make my way back to join the rigging grips and the set dressers to set up for the next day. Since we went late yesterday, the crew doesn't arrive until 3 PM today and once again are not expected to complete the scene before sunrise. Even though I should leave at 8 PM, I stay until 2 AM and then side-track to the office with the hopes of finishing some paperwork for an hour before heading home. I am kind of tired, but what the heck.

It's Wednesday and I am once again joining the gang at 8 AM, only this time things are really crazy and I find myself still there at 4 AM on Thursday—I am there for twenty hours. I head home, first stopping at the office to complete more paperwork, only to turn around again at 7 AM to meet the good ol' gang at the lampposts. The production secretary, who stays in the office overnight (for office stuff that comes up during the shoot) thinks I'm losing my mind.

Thursday, is it Thursday? I should leave at 8 PM but in fact I never leave. By the time they wrap, the sun is rising and I have paperwork to do, and I have to be back here in two hours anyway. So I stay. After some point you're not tired anymore, you get your second wind, right? It's raining and during the chaos I see my friend Larry, who has come in from Boston for the weekend to visit me. I've had to ask my family and friends to entertain him for me since there are no days off for me this week. Fortunately for me, he smiles and seems to understand.

It's Friday now; we're filming at night on a busy street. Did I mention it's a Friday night shoot? There are bars on this street. Are you with me? Among the thousand other things I'm asked to do, I am asked to help the P.A.s **lock up the set** since there are so many streets to cover and not enough people to cover them. On any other day I would-n't mind, but around 4 AM (you didn't think I'd leave at 8 PM, did you?) there are some really drunk locals heading home, and they're ready to puke on me. I manage to contain them, although one drunken woman doesn't listen, and if I grab her I'll be covered in vomit. I turn around to stop another person from crossing and the next thing I know, the drunk woman has crossed the street and ruined the shot. I had no choice but to watch her go. I couldn't stop her. Meanwhile, a different drunk woman is screaming vulgarities at my co-worker, so I guess we're all having the same kind of day.

I leave at. . . well, I don't know what time it is but it's been a twenty-hour day so you do the math. I sleep, I think. Then I go to the next location. It's a daytime thing and we're in a quiet museum. All I know is that I'm with the sheriff of the suburb and I think I just fell asleep mid-sentence, while I was the one doing the talking. That's not good. I get into a fight with a co-worker (the one who was being screamed at on the street next to me last night); she's just as tired as I am. I'm not sure what the fight is really about. All I know is that we're screaming at each other. I get off work with the rest of the crew at 9 PM. I drive home in a daze. I actually use my handy cell phone that I got "for emergencies" to try to return a call to my friend in New York who called me three days ago and thinks I am blowing him off. While we're talking I realize I'm driving in the wrong direction. After three tries and three exit ramps, I make it home. I sleep. . . until 5 AM when it's time to go to work.

The locations department is also known for having to come up with the most bizarre needs for the crew. Because, in the mind of a crew member, when there is a question, you should ask the locations department; after all, we're *on-location,* right? So it is not unusual to hear this conversation over the walkie-talkie:

"Locations, come in."

"Go for locations."

"Yeah, Mitch, we need a heat lamp over here."

Often this conversation ends with Mitch, the location assistant, looking perplexed at why he is being asked to do this task, and where to begin to solve the problem. Somehow Mitch will miraculously find a heat lamp within ten minutes. It is a job for gifted and resourceful people, and for mentally strong people who never get thanked for the miracle heat lamp, or the perfect location.

Location managing and scouting are for people who like to take photographs and are more comfortable driving around or touring the neighborhood than sitting behind a desk. Working in locations is a great way to learn about the other departments, as the locations department interacts with every department head during the planning process, and with the rest of the crew while on-location. It is also a unique way to get to know the producers and directors during prepping or scouting the locations. Working in the locations department also means working with local businesses. These people spend much time on the streets. This department introduces you to new restaurants, clubs, museums, and the many different, colorful people that run and visit them. It also provides a wonderful opportunity to see some beautiful sunrises and sunsets. Just remember that this is not a position for someone who has many personal time commitments; there will be no time for that while you're working. This job is a true test to see how strong your friendships are (and how long your car can last). If they can survive your long hours, they are truly your friends.

TRANSPORTATION DEPARTMENT

Consisting of the transportation captain, the transportation coordinator, and drivers (generally all members of the Teamster's Union), this department provides all transportation required for the production to flow properly. For film and video production, transportation includes vans to shuttle talent or crew to the set, trucks for carrying equipment to the set, trailers for the talent to stay in throughout the day, vans to run errands or to pick up and deliver film or equipment whenever necessary, and the like. This department also finds and coordinates picture cars (cars from the time period of the story, which are seen in the foreground or background of any scene). Not only do they provide the vehicles, they drive them, maintain them, and clean them inside and out. A typical driver will work from at least one or two hours before the crew arrives until one or two hours after wrap. Similar to the locations department, the transportation department is early to arrive and the very last to leave.

1) Transportation Coordinator

The transportation coordinator begins early in the pre-production process (6–8 weeks prior to the time shooting commences, on average) to set up accounts and deals for truck rental, fuel, and other related items with vendors. Working with the director, producer, UPM, and A.D.s, the transportation coordinator maintains the budget for the department and creates the plan for all transportation and vehicle needs according to the span of the project.

Once the number and type of vehicles are assessed, the coordinator will hire crew to run them. Typically hiring one person per vehicle, the coordinator does his or her best to match the appropriate person to each one, taking into consideration personality traits and what the job for that vehicle will require. For instance, one driver will be assigned to the trailer for the lead actor, whereas another driver will be making runs to and from the production office all day. Each situation will put the driver in different scenarios, which requires a person who gets along and works well with cast and crew. The transportation coordinator wants the drivers to get along well with the people interacting with them all day to ensure a smooth-running production.

Once the drivers are assigned and the locations have been chosen, the coordinator will map out the best route to get the trucks from their evening parking places to the set, planning their departure time to ensure that they will be set up or at their destinations at the appropriate time prior to the crew call. He or she will go on the **tech scout** during pre-production to look at the parking situation for the trucks and to assess the best ways to park them, back them into their spaces, and to plan for them to be level when the ground is not.

2) Transportation Captain

The transportation captain starts working on the project after the coordinator, closer to when shooting actually begins. Following direction and planning from the coordinator, the transportation captain runs the day-to-day operations of the department for the duration of the shoot. Coordinating **company moves**, assigning drivers to specific runs or pick-ups, and overseeing the schedule during the shooting day, the transportation captain works with the coordinator and all department heads to assure smooth work-flow for all production matters relating to transportation and vehicles.

Depending on the production design and the era of the film, the transportation captain will also need to budget for and coordinate the picture cars. On a sitcom that is always filmed on stage, this won't be a difficult issue, if it is an issue at all. However, on a feature film taking place on a street anywhere in the world, the captain must ensure that the cars seen in the background of the shot are appropriate and there when needed. This budget will include drivers for the picture cars, as well as paint or materials like decals to change the look of the vehicles for the scene.

Another aspect of transportation for the captain to budget and plan for are any vehicles used in stunts. When a car is blown up, the transportation department provides that car and budgets for the car and its damage costs.

The transportation captain oversees the department and works with the other department heads to plan for all transportation-related equipment and drivers for each shooting day of the production. It is a massive job that requires attention to detail, organizational skills, multi-tasking, and the ability to work well with others.

The duties of the transportation captain and coordinator will vary depending on their relationship to one another and the scope of the project. Where one coordinator may delegate all of the paperwork to the captain, another may prefer to do it alone. On many large-scale productions there will be a co-captain and possibly one or two picture car coordinators to alleviate some of the overflow from the captain.

It is important not to underestimate the significance of this department. Without a person to coordinate all of the transportation issues and to provide such transportation, there would be no equipment or talent on-set to make the movie. Drivers also get to know many cast and crewmembers, depending on which vehicle they drive. It can be a great opportunity to get to know how the other departments work and to get to know the people running them. Within the transportation department many people will remain as drivers for a very long time, unless they move up in responsibility to become a captain or eventually a coordinator. Drivers may work on trade shows or special events if film productions are not readily available. This may be the case in a smaller town that does not always have a steady flow of features or television programs passing through.

On a non-union or low-budget project, production assistants will often double as drivers in the transportation department, most often driving cube vans or small trucks. In this case, it helps to have truck-driving knowledge on your resume!

CHAPTER 15

The Rest of the Crew—

Miscellaneous Trades

SET MEDIC

The set medic is a medical person, usually an EMT, sometimes a registered nurse, who chooses the leisure world of the movies over the insane hospital E.R. In some cases this person works on films during off-hours or as a second source of income. The set medic is on-site at all times during the shoot in case a crewmember has an emergency medical problem, or more likely an accident on the set. The medic sits a lot. He or she sits on the sidelines waiting for someone to get hurt. With the exception of the hypochondriac crewmember, the medic is hopefully only busy during the cold and flu season. During this time, he or she is constantly pumping out vitamins or Echinacea (or taking the temperatures of crew members who are truly sick but also fear losing their jobs so they never go home or call in sick). Sadly, there are the occasional accidents that send a crewmember to the hospital and require a little more attention from the medic. We all hope that the medic has very little to do, because that means everyone is safe and healthy.

PUBLICITY DEPARTMENT

1) Unit Publicist

This is a person who works in publicity, whether it is for film, magazines, or sporting events. This person is hired to work with the producers for various reasons. In a big-name celebrity movie, this person may coordinate constant photograph sessions for photos to be used later in magazine articles. Similarly, the unit publicist organizes all of the publicity stunts and interviews related to the movie for the actors involved. Heavily involved in the publicity, this person deals with the actors, managers, agents, producers, director, and studio to carry through the grand plan for promotions. Depending on the scope of the project, publicity may be coordinated through the studio rather than by hiring a freelance person. In that case the job is a full-time, corporate position within that studio or network.

2) Still Photographer

This person takes publicity photos during the daily shoots. An experienced photographer is personable and able to handle actors' mood swings. The still photographer works with the unit publicist and the A.D.s to coordinate the appropriate time to take pictures of actors or activity on the set.

SPECIAL EFFECTS (SFX)

Usually these people run their own special effects business, consisting of explosives, rain machines, snow and fog machines, and/or any other special effect you can think of. SFX people or their companies are hired by the producers either for a specific scene or possibly for the duration of the project, depending on the effects needed. Generally these people like to tinker with toys. They are willing to get dirty to make movie magic. The SFX coordinator will break down the scenes into what effects are needed, working with the director to establish the best tricks for the scene. Collaborating with the production coordinator, A.D.s, and art department, the SFX people strive to make their effects fit into the scheduling and the continuity of the scenes. Also, they will work within the budget created during pre-production to purchase or rent equipment that makes the effects possible. If you are an organized team player and enjoy making models and blowing them up, check your local listings to see if a special effects company exists in your area—this job may be for you!

Happy New Year

It was a cold, typical Chicago February night. The only thing missing was snow. It was unlucky for us, because the scene called for a steady snowfall. We were shooting a New Year's Eve scene for *The Hudsucker Proxy* where partygoers were to run through the financial district of Chicago (cleverly disguised as New York) during a snow shower. To make it happen, the special effects crew was brought in to create the snow. There are several ways to create snow; this crew chose to use a type of shredded paper-like material. We closed down the entire financial district to cars and pedestrians for two consecutive nights and obtained special permission from the Federal Reserve (among other prominent buildings) to have the lights left on in the evenings in order to enhance the mood lighting and realness in the scene. In order to shut down such a large and prominent area in the city, we had rules and restrictions to obey during the shoot, one of which was to be completely open to traffic and out of the way by rush hour at 6:30 AM. With the rules in mind, and the actors, cameras, and lights in place, we filmed the scene. The snow was very realistic looking on-camera and the scene turned out beautifully. What did not turn out beautifully, however, was the financial district. At the end of the shoot each night, there were piles and piles of tiny shredded pieces of paper up and down the streets and sidewalks, in alleyways and doorsteps. Always needing to leave a location cleaner and looking better than it was found, the locations department had to see that the mess was disposed of by the time rush hour began. So every morning at 5:30 AM (having worked all night), a handful of us along with a few hired helpers swept the streets of Chicago using brooms, dustpans, and garbage bags to clean up the snow. It seemed strange to shovel snow with a broom, but on the bright side I don't think the streets of the Financial District will ever be that clean again.

STUDIO TEACHER

The studio teacher is a licensed teacher who works on set only when there are actors who are minors working that day. This person is strictly there to teach the child actors while they are waiting to film their scenes. The teacher may change daily or weekly, depending on the age of the children on a given day of shooting. A teacher by trade, this person is required to have elementary and secondary school credentials. The rules for eligibility may vary for productions, depending on state regulations and child labor laws for the state in which the filming is taking place. The studio teacher is a child advocate, looking out for his or her pupils. The teacher works with the 2nd A.D. to make certain that all child labor laws are followed. He or she is knowledge-able about production from having worked around sets with child actors, but is not a production crew person by trade.

Child actors tend to be more mature than others in their age group since they are constantly in an adult environment and not in a public classroom setting. Their maturity levels may be high, but so might be their ego levels. A studio teacher has a unique student body to guide.

☛Note—Sometimes the kids are the easy part of this job, and the parents cause undue stress. Working with bossy parental managers is a skill in itself, requiring patience and a flair for friendliness.

CHAPTER 16

The End of the Chain—

The Post Production Department

Post production deals with developing, editing, adding music, and everything else that goes along with piecing the show together after it's been shot. This department is made up of producers and editors that work with the show's other producers and the director to make the program or film complete. On feature films and television series, this department is usually based in Los Angeles or possibly New York. Hollywood types have not learned to trust other big cities for much of its feature film post production, and unfortunately, no other smaller cities appear (in the eyes of the producers) to truly have the capabilities of handling all that there is to handle. As for commercials, videos, and films needed for special events, post production or editorial facilities are found locally in each major city, possibly only sending out film for development if necessary. Although for different types of projects the post production process is similar, they may have different positions in place to oversee this process. Post production is a separate entity from production (the basis of this book), but it is important to understand how the two areas tie together to complete the final picture. Broken down, the post production department is generally made up of the following positions on a feature film or television show:

1) Supervising Producer or Producer

Sometimes the title is different, but there is generally a producer in the department. This person oversees the post production budget, coordinates various creative entities, and is the responsible person for the final product. The producer is in constant communication with the production's producers to carry through the goals for the project once it has been shot.

2) Associate Producer (A.P.)

When the budget allows for a person to assist the supervising producer, the associate producer works with him or her to oversee the post production process. Responsible for the film once it has left the camera and the set, the A.P. coordinates the various film and sound processes that take place after shooting. On many occasions lines are "**looped**" or sort of dubbed in later by actors, if there is a problem with the sound for a particular scene. On a feature film or television series, the associate producer organizes and oversees this looping. He or she will work with the sound mixer to make sure ambient sounds and dialogue necessary to each scene have been recorded. The A.P. will also coordinate the film and sound processing with the labs, as well as coordinate the editing schedule with the studio, facilities, producer, director, and editors. He or she also oversees all music and playback (video, film, or other performance clips that are used in a given scene) and their clearance to be used within the scene. On a television series the A.P. also picks all of the publicity clips for specials and/or commercials as needed, such as clips used on *Entertainment Tonight* or awards shows. Similar to the POC role (although not usually as frantically paced), this is the go-to person who coordinates all aspects of the post production department under the supervising producer.

3) Post Production Coordinator

Similar to the art department coordinator, the post production coordinator assists the associate producer and coordinates the distribution of any information or materials within the post production department. Overseeing the process of film getting to the labs and then to the editors, and the final product getting to its end destination, the post production coordinator is in the thick of it all.

A job for an organized person who can handle stress, deadlines, and a fast pace, the post production coordinator will often have experience working as a production secretary or APOC in a production office. Dealing with editorial staff but also working with producers and outside vendors, the post production coordinator has strong communication skills and is able to get things done.

4) Editor

Just what it sounds like, this person edits the film after it has been developed. The editor is a creative and skilled person who pieces the film together to tell the director's story. Based on information supplied by the camera loader and script supervisor, and having had conversations with the director and producers, the editor tells the story. He or she works daily while the film is still being shot to piece together the footage from the previous day's shoot and to edit as much of the story together as possible before production is completed. After production concludes, the editor continues to work closely with the director and the rest of the post production team to complete the project. Editors may work with film negative or, more likely, with video after the film has been processed and is transferred to tape. In either case, the editor is knowledgeable in how to use the equipment needed for this craft. Use of editorial equipment is taught in many universities and technical schools nationwide and across the globe. Although it is possible to learn the technical work by assisting an editor and learning from watching, there is more to editing than technical skill. Having a sense of storytelling and the creativity to do it well is essential to this position.

5) Assistant Editor

Each editor has an assistant, sometimes more than one. This is someone who is also trained or in the process of training to edit, but is actually doing whatever the editor needs, which may also include paperwork or other miscellaneous tasks. The assistant editor stores all of the film negative, keeps a record of each roll or scene, and performs many other tasks related to the editorial process as needed from the editor. He or she also maintains the editorial equipment and deals with any equipment problems that arise.

6) Post Production Production Assistant (Post P.A.)

Once again, here is an opportunity to get your feet wet in the industry. In this case it is in post production. The post P.A. is very much a runner position. A post P.A. picks up the developed film and delivers it to the editorial staff. He or she also runs between vendors to pick up or drop off music or other elements needed for the final picture. And of course, as in any P.A. job description, there are lunch and coffee runs, and any other request that may come up during the workday (or night, as it may well be). Generally the post P.A. aspires to work as an editor and has the opportunity to learn from the assistants and the editor when not running errands. This is also another opportunity to get a foot in the door and to meet people on a production. An ambitious post P.A. will use this role to learn about other departments in addition to his or her own.

On large-scale projects there are other editors involved to edit sound and special effects for the film. There are also other post production positions, which include music, video effects, and so on. By working in a post production entry-level position, you will be exposed to this area of the business and will be able to learn about the other opportunities available if this should be your area of interest.

So now you have an overview of your many career options in film and television work. Once you have joined a crew you will have an even better understanding of each person's role. You may be wondering why you should waste your time learning about the craft service person's function when all you want to do is direct. It is simple. You need to have an understanding of the whole picture and everything that goes into it. Cross-training is important. It helps to be familiar with other positions, to be able to do them if necessary, and to understand them because you will inevitably interact and work with other departments as a team while you are on a crew. Every job on a production is important or it simply would not exist. A producer would not want to spend money on something that is unnecessary. Of course each person will tell you that his or her department is the glue holding the whole production together. This proves that each department plays an integral role, and every person has an impact on the final outcome. Most likely you will weed through these positions to discover another love or a talent that you didn't even know you had, one that you can incorporate into your career.

In your free time, when you take a trip to the movies or watch your favorite television show, stay for the credits and check out how many people it took to make it all possible. They each make significant contributions to the production, and each are critical to the crew. Every position has its slow days and hectic days. When one department is crazed and overworked, another may be sitting around waiting all day. They each bring their own unique drama and excitement to the production.

Studios and permanent production companies also have their own full-time staff positions, which may provide opportunities to help you find your way into production. Don't knock the fabled mailroom start—it can really work. Using the information provided in the following chapters, you will gain the knowledge that you can apply later to non-set production opportunities such as these. Just keep an open mind and the possibilities for opportunities in this business are endless.

CHAPTER 17

The First Step—

Setting Goals

Life Decisions

But where does a person start looking for a job? And how? First you need to make a few personal life decisions. These can always change, but you need to have made a few decisions to get yourself in the right frame of mind. The first question to answer is, "What is my goal?" Think about your long-term goal. If any time has passed, it probably has changed since you made your goal list in chapter 2. Do you want to be the world's greatest director of action movies? Are you aiming to be the first cameraperson in space? Think about where you would like to be or what you would like to have accomplished by the time you retire. Remember that no goal is too high. You can be whatever you want to be when you have the right attitude.

Now think back to the time that you decided on your life goals. Did you want a family? Three dogs and a summer home? Or were you planning to be a wild, single person forever? Tie the long-term goal into the life goal. Don't forget to prioritize and to remind yourself of what is truly important to you.

Exercise in Imagination

Close your eyes. Picture yourself twenty years from now. Are you married? Do you have kids? Do you live in your old hometown? Do you have an upper-class lifestyle or are you living small? When your friends see you at your reunion are you proudly talking about the Oscar you won or are you showing them pictures of your family? Maybe both? Now picture yourself in the exact opposite way. If your original plan was a family in a house with a white picket fence and a stable job, try to picture just you with your Golden Retriever in a rented apartment with an award on the shelf with your other knickknacks.

Use your own ideas to create a few possible versions of your future. Think about each scenario for a while. Which things are you the most proud of and which are you secure and happy with? More importantly, which aspects of these scenarios are unpleasant to you? Which ones have you saying, "I don't have to worry about that because of course it will work out the right way"? Pull out your sheet from chapter 2 and add your new goals. Use this sheet as a reference to help you focus when you are feeling lost or unsure.

Think about your short-term goals. Do you want to start making your epic feature now? Or are you interested in goofing off for the summer before you begin your rush-hour commute? Once you have begun your quest for your long-term goal, give yourself an outline of a plan for how you think you will get there. The plan doesn't have to be permanent—it can change. At least it will give you an idea of where you want to be looking for your first job.

When you have decided on your goals, you need to put them into perspective. To accomplish your first step, do you need to be in a major market or big city? Are you already in the right place, or will you need to move to accomplish the goal?

Markets and Opportunities

Be realistic. If your goal is to work in television such as on sitcoms or dramas, you will need to move to Los Angeles or New York City. You will need to move there with the intention of staying if you really hope to prosper in that aspect of the field.

If your goal is to work in broadcasting for television or radio, you can live almost anywhere. Smaller markets tend to hire newer and less experienced (also known as less costly) employees. They also tend to have more turnaround, since people continue to move from smaller to larger markets when they are ready to move up. In addition, at a smaller market you are likely to gain more hands-on experience, as opposed to the larger markets where union members have positions for most tasks.

If you are interested in filmmaking, you can do that anywhere as well, but certain towns draw more feature film work than others. In the following chapter we will take a look at the different production work options that can be found in cities across the U.S.

A Different Time Frame and a Different Pace

Other factors to keep in mind are the pace and stress levels of the various types of production out there. A feature film is an approximately two-hour story that takes several months to a year to shoot. On the other hand, a television program is a 30–60 minute story that takes 5–10 days to shoot. A mini-series is essentially a six-hour story that takes approximately three weeks to shoot, and a commercial is a 30–60 second story that takes 1–3 days to shoot. Yet for any of these options, the same steps are taken to make the production complete. Most of the same crew positions are necessary, and the process is the same except for the pace. Obviously, productions with shorter deadlines will require faster maneuvering to accomplish the goal.

In addition to a faster pace, the job duration is different for each type of production. A feature film makeup artist may be employed for three months, whereas the same position on a commercial may only be employed for one day. Turnaround and unemployment are much more frequent for commercials and mini-series than for films and television series. Combined with the frenzied pace of the production, these factors lead to very high stress levels.

If you are a person who has trouble in highly stressful situations, it will be important for you to consider these factors when choosing which route to follow in your pursuit of production work. Other options such as corporate video, documentaries, and special events may be more suited to people who cannot handle the stress of such a fast-paced and unstable environment.

Take the time to stop and think about your career plan. Think about your different likes and dislikes, and what you might enjoy doing on a daily basis. Research your interests, and the places that have those opportunities, to help you make a decision as to where to begin your job hunt.

CHAPTER 18

The Cities, Big & Small—

Understanding Residential Location Options

Whether you live in a farm town or in a major metropolitan area, chances are that there is some aspect of the entertainment business present there. In a smaller town there may be less variety, but opportunities do exist. By being ambitious you can create new avenues for yourself. Where to physically live to build your career, or at least to get your career started, is a decision that you will need to make. This is a great way to make use of the Internet. Learn about different areas and weigh their pros and cons. In this chapter we will review the major cities that have the most opportunities for production. However, you may discover that other cities hold other values for you and your career path, and that's great. This overview is just to give you an idea of what is out there and some things to consider during your research.

New York

New York City is a very vibrant and dynamic city. It has a lot of hustle and bustle. Here you will find several soap operas and talk shows such as *The View* or *Late Night with David Letterman*. You will also find many magazine or news programs, including *Today*, *Good Morning America*, and *Dateline*, to name a few. New York also houses the headquarters for the major broadcast networks, Viacom (owner of Nickelodeon and MTV), HBO, and other cable networks that produce many of their programs in or around the city. As for feature films and television series, the business in New York fluctuates. Presently, shows including *Sex in the City*, *Ed*, *The Sopranos*, three *Law and Order* series, and a number of cable station original programs are filming in New York and/or New Jersey. However, there are fewer shows shooting in the New York area than in Los Angeles. Movie makers will often shoot a few features in Manhattan and realize the following year that so many movies were filmed there that they need to shoot the next project somewhere else, just to offer variety to the audiences. This is the problem that many easily identifiable cities face.

To work in New York as a P.A., you will undoubtedly need to learn the city streets (and city driving skills), and you must be comfortable in a fast-paced traffic environment. Along with mastering bridges and tunnels, you will need to master driving a van or cube truck, as you will need to move people and props across the city at one point or another.

A Trip to Coney Island

On a popular Finnish series that came to the U.S. to film in New York, Kim was required to drive the actors and producers around in a large van all over the city, day and night. Starting with the airport and making her way to every major tourist attraction, it was a long, harrowing day. At Coney Island she was challenged with **locking up** an area crowded with freaks and tourists during filming before hopping back into her van. The van was later renamed the "moving bar," as the guys were drinking and smoking in the back between stops at each film location. Occasionally, Kim would need to pull over on a bridge or in the middle of the Jersey Turnpike for someone to urinate on the side of the road. It was around 3 AM when she heard a shout from the back of the van: "Vee are out of vhite vine." Alas, Kim began her quest for white wine in her large, clumsy van in the wee hours of the morning. Always carry a map, and when you find a liquor store open at 3 AM, write down its name and location so you can find it again next time.

On the positive side, if a movie is written for New York, there are no American cities that can replicate the streets, architecture, or pace of Manhattan (without repeating and re-using locations constantly), and therefore they probably will need to film at least the exterior scenes in New York. It is not easy or cheap to replicate New York exteriors in Los Angeles.

As for moving to live in New York, it can be as simple as a physical move to anywhere else, but it may require a change in lifestyle. Living expenses in New York are outrageous. An apartment is often extremely small, yet very high priced. A bedroom in a one-bedroom apartment in New York City is most likely the size of a large closet in a one-bedroom apartment found in Los Angeles for the same price. The same rule applies for food and many other living expenses. In return, some jobs may have a higher pay scale but that will depend on the company.

The conveniences in New York also differ from those in other large cities. Groceries are often purchased at small shops that specialize in a type of food. For instance, a person may shop in a deli for meat and a fruit stand or small grocer for fruits and vegetables, whereas other cities have large one-stop supermarkets.

Many people living in Manhattan cannot afford parking or do not want the hassle of parking a car, and the streets are extremely congested with taxicabs. People there tend to use public transportation such as the subway, trains, or buses. Others will take cabs. Often, people just starting out in their careers will choose to get rid of their cars or will park them in a neighboring borough where street parking is more available.

Depending on your personality, you may love New York. It has a lot to offer as far as culture and energy.

Chicago

I may be biased because I'm a resident Chicagoan. But I do know both the pros and the cons of my fair city. Chicago is a beautiful town. Similar to Boston in friendliness and size, it is a smaller combination of New York and Los Angeles. Nicknamed "The Third Coast," Chicago can be cheaper than both as far as cost of living, although it is not too far removed from Los Angeles in this respect.

On the positive side, Chicago is very friendly and very social. The winters are very cold, and therefore the people run outside at the first sign of sunshine in the spring and stay outside until the next snowfall. Aside from the festive outdoor atmosphere, it is also friendly inside the workplace. Business people are a little more down-to-earth and laid-back in Chicago than in New York. The film and television community is close-knit, as its members understand that their work situation is based on drawing productions from other states or from Canada. Therefore, the people in the industry need to band together to keep the work coming. They put forth all of their effort to show the out-of-towners what hard work is all about. To work in Chicago for most people requires a very hard-working mentality; no slackers will survive.

Chicago is a very easy city to maneuver either with a car, public transportation, or walking (which is unheard of in Los Angeles).

Despite its famous skyline, Chicago has a very "Any Town, USA" look to it, since there are both urban and rural neighborhoods (even farms) within reasonable driving distances. It also has great beaches and is situated along the shore of Lake Michigan. But similar to New York City, movie-makers may decide that in a given year the general public has seen too much of the same city skyline and decide to film elsewhere for a different look. Add this scenario to Chicago's famed cold winters, and you'll find that the Windy City has high and low seasons, or even high and low years, for filming. During a slow season, finding crew work can be very competitive. There are seasoned professionals who have been working in this field within Chicago for many years. Therefore, breaking into Chicago's crew scene from another state, or as a newcomer to the industry, may be more difficult.

Mention Chicago and most television viewers will think of Michael Jordan and Oprah. Oprah has been taping shows in Chicago for decades. Also taping in Chicago is *The Jerry Springer Show*. With many of the greatest advertising agencies residing in the city, Chicago was once the largest commercial market in the country. Although this business has somewhat slowed, the agencies are still here and the city is working to bring commercial production back up to its potential. Chicago's other production work includes feature films, cable series, commercials, local television broadcasting, and industrial videos. Some artists do come to the city to film their music videos, but they are few and far between. The city's production community is hopeful for a sitcom to follow the loss of the recently canceled *What About Joan*, but presently there are no television series and few feature films being produced in Chicago.

Did you know that some very famous movies were filmed in Chicago? *Road to Perdition* is the most recent success to join the list. Hometown to John Hughes, *The Breakfast Club*, *Planes, Trains, and Automobiles*, *Home Alone*, and (who could forget the ultimate guide to Chicago) *Ferris Bueller's Day Off* were all shot in the Windy City. Of course, everyone knows that the famous *Blues Brothers* takes Jake and Elwood on a wild ride through the city, as does *Risky Business*, *Backdraft*, *Chain Reaction*, *My Best Friend's Wedding*, and *Ali*, to name a few. Some movies like *The Hudsucker Proxy* are misleading, as they create the illusion of New York City's exterior while in fact it's Chicago you're seeing.

Los Angeles

Southern California is sort of in its own little world. Los Angeles is filled with people who, like you, are trying to make it in "the biz." It has its own personality, which is very different from the rest of the country, and the world for that matter. From the industry perspective, there are two kinds of people in Los Angeles, people who moved there to work in the entertainment business and California natives. One tends to think that the entertainment people outnumber the natives.

The city itself does not seem to be that large compared to New York and Chicago. However, when referring to Los Angeles, one assumes "Los Angeles" to encompass not only the city itself, but also all of the suburbs within an hour's drive from the downtown area. Therefore, cities including Burbank, Santa Monica, Hollywood, Sherman Oaks, and Pasadena are also included under the "Los Angeles" umbrella. This being the case, the city becomes very large and very spread out. People commute from all over the place, as in any major city. However, Los Angeles is unique in that many of these people are working in production, which has unusual hours. Therefore, the rush hour commute can actually fluctuate and may become heavier during a different hour or different stretch of highway from one day to the next. (At least that's my explanation for the weird traffic patterns in L.A.; if that isn't it then I'm stumped.)

Because the people are generally spread out, in addition to the hassle of finding parking or having to valet park everywhere, many find themselves sticking to their own neighborhoods in their free time. Besides, for the average person, regularly going to nightclubs is difficult to afford. Usually it's the celebrities who find themselves pushed to the head of the line and having no cover charge, and therefore they are the people most enjoying the nightlife of the trendy Hollywood scene. Of course there are plenty of ordinary people who do try to be trendsetters in Hollywood. It's just not always as glamorous as it is portrayed in the movies.

On the bright side, it's always sunny and relatively warm in Santa Monica, South Beaches, and West L.A. It's a little smoggier and muggier in the valley but essentially always nice weather compared to the rest of the country. California's climate is the key to why people stay. You can drive to the mountains to snow ski, or pull out your surfboard to ride the waves.

For entertainment-related business in the United States, L.A. is the place to be. There are many jobs in a variety of areas. Sitcoms, features, documentaries, industrials, commercials, dramas, reality shows, broadcast news, award shows and specials, you name it—they all exist in L.A. However, because it is a mecca for entertainment, many people are competing for the same jobs. With such competition the pay scale is low. The employers know that there are many people looking to get their start, and many willing to do it for little or no money, so that's what they pay.

In L.A., different from in smaller markets, the turnaround rate for P.A.s can be lower. In smaller markets people are constantly moving up or out of the position, whereas in L.A. more people are likely to stick to their position for lengthier periods of time. A person may decide to be a professional P.A. He or she will be the best P.A. possible, and make a long-lasting career of it. This scenario throws in another obstacle for the first-time job seeker as it makes for more competition for entry-level positions. However, there are a lot of places to look for an opening. If you steer away from the popular mainstream network shows and look into cable, film, or video, you will have many opportunities at your fingertips.

San Francisco

Home to George Lucas' Lucasfilm and Skywalker Sound studios, as well as Pixar and other major animation houses, San Francisco and its surrounding area are a major hub for graphics, animation, and special effects. A beautiful city, the climate is a favorite for West Coast transplants. A hilly region located on the ocean, the area provides both rural and urban settings, which frequently attract features and visiting television series.

The South

Southern states, including Georgia, Florida, Tennessee, and the Carolinas, have very strong production communities. These states provide opportunity to work in the entertainment business while living in a clean, pretty, and more residential area. The South is definitely a slower paced, friendlier atmosphere than the big cities. The people would rather chat about their weekend than scream and yell over deadlines. This type of climate is helpful in maintaining a balance in your life as you prosper in this business. Bigger productions tend to bring key positioned crew people in from L.A. or New York when filming in smaller towns, but good local people can make a niche for themselves in this business when choosing to live in smaller communities such as these.

Atlanta

Atlanta is a small town that is constantly expanding into a bigger city. There is definitely a Southern way of life there but with all the East Coasters and Midwesterners that have moved in, there is a sense of city life and hustle and bustle just waiting to take over. It is a beautiful city in most areas, with trees and flowers. Smog is a foreign word here.

As for feature film work, there isn't much of it in Atlanta. There is a studio that gets work for films, such as *Fried Green Tomatoes*, and some commercials. Similar to Chicago in pace, although not as busy, Atlanta has on and off seasons where the work is either dead or pouring in. It has a decent commercial and industrial market, however, with very capable film crews residing in the area. Home to Ted Turner and the Turner networks, including TBS and CNN, there is a strong broadcast television presence here as well. Atlanta is a nice place to live (minus the steamy hot summers) but not a mecca for filming if you're looking for variety. There is work, though, and it can be found if you're looking for quality of life along with your profession.

Florida

Orlando and Miami stand out as leading production communities for the state of Florida. With the numerous theme parks in Orlando, children and family-oriented production (especially live shows and special events) are prevalent in this area. With the ocean and the different climates provided in this state, many television and feature film productions take place here. Contacting the local film commissions will give you a sense of the opportunities and the work atmosphere to be found.

Wilmington

Wilmington, North Carolina has maintained a steady flow of production work over the years. Its green, lush beauty provides a look that studios can't seem to resist. Wilmington has grown to become a strong and respected city for production. It may not yet be a film center comparable to Los Angeles, but with continuing series such as *Dawson's Creek* making their home here, it does have a reputation for providing scenery as well as strong production crews and resources for feature films and national commercials.

Texas

In recent years, Austin has emerged as a growing producer of independent features. Serving the Southwest market, there are also commercials and industrials produced here. With celebrities buying ranches and homes here away from the spotlights of Hollywood, the current trend shows Texas slowly becoming a popular place to film.

Tennessee

Home to the Grand Ol' Opry and the Country Music Hall of Fame, Nashville is a music hub for the nation. Appropriately, it has a strong film presence, mostly geared toward music videos, although commercials and industrials are filmed here as well. Knoxville also has a production community for industrials in addition to programming for cable stations such as the Food Network and HGTV.

Other small and mid-sized cities to consider are Seattle, Las Vegas, Minneapolis, Milwaukee, Philadelphia, and Pittsburgh. Every state in the U.S. has a film commission (if not more than one); see the appendix for a listing of offices in the area you are considering. These offices can provide you with an idea of the opportunities available to you and will probably have either a film hotline or a resource for you to reference while job hunting.

Relocation Story

When Brook decided to move to Monterey from Atlanta, she contacted the local film commission for their production guide. She used her own organizational system to call the companies listed in the guide to send her resume to companies in Monterey. She found herself a job at a documentary company and thanks to her local resources, continues to successfully work as a producer within this small production community.

Some pluses to working in smaller markets are:
- More job availability for qualified and senior crew staff
- Healthier lifestyle and home life than compared to a large, fast-paced city life
- Closer-knit film communities that work together, sharing job opportunities and information with each other

Oh Canada

During the last decade, Canada (most specifically Toronto, Vancouver, Montreal, and Calgary) has become a major draw for filmmakers. Mostly due to the strong exchange rate for the American dollar, and different tax laws, it is thought to be cheaper to film in Canada. We will not discuss that option in this book because if you are an American reading this book, you should not film in Canada unless it is necessary to the action and visual look of the film. More Americans need to support their film community, and we need to do this first by keeping production inside the U.S. The U.S. economy suffers when film production continues to move to Canada, as many businesses outside of, yet related to, the production industry are affected. Ah, but that's a chapter for a different book!

Many professionals working in hiring positions for smaller markets are constantly looking for good support staff. Often a film producer working in a smaller market will bring crew members in from out of state, because good local talent may be hard to find. If you are able to shine and stand out in your small-town community, you will go far.

Whether it is a large or small market, you will need to decide which one is most appropriate for you in your chosen career. Do your research. Take into consideration your personality and your closeness to friends and family while you decide where your first job should be located.

CHAPTER 19

The Decision—Adjusting Your

Life to Staying or Going

You've gotten an overview of the major cities of the U.S. and how they tie in to the production world. Hopefully you will visit any city that interests you before making a permanent move. Of course, in addition to job opportunities in these cities there are other aspects of your life that you need to consider when deciding where to reside.

Family

Will your family make you crazy if you leave? Or are you currently away from them and have an opportunity to move closer? Make sure you have a talk with them before you move. Your family may be the only consistency you will have in this life, so don't discount them. Mom and Dad have been around a long time, and although they may know absolutely nothing about your dream career, they probably have some sort of moving advice and definitely an opinion or two to share. They may be more accepting of your final decision if they know that they were able to participate in the decision-making process.

If you have an opportunity to move closer to a relative who you don't see as often, such a move could be a great relationship renewal. Look at every opportunity that you can take advantage of in your new life. You need to think about your move very carefully. Of course, anywhere that you end up is only as permanent as you make it. You can always move elsewhere.

☛Note—It is unlikely that a production company will decide after a phone call interview to hire you from out-of-state, especially if you will only be working there for a limited time period such as a summer internship or a freelance position on a feature film. It doesn't matter if you tell them that you'll move to their city in a heartbeat. There are so many people who already live in the bigger cities and are trying to break into the business; they will have no need to hire an out-of-towner. Your best bet is to save the move for a period in your life when there are no time constraints affecting your future. Once you are out of school or have left a job, you will find that it will be an easier time to move. Moving first will show the employer that you are serious and that you truly want the job. Exceptions may be made in smaller markets where fewer residents are applying for internships or in markets where students from local schools (who essentially are residents for the semester) apply for positions.

Friends

Do you have friends where you are moving? Are you a people person who will make friends anywhere? Are you shy or a home-body? These are important issues to address when you are moving. Moving for work is one thing, but when you get to your new home you don't want to suddenly realize that you are lonely or lost with no one to call. If you don't know anyone there, do you have friends that do? Ask around. Chances are you will meet people eventually, but it is nice to move some-where and to have an emergency contact if the unexpected happens. For some people, moving is extremely difficult socially. There are some people that are very shy and end up very unhappy when they move somewhere new. Be honest with yourself and think about whether or not you can leave the life you have behind in order to tread new waters. You may be surprised that you can accomplish things that you never thought you were capable of doing.

Rushing

A major factor in determining when to move is time—how hectic will your life be if you move right now? Are you trying to do it within a week's time span or do you have some time to live where you are while you make the necessary arrangements? If you are planning to pack up and move tomorrow, I strongly advise you to stay home. Rushing somewhere and moving with no notice is stressful for all parties involved and is not the way to start off on your new adventure. You want to be able to think rationally about your new home and your plans; you don't want to be frantic during job interviews. Take it slow if you can.

Money

Moving anywhere takes money. Even if you have no belongings to move and you have friends' couches to sleep on, you will of course need money. This is one of the benefits of staying with Mom and Dad when you first graduate from college. Living at your old homestead may allow you to work without paying rent and to save up for when you do decide to move out. Your parents will probably have trouble letting you go anyway (even if they don't admit it), so it can't hurt to stick around at least for a little while.

Should you decide that moving is a better option, or perhaps your only option, just make sure that you plan for all of your costs. If you have friends living in the area you have chosen, it's a good idea to call them to get an idea of the costs of living there and what neighborhoods are appropriate for your income. Remember, if you're moving to New York City or San Francisco, they are both very expensive.

Where to Start

Here you go. You made the decision and now you need to act on it. First, make a budget and a timeline. How much money can you spend on the move? Can you afford to hire movers? Do your research. Moving-related expenses include:

- Movers or rental truck
- Shipping service for your car if you fly
- Packing boxes
- Packing blankets
- Packing tape and tape gun
- Storage (Will you be leaving anything behind? Will you need to store your stuff once you get to your new home?)
- Gas or plane ticket
- Hotels at the destination and/or along the way (or treating your friends to meals in exchange for letting you sleep on the couch)
- Food along the way
- Souvenirs from the scenic route
- Phone bill to prepare for the move
- Security deposit for your new place
- Furniture for your new place
- Start-up costs (gas, electric, cable, telephone, etc.)
- Cell phone connection and pager
- Car rental or purchase
- Phone bill that will be heftier now that you are living far from friends and family

You'll also need to plan on being out of work for at least a little while. You don't want to get a part-time job right away. Wait until you get your bearings to give yourself time to send out resumes and fit in interviews. Or, you can take a job right away just to make ends meet, but take one with flexibility so you can go on interviews when they come your way. In the meantime, make room in your budget for food, stamps (don't laugh—they add up!), stationery, resumes, and copies of your resume. You may have some contacts in your new city. If so, plan on business lunches to meet them for informal interviews or job search meetings.

If you're moving to L.A., Atlanta, or similar cities that are spread out, plan on spending a little more on automobile gas since you'll be doing more driving to get to the interviews. If you're moving to New York, plan on taxi cab or subway fare. In any city, plan on buying a map and getting to know the layout. Having a good map is mandatory for success as a P.A., as you will be running errands all over town.

☛Note—If you decide to move to L.A., spend your first $40 on a Thomas Guide. It is the essential map for navigating the area, and a must-have for anyone in production. Found in any travel store or L.A.-area bookstore, this should be the first thing you buy when you step off the plane. Production assistants and other crew people are so reliant on the Thomas Guide that pages from the guide are often listed on **location maps** to and from the shooting locations in Los Angeles.

The more you "fit in" as a local, the easier it will be to find a job. But the time you spend and the stuff you buy to acclimate yourself to your new territory will add up. It's helpful to research the costs before you make the move.

As for a timeline, you will need time to physically move yourself to the new town, find an apartment, buy furniture, find places to call for work, and go on job interviews. You may luck out and find something right away. Realistically, you'll need at least 3–4 weeks; for some people (especially for a first job) it can take months.

What to Pack

There are two ways to look at a work-related move. On the one hand, it is a trial-and-error test. You may like your new locale or you may not. This relocation may be short-lived if you decide to return to your hometown.

On the other hand, this change is to be your new start on life, your beginning and renewal. In order to truly succeed and to accomplish your goals, it is important to be determined and to think positively. With this mindset, you should choose to look at this move as permanent. You know deep down inside that you can always return home or head elsewhere. If you are looking at this move as a permanent one, you are more likely to succeed. Viewing this relocation as a wonderful opportunity in your life will cause you to have a positive and happy outlook, which is half the battle in finding work and maintaining happiness in a new environment.

Keeping this idea in mind, you need to pack for a permanent stay. Remember that you are not moving to another planet. There will be supplies like toiletries and garbage bags wherever you go. Try to only pack the necessities. Obviously, pack clothing necessary for the climate. Hopefully you can find a storage location (or a family basement) to hold the things you don't want to drag around with you before feeling situated. Of course make yourself comfortable, bring the things that keep you happy and that you use in your everyday life (such as CDs or a favorite teddy bear). Just be careful not to overpack with trivial pieces like the big stack of wire hangers from your closet. You can probably find those at your new destination and it will cost you more to ship them somewhere than to buy them later.

Stress Management

Moving is stressful for most people. You may think it will be easy, and hopefully it will. However, there are many details to research and many decisions to make. Try not to get too tense; it's just not healthy. Keep reminding yourself that any move you make can be as temporary or as permanent as you want it to be. You should have an "I'm going to succeed here" attitude, keeping in mind that should things not go as planned you can always turn around and go back to where you came from. There area no final decisions being made here, only optimistic ideals. If you find yourself getting stressed, try to manage it. Stop to breathe. Sit in a park and relax for a while. Take a hot bath. Do anything to ease your mind. You want this move to be positive and it is not going to be if you're upset before you even get there.

House Hunting

If you are not able to stay with a friend while you search for housing, there are a few cheap alternatives. Again, it helps to research before you physically move. Surfing the Internet for that city, or for housing in general, will most likely turn up options and will probably give you an idea of what to look for and what to expect upon arrival. Contacting a local apartment finder company via the Yellow Pages or the Internet is a great way to look for housing in a new town. These people will assess your needs and find you an apartment that is in a decent area and around your price range. You can at least meet with them to get an understanding of the good and bad neighbor-hoods in the area, even if you decide not to use their hunting services. Some cities charge for apartment finders and others do not; it's all a matter of researching your new town. There are also roommate-finding services that may be helpful to you. This way you find a new friend and someone to share the moving costs with you.

Deciding to Stay

For those who choose to stay in their hometown, there are still emotions to deal with and decisions to be made. Do you live with your family for a while or find your own place? If living with your family is an option, it is a great money saver. You may need to adhere to different rules and guidelines that your family has established under their roof. You will probably want to explain to them your plan, when you have one, for job-hunting. This way you will start off with open communication lines, which are important for sharing space.

You may choose to live on your own and find a way to make ends meet, or perhaps you will choose to find a roommate to share the costs. Living alone will give you more freedom and perhaps ease the stress of a new job or a job with odd hours. Working in production will have you leaving very early and coming home very late. This can be difficult when living in another person's house and having to be quiet or to sleep when others are not. But if having company is important to you, the odd-hour schedule can be managed; it's all up to you to make it happen smoothly.

Think about your options and find one that will best suit your needs. Consider the distance from your job prospects. It may be wise to find the job first and then look for a new home in the same neighborhood, if that is an option for you.

Couch Potato Syndrome

If you are living with your parents or other close relatives, it is very easy to fall into a trap of staying at home and lounging around. Now is the time to set up your plan for job-hunting. Be realistic and determine a future date by which you will be working or at least making progress in your search. Start by setting a date to complete your resume by, then a date to send out letters, a date to make additional phone calls, and so on. It will ease your mind to have a plan, and ease your parents' or relatives' minds that you are in fact looking for work and not just loafing.

The Friendly Midwest

From Iowa City, Toledo (Iowa) is approximately a forty-five-minute car ride through cornfields. It is a hard commute when you're working long hours and into the night. It can also be magical to watch the lightning bolts streak across the plains. But people who watch a lot of films may instinctively connect corn fields with the thriller *Children of the Corn*. At least I did, and my mind often started to play nasty tricks on me during my long drives.

While working on *Shimmer*, one of the crew members suggested that I phone a woman who lived in a house near the production office. She was rumored to be looking for tenants to live in her attic. The rumor proved to be true. A friendly woman, she was looking for company and a way to help the movie people. Plus, she made a profit off of my twenty-five dollars a week to rent her bed and to keep a roof over my head. Not a bad price for a friendly home that cut my commute by forty minutes! Not to mention, I got to trade in my friends' couch for my own bed.

On *Rudy*, I was passing out filming announcements at Notre Dame when I met Brenda. An employee of the university, Brenda made a similar offer to my Iowa lodger's and I found a place to stay for months on end while we were filming. I also made a new friend and had a smiling face to greet me as I came home from a long day of filming in an unfamiliar place.

The hospitality of strangers is often found at production sets, especially in small towns. It brings the country together. What a wonderful way to discover that kindness exists, and that there are warm and giving people out there to meet.

Once you have made your decision, and perhaps have made a physical move, your next step is to prepare to sell yourself. It is time for your resume.

CHAPTER 20

The Production Resume—The Format

They Don't Teach You in School

Once you've found a place to live, you are ready to start the job-hunting process. Finding a job can be tough. By using creativity and assertiveness you can be anything you want to be.

First, you need to decide what type of work you are looking for at this point. Again, think about your short-term and long-term goals and your skills. Are there skills you would love to pursue? Are there skills you are looking to enhance? Is there something you've always wanted to try? Make a list of things that you are interested in doing. Look at the list to see if there are any repetitive themes or jobs that are similar or related to each other. It may help to go to the library to further research the options in the craft, and to look at job titles and businesses that perhaps you had never considered or even heard of before. Once you have narrowed down your area of interest in the field, it is time to start the hunt. The first stage is writing your resume.

Resume writing can be difficult and tedious but it is the first impression you make on the prospective employer, and it may be the decision-maker on whether or not you have a chance to get in the door. However, a resume is not the only determining factor. The cover letter, phone calls, and references can all play a major role in winning an opportunity to meet for an interview. We'll get to those in a moment. Let's start with the resume.

Generic Resume

With the ease of typing on a computer, you will benefit from having a resume that is geared toward a specific company or position, rather than the old-fashioned generic CV that you send to the masses. It is recommended that you save each version of your resume with a different title. Save it as something you will easily remember, such as the name of the company that you are sending it to. This way you will easily track all of your different resumes and you can gear them to specific jobs. With only a limited work history, you may not be able to aim each resume to a specific company, in which case a generic one will suffice. If you do not have access to a computer, you can rent one in a business center such as Kinko's. In this case, you will want to have much of your resume pre-planned on paper in order to cut back on the hours you will spend typing, cutting, and pasting on your dime.

A resume is basically a sheet that the employer can glance at quickly to determine your background and to assess whether or not you will be a good candidate for a position in the company. It is meant to be short—a summary of your background. It is important to leave it as a summary and to save the long details for your interview so you have something to talk about.

It is a good idea to have a preliminary resume ready to go at the very start of your job search. Once you have it on your computer, you can always go back to tweak or mold it to fit a specific job opportunity. Having a generic resume ready to go at all times is important. Resumes often take a long time to work on, and if an employer is looking to have one from you immediately you want to be able to send something without having to waste hours rebuilding yours.

Production Resume

The television, film, or radio production resume is very different from the corporate or business resume. You can buy many books on corporate or standard business resumes; however, this is the only book that discusses the production resume.

The resume that is aimed at a production position needs to be very short and to the point. Once you have industry experience, your resume will simply be a list of your production credits and references with no descriptions or bullet points. Once you have experience you will not necessarily need a resume to get your next job. At that point, most production people are hired by word-of-mouth and recommendations through networking. When you are ready to submit a resume, it should be only one page in length.

Header

Every resume's header should include your name, telephone number, pager number, or cell phone number if you have one. A production position will likely be a quick-to-come, quick-to-go position. If you aren't home when the employer calls, he or she will move onto the next resume in the stack. In contrast to an applicant for a business job, an applicant for a production job who has a pager and/or cell phone will have an extra chance for the position by being accessible when the job is available.

As on any CV, it is standard for your home address to be at the top of a production resume. If you are sending your resume in from out of state and do not yet have your future address, try to use a friend's address and phone number. Just give your friend some warning that job calls may come there. If a prospective employer sees an out-of-state address on your resume, he or she will most likely not read any further. Chances are that the job is available immediately and the employer will not want to wait for you to move to another state for you to fill it, let alone wait for you to arrive for an interview. Should you have no friends in the area to which you are moving and have no forwarding address, you may want to write "Temporary Address" next to the address at the top of your resume, to give them the impression that you are not out of state full-time. They will still be hesitant to consider you for a job far from your home, but you might get lucky and find someone who will give you a chance.

Sample Header:

JOE SCHMOE Jr.
Temporary Address:
1234 Prairie Road
Your Town, Alabama 55555
(555) 555-5555 (home)
(555) 555-6666 (pager)

You can be creative with the header, just don't make it so creative that you can't see the main point: who you are and where you can be reached.

Body

After the header, the rest of the information is simply work experience. In a business resume, you will see examples that show schooling and statistics about your education. Educational background is not always important on a production resume. In fact, as we covered in earlier chapters, anyone from any background can work in production. It helps to have a background in the area that you want to work in, but it is not always crucial. However, if you do have college experience, listing it on your resume is another opportunity to catch someone's eye. Sending your resume to someone who also graduated from your alma mater is one more commonality and could influence his or her decision about whether or not to consider you for the position. Therefore, on a production resume your education may not be the most important information, but it does serve a purpose. For this reason it is helpful to have it on your resume—just put it at the bottom of the page instead of at the top.

London Calling

While production coordinating on *Pizza Wars*, an independent feature film, I was flooded with resumes from recent college graduates looking for any way to get a foot in the door.

I had lucked out by finding this particular film after calling a job hotline and consulting an area film newsletter. Somehow I quickly worked my way up the chain and was hiring crew members. After a short while, the resumes started to look the same to me. Everyone was new, just starting out, and had a variety of talents to offer to our production.

Then I saw Kim's resume. It listed something that I could connect with. Kim had spent a semester of college in London, the same semester that I had spent there. I wanted to meet her and to share our stories of living abroad. I called her and gave her a telephone interview. Because we connected on paper via her resume, and then over the telephone, I saw her stand out from the stack of other qualified candidates. Thus began Kim's first position on a feature film, as I hired her to run the art department.

Kim went on to later become a television producer in New York. By including her semester abroad in her resume, she caught the attention of an employer. You never know what key information will be the eye-catcher.

Experience

Again, you are gearing your resume to a specific job. Think about what that job may require as far as skills and experience. As mentioned earlier, a production resume tends to look more like a checklist than like a business resume. Start by making a list of movie or television titles that you've worked on or names of companies in the industry that you've worked for. If this is your first job, you probably have little or no practical work experience in the business to lend to your resume. If you have experience on student films or school productions, list them individually. With no previous industry experience, start by listing regular non-film jobs and we'll work on other ways to tie them to the job you're after. Once you have your list laid out, you can expand the information to fit the page.

Example:

JOE SCHMOE, Jr.

1212 N. Park Avenue, Atlanta, Georgia 33333
(440) 555-5555 (home) • (440) 555-5556 (pager) • (440) 555-5557 (cell)
E-mail: jsjr@network.net

WORK EXPERIENCE:

Production Assistant	G Productions/Producer Scott Gordon	2001
	The Cuba Story/UPM Larry Jones	2000
	Ice Cream Studios	1999
Cable Runner	*Bombers Football*/Ithaca College Television (ICTV)	2000
	My Friend's Dog/Student Film	1999
	Helicopterland/Student Film	1999
EDUCATION:	Ithaca College B.S. Finance, Minor in T.V./Radio	2002

With your list in order, you now have the skeleton of your resume. Next it's time to expand the list to fit the page and to expound on each experience briefly. If you are just starting out, you will need to be creative with how you list your experiences and group them together.

Separate your list into categories. You can tie together similar job positions if you have several listings for one position, or you can divide your work history into groupings by date or by type of business if they are not all film-related.

A production resume will generally take the shape of a list grouped by job titles as a person gains more experience in one area of the business. For example, a 1st A.D. who has worked on a number of projects will have a list of 1st A.D. experiences and likely a few 2nd 2nd A.D. experiences that led to this higher position. In this example, his or her resume will show two groupings in the body of the page:

Example:

JOE SCHMOE, Jr.
1212 N. Park Avenue, Atlanta, Georgia 33333
(440) 555-5555 (home) • (440) 555-5556 (pager) • (440) 555-5557 (cell)
E-mail: jsjr@network.net

WORK EXPERIENCE:

1st A.D.	*My Cat Jumped*/Director Jane Doe	2001
	The Wonderlings/Director John Doe	2001
	The Happiness Club/Director Mike Mudd	2000
	Battlebots Come Alive/Director Dennis Smith	2000
	Hart To Hart Lives/Director Jennifer Powers	2000
2nd A.D.	*Rocky VIII: The Next Generation*/ Director Mikey Smith	1999
	Kids R Us/Series Director Helen Doe	1999
	Rick Springfield: The Rise of a Legend/ Director Noah Drake	1999
EDUCATION:	Ithaca College B.S. Finance, Minor in T.V./Radio	2002

Another suggestion is to group by date. In this scenario, you are simply listing your credentials in chronological order. This is a better option for a resume layout if you don't have enough experience to create a strong grouping by title. Beginning with the most recent experience and going back in time, you are expressing your work history as a timeline of sorts.

Example:

JOE SCHMOE, Jr.

1212 N. Park Avenue, Atlanta, Georgia 33333
(440) 555-5555 (home) • (440) 555-5556 (pager) • (440) 555-5557 (cell)
E-mail: jsjr@network.net

WORK EXPERIENCE:

October 2001	Set Production Assistant/The New Guy
August 2001	Office Production Assistant/ *Harper Valley PTA Returns*
June 2001–July 2001	Sales Associate, Dairy Queen, Inc. Dunwoody, Georgia
April 2000–April 2000	Executive Assistant, Technophonics, LTD.
February 2000	Cable Runner, Ithaca College Television (ICTV)

EDUCATION:	Ithaca College—2002 B.S. Finance, Minor in T.V./Radio

When showing work experience that obviously correlates to the film business, your list can remain as-is with no further description or bullet point to back it up. In this situation, the person reading your resume will know the job description from experience. Unless a job had unusual duties or something of special significance to point out to others, it can remain a simple list. However, work experience that is not related to the film industry, or which consists of unusual titles or duties, will need a quick sentence or bullet point to explain its importance to the reader.

Example:

JOE SCHMOE, Jr.

1212 N. Park Avenue, Atlanta, Georgia 33333
(440) 555-5555 (home) • (440) 555-5556 (pager) • (440) 555-5557 (cell)
E-mail: jsjr@network.net

WORK EXPERIENCE:

June 2001–July 2001	**Sales Associate, Dairy Queen, Inc.** **Dunwoody, Georgia** • Assisted owner in maintaining and operating daily activities • Coordinated delivery of product • Interacted with wide variety of customers • Provided customer service
April 2000–April 2000	**Executive Assistant, Technophonics, LTD.** **Groton, Georgia** • Assistant to CEO of international company • Heavy phones • Dictation • Heavy typing
February 2000	**Cable Runner, Ithaca College Television (ICTV)** **Ithaca, New York** • Ran cables for *Bombers Football* telecast • Assisted camera operator in field shoots • Managed crowd situations during live shoots
EDUCATION:	**Ithaca College 2002** **B.S. Finance, Minor in T.V./Radio**

Skills

After listing your experience, try to add a section for related skills or activities that may separate you from the other candidates. Perhaps you are proficient in another language, a type of software, or with computers. These are skills that will make you a better choice for some positions and they need to be on your resume for the prospective employer to see.

If you worked with cameras or other technical equipment in college, list the specific type of equipment that you used. Having this noted on your resume will let

THE PRODUCTION RESUME—THE FORMAT THEY DON'T TEACH YOU IN SCHOOL ➢ **123**

the reader know that you are well-educated and qualified for a specific position that has opened up. You may even apply for one job but have an employer call you for another that you didn't know existed, just because he or she saw your skills on your resume and thought you might be interested. This is rare but it can happen.

Example:

JOE SCHMOE, Jr.

1212 N. Park Avenue, Atlanta, Georgia 33333
(440) 555-5555 (home) • (440) 555-5556 (pager) • (440) 555-5557 (cell)
E-mail: jsjr@network.net

WORK EXPERIENCE:

Production Assistant	G Productions/Producer Scott Gordon	2002
	The Cuba Story/UPM Larry Jones	2001
	Ice Cream Studios	1999
Cable Runner	*Bombers Football*	
	Ithaca College Television (ICTV)	2001
Grip	*Helicopterland*/Student Film	2001
	Stanley's Room/Student Film	2001

SPECIAL SKILLS:
Typing, phone handling, computer (Mac and PC), Word Perfect 4.0, Windows 98, Adobe Photoshop, ACT!, Sony DVcam, Wheatstone Audio Board 2002. Can drive a cube truck and carry six coffees at once.

EDUCATION:	Ithaca College 2002
	B.S. Finance, Minor in T.V./Radio

The layout of the resume is up to you. This is not a step-by-step guide to writing a resume. This is simply an explanation of how this type of resume differs from others, pointing out those differences.

Have you perfected your production resume? Good. Now go back and proofread it three more times. A misspelling on a resume is a sure-fire way to have it thrown out. If you can't be efficient enough to have a perfect resume, then how can you be trusted for the job? Take your time and be certain it is perfect before you move on to the next step.

Your resume is a snapshot of your experience. It summarizes your background and your qualifications for the position you are trying to get. A production resume is a short list, descriptive enough to explain the importance of each experience yet brief enough to be a quick read. Once you have more production work under your belt, your resume may grow to take up several pages. But as a new kid on the block looking for entry-level work, anything longer than one page will seem too long (and too pretentious) to the employer, and will likely be passed over. Your cover letter, and more importantly your interview, is your opportunity to expound on your background and qualifications for the position.

Standing Out

There are many people who are looking for their first job in production, and most have the same or similar backgrounds. Production companies see the same resumes constantly and will weed them out for many different reasons. This may lead you to believe that the more creative your resume is, the more it stands out from the crowd in the reader's eyes. However, there is a point at which you are too creative and the prospective employer will not want to be bothered by reading that type of resume either. One producer interviewed said he immediately rejects resumes that are "too cutesy," feeling that a person spending so much energy on the appearance must have something to hide.

Odd Shapes and Sizes

Jackie received a basketball with a photo taped to it and "Someone who is on the ball" written across it as an attention-grabber for a resume. Admittedly, it did grab her attention and she did call the applicant. It was more out of curiosity than anything else. Although it worked in this case, it was a risky move and Jackie does not call applicants who use highly unusual methods very often.

CHAPTER 21

The Job Search—How to

Job Hunt for the First Time

Now you have a resume, but where do you send it?

Obviously, there are hundreds of websites, manuals, listings, newspaper ads, and so on that will give you leads for job opportunities in your area of interest. It can be overwhelming when you are not sure where to begin. Each position may have different opportunities for job seekers to get their start in the industry. For more technology-driven jobs such as the camera department or the sound department, it may be best to begin by working in (or donating your time to) a gear rental facility. You can also offer your services to a student or independent (low budget) film. In skilled professions that require technical training, these areas of opportunity often are starting points for future D.P.s or sound mixers. No matter which methods you choose for beginning your career path, you will need to search for that opening.

There are different outlets available for job searching in film as opposed to television or video programs. But once you find contact information for a possible position, the application process is generally the same. In this chapter I will reveal to you my main strategy for job hunting in production. It's not a secret; anyone can do it and probably many people do. I believe that I take a few extra steps that ensure better feedback and more opportunities. If you follow all of the steps, you can have that assurance too.

The *Reporter* Method

In concept, the job-hunting technique I call "The *Reporter* Method" is very simple. *The Hollywood Reporter* is an industry magazine for television and film production. It is generated in Southern California and caters to the industry. It is not your typical pop-culture, entertainment magazine like *People* or *Entertainment Weekly*. Instead, it is ranked with *Variety* as a leading trade magazine serving the producers and executives in the entertainment business. Most people trying to get work in production read *The Hollywood Reporter* and *Variety* (and browse their Web sites) for the classified ads, which are solely geared to the entertainment industry. Of course you should look at these ads during your job hunt. As easy as it may seem to send a resume to a job listed in a trade magazine, it is not always the easiest way to get noticed. They are magazines that a large percentage of the entertainment industry professionals read to keep up on the day to day production ins and outs. Similarly, there are now a few Web sites available to search for production work via the Internet (see appendix, p. 192). Subscription services like www.productionweekly.com can provide up-to-the-minute job listings in the industry. I have found that the way I used *The Hollywood Reporter* to find work actually helped me more often than answering an ad, and this system enhanced my organizational skills. I use *The Hollywood Reporter* in my examples here, but it is the system, not the magazine, that is the key. Applying these tips to any job posting will lead to results. It's not only *whom* you call, but also *how* you call that gets your foot in the door. Let me explain.

This process is geared toward looking to work on a television or film production, most likely in L.A. or in another major city. If this is not your immediate intention, you can apply the basics of this plan to a magazine or listing for a position in your area. *The Hollywood Reporter* and www.productionweekly.com contain job listings located in L.A. or New York, but keep in mind the basic premise of what you read here, and you can apply it practically anywhere. The important lesson of this process is to understand and practice the organization behind it. Successful job hunting is just a matter of being organized and patient.

Find your copy of the Weekly International Issue of *The Hollywood Reporter* that contains the television production listing. It comes out during the third week of every month. Unfortunately, if you don't live in Southern California, this may be difficult to obtain. Check around at magazine stores or theater and entertainment specialty bookstores. In California the magazine is a daily publication, whereas other states and countries will only receive this Weekly International Edition, which hits the stands every Thursday. You can also register online at www.hollywoodreporter.com to have access to the listings via the Internet. The issue is a weekly overview of the goings on in the business for that week. It recaps the movie earnings, tells the news of the day, and lists updates to feature films and televisions production for that week, among other pertinent news. The film and television production listings are of particular interest to anyone reading this book. They provide all the information you need for pursuing employment for any major broadcasting, television, or film production in the world. This is where we begin our search with "The *Reporter* Method."

If you are only interested in television production, refer to the television section as mentioned above. If you are only interested in films in production, refer to any Weekly International Edition. Since they are very similar in nature, you may extend your search to cover both areas. Of course if you are interested in another aspect of the industry such as television news or corporate communications, just apply the organizational structure from this chapter toward other listings or job outlets.

Feature Film

The Film section of the Weekly International Edition is broken into four parts: films in development, films in preparation, films in production, and international films. They are not listed alphabetically in each section, but in chronological order. Read through the selections carefully and get to know what is out there waiting for you. For our purposes we will concentrate on national films, although the same idea will apply to international listings and any other job resource in the industry.

Development

The films listed in the development category have very short listings. Since the films are only in development and not yet in production, there are very small staffs involved and very little information to be found via media outlets such as trade magazines. Nonetheless, there are listings for them, and a clever researcher can find out what he or she needs to know. The development stage is a great place to make an initial contact. During this period in the project, things may not be as frenzied as they are during a shoot, so any friends you make who are involved with a production at this stage will more likely have your attention for longer at this point than they will later in the schedule. There are little to no crew hired, so you may be the first resume in the stack. On the other hand, the producers may not yet have the funding, or perhaps they have the funding but are not considering applicants at this point. In this case, your call may not land you a job right away. It can open the door to meeting a new person though, and that is what this business is all about.

Preparation (Pre Production)

The early stages of pre production for a film are when you need to interview. Pay close attention to the date listed by the title; it may be outdated and they may have already started shooting. Either way it can't hurt to call. You never know when someone has quit or been fired, and timing is everything.

Production

By the time a film is listed in production, it is already shooting, and a call from you will most likely be too late. Unless someone has moved out, there will be no room for a new hire.

Television

The monthly listing of television programs in production is just that, a listing of the basic information to all current productions. It includes broadcast and cable programs, both large and small, that are airing nationally and internationally.

production charts

APRIL 16-22, 2002

Week 16

Shaded ...... New Listing
★ ...... Change in Listing

Galidor: Defenders of The Outer Dimension (Fox) Series
ExPrd., Jacques Pettigrew, Tom Lynch; Prd., Marie-Claude Beauchamp, Michel Lemire; Dir., George Mihalka, Giles Walker, Jim Donovan; Wrtr., Tom Lynch; PrdEx., Ken Katsumoto; Publ., Gerry Porter, Marie Christine Dufour

Columbia Pictures Television
9336 W. Washington Blvd., Culver City, CA 90232 - 310-202-1234

Days of Our Lives (NBC) Soap
ExPrd., Ken Corday, Tom Langan; Supv Prd., Steve Wyman; Prd., Sheryl Harmon; Cstg., Fran Bascom

The Young and the Restless (CBS) Soap
SrExec Prd., William J. Bell; ExPrd., Edward Scott; Prd., David Shaughnessy; Coord Prd., Nancy Ward; Cstg., Marnie Saitta; Publ., Frank Tobin

Columbia TriStar TV Distribution
10202 W. Washington Blvd., Culver City, CA 90232 - 310-244-7411

Ricki Lake (SYN) Series
(In assn w/ The Garth Ancier Co.)
ExPrd., Gail Steinberg; CoExPrd., David Shenfeld; Dir., Bob McKinnon; LinePrd., Susan Sobocinski

Columbia TriStar Domestic Television
9336 W. Washington Blvd., Culver City, CA 90232 - 310-202-3788 Fax 310-202-3766

Dawson's Creek (WB) Series
(In assn w/ Granville Prods.)
ExPrd., Paul Stupin, Tom Kapinos, Greg Prange; CoExPrd., Jeffrey Stepakoff, Gina Fattore; Prd., David Blake Hartley; CoPrd., Rina Mimoun; Cstg., Patrick Rush

Family Law (CBS) Series
(In assn w/ Paul Haggis Prods./CBS Prods.)
ExPrd., Paul Haggis, Stephen Nathan, David Shore, Fred Gerber; Prd., Gary Law; CoPrd., Hilton Smith, Tommy Moran, Jan Nash; AsPrd., Max Mayer; Cstg., Mary Jo Slater; Publ., Jennifer Schmitz

The Guardian (CBS) Series
(In assn w/ David Hollander Prods./Gran Via Prods./CBS Prods.)
ExPrd., David Hollander, Mark Johnson, Michael Pressman; CoExPrd., Vahan Moosekian; Supv Prd., Sara Cooper, Michael R. Perry; Prd., Jimmy Miller, Peter Parnell, Alfonso Moreno; Cstg., Jeannie Bacharach

Jeopardy! (SYN) Game Show
ExPrd., Harry Friedman; Prd., Lisa Broffman, Gary Johnson, Richard Schmidt; Dir., Kevin McCarthy; Wrtr., Steven Dorfman, Kathy Easterling, Billy Wisse, Steve Tamerius, Debbie Griffin, Jim Rhine, Michele Silverman

The King of Queens (CBS) Series
(In assn w/ Hanley Prods./CBS Prods.)
ExPrd., Michael J. Weithorn, Josh Goldsmith, Cathy Yuspa, Kevin James, Tony Sheehan; CoExPrd., Jeff Sussman; Prd., David Bickel, Annette S. Davis, Rob Schiller; CoPrd., Ilana Wernick, Chris Downey; Cstg., Meg Liberman, Cami Patton

Odyssey 5 (Showtime) Series
ExPrd., Manny Coto, Tracy Torme; Supv Prd., Larry Gross; Prd., Jim Michaels; CoPrd., Adam J. Shully; Wrtr., Lindsay Jewett Sturman; ExStory Ed., Edithe Swensen; PrdEx., Andy House; Cstg., Stephanie Gorin, Eric Dawson; Publ., Steven Clark

Residents (TNT) Series
ExPrd., R.S. Cutler; Supv Prd., Dan Partland; Sr Prd., Ted Skillman; CoPrd., Gina Kwon, Amy Veltman, Christine Noe, Keith Hoffman; LinePrd., Patty Gary-Cox; AsPrd., Belisa Balaban; PrdEx., Susan Nessanbaum-Goldberg; Publ., Steven Clark

Ripley's Believe It or Not (TNT) Series
ExPrd., Dan Jbara; Supv Prd., Dennis Lortz; Sr Prd., Roman Rosales; Prd., Phil Davis; CoPrd., Kathleen Burns; LinePrd., Jack Martin; AsPrd., Gail Smerigan; Dir., Paul Nichols; PrdEx., Susan Nessanbaum-Goldberg; Publ., Steven Clark

Russian Roulette (Game Show Network) Series
ExPrd., Gunnar Wetterberg; Supv Prd., Michael Metzger; Coord Prd., Howard Baver; Dir., Lenn Goodside; Wrtr., Arnie Meissner, Stephanie Wilder, Doug Armstrong; PrdEx., Susan Nessanbaum-Goldberg; Cstg., Mark Saks, Delia Frankel; Publ., Steven Clark

Street Time (Showtime) Series
ExPrd., Stephan Kronish, Richard Stratton; Supv Prd., Nicholas Grey; CoPrd., Lois Johnson; AsPrd., Gary Mueller; Cstg., Susie Ferris; Publ., Steven Clark

Strong Medicine (Lifetime) Series
ExPrd., Whoopi Goldberg, Tammy Ader; CoExPrd., Jeremy Littman; Prd., John Flynn, Rick Alexander; CoPrd., Joe DeOliveira, Lone Zerweck; AsPrd., Tom Leonardis; Story Ed., Robin Katz, Jim Symons, Lynn Leonhard; PrdEx., Andy House; Cstg., Lori Sugar; Publ., Jennifer Schmitz

Wheel of Fortune (SYN) Game Show ✓
ExPrd., Harry Friedman; Prd., Karen Griffith, Steve Schwartz; Dir., Mark Corwin

Worst Case Scenario (TBS) Series
ExPrd., Craig Piligian; Supv Prd., Ronnie Weinstock, Chuck Bond; Prd., Lauren Brady; Dir., Cole McKay; PrdEx., Susan Nessanbaum-Goldberg; Cstg., Michelle Mock; Publ., Steven Clark

Comedy Central
2049 Century Park E., #2295, Los Angeles, CA 90067 - 310-201-9515

The Daily Show (Comedy Central) Series
ExPrd., Madeleine Smithberg; Supv Prd., Rob Fox; Dir., Scott Preston; Hd Wrtr., Chris Kreski; Talent, Hank Gallo

South Park (Comedy Central) Series
ExPrd., Anne Garefino, Deborah Liebling, Trey Parker, Matt Stone; Wrtr., Trey Parker, Matt Stone; ExChrg Prd., Deborah Liebling

Court TV
600 3rd Ave., New York, NY 10016 - 212-973-6754

★ Catherine Crier Live (Court TV) Talk Show
ExPrd., Rita Barry, Emily Barsh; Dir., Dominic Palumbo; ExChrg Prd., Marlene Dann

★ Hollywood at Large (Court TV) Series
ExPrd., Steve Bronstein; Sr Supv Prd., Marvin Daye; Prd., Michelle DuMont; AsPrd., Michelle Stolls; Dir., Dominic Palumbo; PrdEx., Marlene Dann

Mugshots (Court TV) Series
(In assn w/ Parco Prods.)
ExPrd., Anthony Horn; ExChrg Prd., Ed Hersh

The System (Court TV) Series
ExPrd., Bonnie Dry, Anthony Horn, Robyn Hutt, Carolyn Kresky; ExChrg Prd., Ed Hersh

Curious Pictures
440 Lafayette St., New York, NY 10003 - 212-674-1400

Codename: Kids Next Door (Cartoon Network) Animated Series
ExPrd., Susan Holden, Steve Oakes, David Starr, Richard Winkler; Prd., Bruce Knapp; Dir., Mr. Warburton; Wrtr., Mr. Warburton, Mo Willems; Story Ed., Mo Willems; PrdEx., Khaki Jones; Cstg., Collette Sunderman

David E. Kelley Prods.
1600 Rosecrans Ave., Bldg. 4B, Manhattan Beach, CA 90266 - 310-727-2200

Ally McBeal (Fox) Series
(In assn w/ Twentieth Century Fox Television)
ExPrd., David E. Kelley, Bill D'Elia; CoExPrd., Alice West, Pamela Wisne; Supv Prd., Steve Robin; Prd., Roberto Benabib, Constance M. Burge, Kim Hamberg, Jack Philbrick, Ellie Herman; AsPrd., Rosearn M. Keris, Pam Jackson; PrdEx., Rick Silverman; Cstg., Nikki Valko, Ken Miller; Publ., Stacey M. Luchs

Boston Public (Fox) Series
(In assn w/ Twentieth Century Fox Television)
ExPrd., David E. Kelley, Jonathan Pontell; CoExPrd., Mike Listo, Kerry Lenhart, John J. Sakmar; Prd., Douglas Steinberg, Peter Burrell, Jeremy Miller, Daniel Cohn, Philip Neel; CoPrd., Sean Whitesell; AsPrd., Chuck Conway; PrdEx., Rick Silverman; Cstg., Laura Schiff; Publ., Stacey M. Luchs

The Practice (ABC) Series
(In assn w/ Twentieth Century Fox Television)
ExPrd., David E. Kelley, Bob Breech; CoExPrd., John Tinker; Supv Prd., Christina Musrey; Prd., Pamela Wisne, Joseph Berger-Davis, Jeff Rake; CoPrd., Lynne E. Litt; AsPrd., Steven Lang, Tammy ann Casper; PrdEx., Rick Silverman; Cstg., Janet Gilmore, Megan McConnell; Publ., Stacey M. Luchs

Decode Entertainment Inc.
512 King St. E., Suite 104, Toronto, ON M5A 1M1 - 416-363-8034 Fax 416-363-8919

Angela Anaconda (ABC Family Channel) Animated Series
(In assn w/ C.O.R.E. Digital Pictures)
ExPrd., Steven DeNure, Joanna Ferrone, Susan Rose; Prd., Beth Stevenson; CoPrd., John Manella; AsPrd., Kym Hyde; Dir., Kyle Menzies, Doug Masters; Story Ed., Holly Huckins; Publ., Jacqueline Nuwame

Dick Clark Prods.
3003 W. Olive Ave., Burbank, CA 91505-459 - 818-841-3003 Fax 818-954-8609

The 29th Annual Daytime Emmy Awards (CBS) Special
ExPrd., Dick Clark; Prd., Al Schwartz; Dir., Louis J. Horvitz; Wrtr., Barry Adelman, Ken Shapiro; PrdEx., Bob Bardo; ExChrg Prd., Fran LaMaina

The 37th Annual Academy of Country Music Awards (CBS) Special
ExPrd., Dick Clark, Al Schwartz; Prd., R.A. Clark, Barry Adelman; CoPrd., Ron Weed; Dir., Bruce Gowers; Wrtr., Barry Adelman, Robert Arthur; ExChrg Prd., Fran LaMaina

★ American Bandstand's 50th Anniversary (ABC) Special
ExPrd., Dick Clark; Prd., Larry Klein; CoPrd., Barry Adelman; Dir., Barry Glazer; Wrtr., Barry Adelman; PrdEx., Bob Bardo; ExChrg Prd., Fran La Maina; Publ., Paul Shefrin

Bloopers (ABC) Series
ExPrd., Al Schwartz, Dick Clark; Prd., Barry Adelman; CoPrd., Ken Shapiro; ExChrg Prd., Fran La Maina

Digital Ranch
14110 Riverside Dr., Sherman Oaks, CA 91423 - 818-817-9690 Fax 818-817-9699

The History of Basic Training (History Channel) Special
ExPrd., Robert Kirk, Rob Lihani; Prd., Tom Jennings; CoPrd., Mike Vincenti; PrdEx., Ann Hackett

The History of The Beach (History Channel) Special
ExPrd., Robert Kirk, Rob Lihani; Prd., Laura Verklan; CoPrd., David Cargill; PrdEx., Ann Hackett

Latinos & the Medal of Honor (History Channel) Special
ExPrd., Robert Kirk, Rob Lihani; Prd., Arthur Drooker; CoPrd., Teri Scott, PrdEx., Ann Hackett

Mail Call (History Channel) Series
ExPrd., Robert Kirk, Rob Lihani; Prd., Ann Hackett; CoPrd., David Cargill, Tara Craig, Teri Scott, Martha Sloan, Mike Vincenti

Sniper (History Channel) Special
ExPrd., Robert Kirk, Rob Lihani; Prd., Greg Goldman, Tony Long, Andy Papadopoulos, Dan Gagliasso; CoPrd., Mike Vincenti, Martha Sloan, PrdEx., Ann Hackett

The Long Grey Line: The Spirit of West Point (History Channel) Special
ExPrd., Robert Kirk, Rob Lihani; Prd., Arthur Drooker; CoPrd., Teri Scott; PrdEx., Ann Hackett

DreamWorks Television
100 Universal City Plaza, Bldg. 477, Universal City, CA 91608 - 818-695-5000

The Job (ABC) Series
(In assn w/ Touchstone Television/Apostle Pictures/The Cloudland Co.)
ExPrd., Peter Tolan, Denis Leary, Jim Serpico, Lauren Corrao; CoExPrd., Rick Dresser; Prd., Kerry Orent; Coord Prd., Leslie Tolan; Cstg., Avy Kaufman; Publ., Mozell Miley

E! Entertainment Television
5750 Wilshire Blvd., Los Angeles, CA 90036 - 323-954-2400 Fax 323-954-2662

Behind the Scenes (E!) Series
Supv Prd., Art Lovell; Prd., Chris May, Frank Moran; Talent, Eliza Cost, Karen Rhee, Rich Pisani; ExChrg Prd., Edward Zarcoff

Celebrity Adventures (E!) Series
ExPrd., Gary Snegaroff, Scott Woodward; Supv Prd., Shannon Keenan; Prd., Mike Demers; PrdEx., John Rieber; Talent, Eliza Cost; Publ., Diane Morgan

Coming Attractions (E!) Series
Supv Prd., Art Lovell; Prd., Amy Ikeda; Dir., Cynthia Zoller Malone, ExChrg Prd., Edward Zarcoff

E! News Daily/E! News Weekend (E!) Series
ExPrd., Peggy Abraham; Dir., Cynthia Zoller Malone; Talent, Jill Lascher, John Wood, Lisa Rowan, Rich Pisani, Juliette Knight, Camille Anderson; ExChrg Prd., Gary Snegaroff; Publ., Elena Girard

The E! True Hollywood Story (E!) Series
ExPrd., Mark R. Harris; Supv Prd., Andreas Kanonenberg; PrdEx., Betsy Rott; Talent, Barry Nugent, Marcia Landsdown, Karyn Wulburn, Stacie Gottsegan, Lillian Mizrahi, Kelly Greenleaf; Publ., Diane Morgan

Extreme Close-Up (E!) Series
Supv Prd., Nick Sotirakos; Talent, Karen Rhee; ExChrg Prd., John Rieber

Howard Stern (E!) Talk Show
ExPrd., Robin Radzinski; Prd., Jon Bilicki, Doug Z. Goodstein, Mike Gange; Dir., Scott DePace, PrdEx., Gary Snegaroff

Nearly Famous (E!) Series
ExPrd., Jeff Shore; Supv Prd., Mark Harris; Prd., Emily Puk; Publ., Cindy McLean, Kim Pinsker

RANK (E!) Series
ExPrd., Deana Delshad Schwartz; Supv Prd., Nick Cates; Prd., Stefania Di Mambro, Maggie Welter, Erin Zelie; AsPrd., Michael Ambers, Fred Charleston, Jenna Girard, Jacob Isenberger; Wrtr., Michael Seligman; PrdEx., Betsy Rott, John Rieber; Talent, Eliza Cost, John Wood, Rich Pisani, Kendee Yamaguchi, Carla Steiner; Publ., Elena Girard

Revealed with Jules Asner (E!) Series
ExPrd., Gary Socol; Supv Prd., Barry Grey; Prd., ...

38 www.hollywoodreporter.com

Television production listings from *The Hollywood Reporter*

Reading a listing for either film or television will provide you with key information to start your search. They will likely list a production company or studio associated with the project and possibly a telephone number. The producer or celebrity talent may also be listed. From here you can assess the type of production. If it is a bigger-budget, blockbuster film, it will most likely be attached to a large studio name with a larger-than-life celebrity name attached. If the production budget is lower, the information provided may seem less familiar.

"I don't care about the budget, I just need a job." Is that what you are thinking? Yes, you need a job, but in order to get one it helps to know something about the company that you are calling. This way, you can assess the possibility that they will need your talent. A lower-budget film will more likely take newcomers or less-experienced crew, paying lower wages in return. The lower the budget, the more responsibility you will likely have as a crew member. They'll take what they can get. Larger budget films will more likely already have regulars and friends lined up for their crew, using experienced veterans in return for higher wages. This is not always the case, but it is a very common scenario.

There is nothing wrong with being ambitious. You can set your heart on a mega-movie and go for it! You never know what may happen. As I said, timing is everything. But for faster results I recommend starting with smaller-scale productions and lesser-known companies. The same is true for television. Sure, it sounds like it would be fun to work for *The West Wing*, but they probably have their returning crew from last year's successful run. A new show that has not made its debut yet probably doesn't have the same stack of a hundred resumes sitting in a file cabinet that a show like *The West Wing* does. Again, they also may not have the pay scale that a popular NBC sitcom does. But getting in early with an unknown show can be an adventure. Who knows? Maybe the show you find will debut as the most-watched show ever! The people who joined the crew for *The West Wing* had never heard of it before and did not know if it would be a success or a bomb, but they landed a job there and they're smiling about it now. As one commercial producer suggested, "Experience is relative . . . don't get snobby about what you're going after." Experience on any production will help you climb higher on the ladder, no matter what the production is. Being selective only narrows your chances of getting your start.

If you do come across a small company or a program that you've never heard of, find its listing in *TV Guide* or look for the company name on the Internet. Make a point of checking it out. Maybe you'll discover an interesting topic or program you never knew existed or a production company that intrigues you. It can be a learning experience just to know what is on TV and what people are watching.

Starting the Search

Now, to begin. Use a highlighter marker to note the listings that are of particular interest to you, and use a dark marker to cross off the places that you have no interest in at all.

Once you have glanced them over, it is time to begin your search. On the top of the first page of a spiral notebook, write down the name of the first production company you are going to call and today's date. Also write the name of the program or film being produced and the phone and fax numbers. Switch to a different pen or to a pencil once that information is recorded. Now you are ready to place your first call. The goal of your first call is to find a contact at this company to whom you can submit your resume and make your first impression. This is a very important phone

"UNTITLED RICH APPEL PROJECT" Pilot / NBC   12-06-01 ★
TWENTIETH CENTURY FOX TELEVISION
10201 W. Pico Blvd., Bldg. 746, Los Angeles, CA 90035
                                        PHONE - 310-369-1000 FAX - 310-369-3242
STATUS - Spring 2002
PRODUCER - Rich Appel
A half-hour single-camera ensemble comedy, set in the world of young U.S. prosecutors in the Foley Square headquarters of the U.S. Attorney's offices in New York.

"UNTITLED ROBERT PALM PROJECT" Pilot / UPN   11-29-01 ★
PARAMOUNT NETWORK TELEVISION
5555 Melrose Ave., Schulberg Building, Room 302, Los Angeles, CA 90038
                                        PHONE - 323-956-5000 FAX - 323-862-1410
STATUS - Active Development
PRODUCER - Robert Palm
A new take on the private eye genre.

"UNTITLED TIM HERLIHY COMEDY" Pilot / NBC   11-29-01 ★
HAPPY MADISON PRODUCTIONS
10202 West Washington Blvd., Judy Garland Building, Culver City, CA 90232
                                        PHONE - 310-244-3100 FAX - 310-244-0074
STATUS - Spring 2002
PRODUCER - Jack Giarraputo - Adam Sandler - Tim Herlihy - Doug Robertson CAST - Jon Lovitz - Norm Macdonald
NBC STUDIOS 330 Bob Hope Drive, Suite C-227 Burbank, CA 91523 818-840-7500 FAX - 818-840-7681
A buddy comedy, about a pair of mismatched roommates.

"UNTITLED TONY JONAS & CHARLES HOLLAND PROJECT" Pilot / UPN   11-29-01 ★
TONY JONAS PRODUCTIONS
4000 Warner Blvd., Bldg. 34, Rm. 100 Burbank, CA 91522
                                        PHONE - 818-954-7111 FAX - 818-954-4101
STATUS - Spring 2002
PRODUCER - Tony Jonas - Charles Holland
WARNER BROS. TELEVISION 4000 Warner Blvd., Bldg. 137, Rm. 2020, Burbank, CA 91505 818-954-6000 FAX - 818-954-7885
About a group of law students.

"UNTITLED YVETTE LEE BOWSER COMEDY" Pilot / ABC   11-15-01 ★
TONY JONAS PRODUCTIONS
4000 Warner Blvd., Bldg. 34, Rm. 100 Burbank, CA 91522
                                        PHONE - 818-954-7111 FAX - 818-954-4101
STATUS - Spring 2002
PRODUCER - Tony Jonas - Yvette Lee Bowser CAST - Gary Owens
SISTERLEE PRODUCTIONS 4000 Warner Blvd., Bldg. 180, Ste 511, Burbank, CA 91522 818-954-7579 - FAX - 818-954-2741
WARNER BROS. TELEVISION 4000 Warner Blvd., Bldg. 137, Rm 2020, Burbank, CA 91505 818-954-6000 FAX - 818-954-7885
A comedy based on a couple who are in a racially mixed marriage.

"VANISHED" Pilot / CBS   01-10-02 ★
JERRY BRUCKHEIMER FILMS
1631 10th St. Santa Monica, CA 90404
                                        PHONE - 310-664-6260 FAX - 310-664-6261
STATUS - March 6
PRODUCER - Jerry Bruckheimer - Billy Devlin - Hank Steinberg - Jonathan Littman DIRECTOR - David Nutter
WARNER BROS. TELEVISION 4000 Warner Blvd., Bldg.137, Rm 2020, Burbank, CA 91505 818-954-6000 FAX - 818-954-7885
The drama centers on the head of the Missing Persons Task Force of the FBI Jack Malone.

"THE WANDA SYKES SHOW" Pilot / FOX   01-10-02 ★
MOHAWK PRODUCTIONS
4000 Warner Blvd. Bldg. 136, Rm 213 Burbank, CA 91522-0001
                                        PHONE - 818-954-7902 FAX - 818-954-3979
STATUS - Spring 2002
PRODUCER - Bruce Helford - Les Firestein CAST - Wanda Sykes
WARNER BROS. TELEVISION 4000 Warner Blvd., Bldg.137, Rm 2020, Burbank, CA 91505 818-954-6000 FAX - 818-954-7885
A comedy about a judge in the nation's capital.

Television production listings from www.productionweekly.com

call, probably the most important call you will make during the process. Many people will call a company only to ask for their fax number and simply hang up the phone. This doesn't really get you anywhere at a large production company except for the long-shot of catching someone's eye at the fax machine. No, what we're doing here is establishing a relationship. We are making a connection with a person at the company that will hopefully *want* to look at your resume or at least will give it to the right person in order to help move you along. This is the phone call that lets them know who you are and that you are important.

How do you do that? It's simple. Be bold and assertive; give the person you speak to a sense of your personality and a sense of determination. When you call, you are not simply looking for a fax number or address. You are not merely asking if there are job opportunities available; you are introducing yourself. Take a deep breath and let's go!

Placing the Call

Dial the telephone number from the listing. Most likely you will get a receptionist. At a studio, this person is very busy and doesn't have time to chat. For a smaller production company you may find a more bubbly person who is eager to make your acquaintance. If you are not using an L.A. or New York source such as *The Hollywood Reporter*, but are using local listings in your hometown, you may find that it is much simpler to find a person to talk to. In any scenario, you want this person to like you so that he or she will do you the favor of putting the next person on the phone with you. (However, if the person answering the phone is a receptionist at a large studio, be quick and to the point—this person has too many other lines ringing and will direct you to another receptionist who you should speak to instead.) With a smaller company, you can possibly afford to be a little slower, but still use your time wisely. No doubt this person is also very busy.

The first question you need answered is, "Where do I reach the production office?" for the program on which you are interested in working. If you are calling a studio such as ABC or Warner Brothers, the phone number you have called is the main line for all of their offices. Each program or feature film in production will have its own office (most likely in a different building) and separate phone lines. You need to be able to call those offices directly in order to make any headway with the hiring staff. So when you speak to the receptionist, ask him or her how you can contact the production directly. In the case of a large studio, you may ask for two or three television shows' phone numbers during the one call. If the receptionist is not too busy, he or she may want to assist you. But don't ask for more than three at a time; the receptionist will get annoyed and will likely not want to help you, should you need to call again.

Once you have obtained the phone number to the specific production office you are looking for, write it down on the same sheet of your notebook, labeling it for future reference. You'll be surprised at how easy it is to forget who you were calling and what the person said when you need that information later. Always write it down.

Now it is time to call the production office directly. This time your goal is to talk to the person who does the hiring. In production companies put together solely for a specific project like a feature film, there usually is no human resources department. They exist in corporate settings such as studios and the staff working at the studio, but not on a specific program. Rather, different department heads hire their own staff for the production. You need to weed through the staff of a show to find the person who will hire you. Most likely if this is your first job hunt, you are looking to be a production assistant either on the set or in the office. Therefore, you need to speak to the production coordinator to interview for the office position or to have her refer you to the assistant director for an on-set position. Either way, this is the person that you most likely need to speak with. This is true for any production, film or television, with the exception that a sitcom may not have a production coordinator. In this instance, a production manager or producer will fulfill that role and should be your goal of this phone call.

The Name Game

If you have any means to find out the name of the coordinator before you call, do it. It is always best to have a person to ask for when you place the call. If you don't know the coordinator's name, you can ask the person who answers the phone with a simple, "Who is your production coordinator, please?" This is when it gets tricky. They may ask, "What is this regarding?" and you can simply answer, "I am looking for employment and was wondering who to forward my resume to," or something of that nature.

If you're nervous, just remember that this person has been in your shoes and will hopefully be sympathetic, as long as you keep him or her on your side. If they are able to give you a contact name, *write it down*. Ask for proper spelling. Then ask if you can speak to that person. Try to get as far up on the chain of command as possible. If the receptionist knows that you are job-hunting, he or she may cut you off at this point and suggest that you send in a resume. If you aren't being totally rushed off the phone, now is the time to let this person know that you are serious and that you know what you're talking about. Say that you understand that he or she is busy and you don't want to waste anyone's time, but that you are interested in introducing yourself so that the coordinator will know whose resume is being received. Just try to keep your call going. This may not get you very far, but you've made your point and the receptionist will most likely remember you the next time you call. Familiarity is key to getting the job.

Small Talk

If you are able to make small talk at any point during this call, make it. Perhaps open your question with a statement such as, "I'm new in town" or "I just graduated from _____ College." If you are able to strike up a conversation and you touch on a subject of interest to the person you're speaking with, you may win him or her onto your side.

This is the same strategy to take with the production coordinator, should you get that far in your pursuit. Remember, these people are extremely busy. You've never seen this kind of busy before. They may not have the time to chat. You have the next ten seconds to state your case and make your impression. If you succeed, you can move onto the next step more quickly.

The Informational Interview

Now that you have the coordinator on the phone, but what do you say? Brief him or her on what your goal is. Remember, your goal is to work on this project! The object of this call is to get a job interview. But if the production is not hiring, maybe someone will meet with you for an informational interview. Rather than size you up for a job, an employer willing to meet with you may be kind enough to listen to your questions about the business, or about the particular production, as you interview him or her. By asking intelligent questions, you can learn more about the field and impress someone who may decide to call you later when a job becomes available.

You want to come in for an informational interview. What is important to express to the coordinator is that you don't want to waste his or her time; you only want the opportunity to introduce yourself in person. You know that you are a good employee, and he or she needs to see you in person to be able to better understand what a good asset you will be to the production. Suggest that when it is a little less busy, you can come by for a brief introduction. This will tell him or her that you are intelligent and are truly interested in working on this particular project. It will impress upon him or her that you are looking to meet the coordinator, not just anyone, and that you have an understanding of his or her demanding job and its time restraints. You will probably be told that there are no openings for employment at the moment, but don't let that stop you! This is a flighty business and people are constantly coming and going. You can still meet for an interview and still send in your resume. Who knows. . . a position may open up tomorrow out of the blue.

A Chat

When sending my resume to *Married. . .With Children*, I started with a phone call. I managed to reach the production coordinator who, fortunately for me, was having a slow day. She took my call and was surprisingly pleasant over the telephone. I opened my conversation with, "I just moved here from Chicago," and that was all it took to get the conversation flowing. As it turns out, this production coordinator had once lived in Chicago, working for *The Jenny Jones Show*. What a wonderful coincidence. We were able to chat briefly about Chicago. She liked the city and hoped to come back to visit in the future. Our chat ended with her telling me that there were no openings on her show and that as a sitcom there were limited positions for production assistants. She gave me some advice to follow in my continuing search for work. I sent a follow-up thank you letter to which she responded, calling me with further advice. She had liked my letters and wanted to help, even though there were no available positions on her show for me. By getting the opportunity to converse with a hiring person on the phone, I was able to make a new contact and to get myself a few more ideas of places to send my resume.

Let the coordinator know that you are sending your resume to his or her attention, making certain that you have the proper fax and/or mailing address before you hang up the phone. As you can see, this is not a simple phone call. But take a deep breath and plunge right in. You will be surprised at how good it feels to successfully reach your goals with each call.

Write It Down

Before you move on to the next call, you have a few notes to add to your page in the notebook. Start with the receptionist or the first person that took your call. Write down his or her name if you can, and add any notes about the conversation. Did he or she tell you they were hiring or to call back in three weeks? Did he or she laugh at your joke about the weather? Did you talk about anything that would stand out from the rest of his or her phone calls? Did he or she give you the name of the next person in line to speak to or behave rudely? Write it all down.

Next do the same for the coordinator or any other person you spoke to. Did you have any outstanding conversation topics? What did he or she tell you about the project, availability for meeting in person, or your interview?

Now continue calling each number on the list of projects you highlighted for as long as you can stand it on a given day. You will most likely get into a groove and get the system down quickly. I told you it was simple. It's just a matter of being organized. Always remember to start a new page in your notebook for each production company, even if you only leave a voicemail message and it only takes up one line of space. You will fill in more of the pages when people return your calls. By the way, if you do leave a voicemail, be sure to note when you left it and for whom in your notebook. This may seem like a lot of work, and it is. It's your full-time job for the moment. Your hard work will pay off in the end if you keep at it.

Broaden Your Scope

Obviously, my explanation of "The *Reporter* Method" focuses on using trade magazine listings for job hunting. However, if you use creativity you are likely to find many other opportunities toward which you can apply this organizational guideline.

Film Commissions

Your first local film source is the city or state's film commission. They are on top of the scene and always know what productions are going on in the area. Filmmakers often begin their pre-production process by working with film commissions to find the right location for filming. Therefore, film commissions also find themselves in hiring positions when drivers, scouts, and P.A.s are needed to take out-of-town filmmakers around the city to scout possible locations. For this reason, some film commissions have a file of resumes handy for hiring, as well as to pass on to the film producers who need to find local crew when they are ready to set up shop in a town with which they are unfamiliar.

Also, film commissions will often have a job hotline set up for crew in the area to check periodically. The hotline will likely list productions that are in town and what crew positions are needed at the time of your call. Contact the commission to ask for the hotline number, or look it up online. In addition to the hotline, most state film commissions have publications that list the local crewmembers and their phone numbers. You will want to have your name and number listed in this publication so as not to miss out on your chance to beat someone else to receiving a phone call for freelance work. Many of these listings can now be found online. Go to your film commission or state tourism's Web site to find any local production guides in which you can be listed.

Film commissions can be very valuable resources to local job hunters. But you have to take the initiative in order for them to know you exist. If you don't send a resume, they can't keep it on file. Suzy Kellett of the Washington State Film Office says that her office remembers the people who take initiative and its members are able to give people chances when they become visible. She meets with producers following the film shoots in her area, and goes over the crew list with them to see if any people stood out as being valuable for future work. Because the film commission is such a valuable tool for filmmakers, and for the community, the commissioner must feel confident in his or her recommendations of crew people. If you stand out as a good, hard worker to the film commissioner, you can gain his or her assistance in helping your career get started. Not every commission will be able to help you in this way, but the only way to find out how they can help you is by asking. Contact your local film commission to inquire as to how they can help you, and how you can help them to bring film work to their city by being a valuable asset as a P.A. (See the appendix for a listing of the film commissions in your state.)

Temping
Temporary placement agencies are not just for corporate secretarial work. Many different types of companies related to the entertainment business hire temps for their offices. Ad agencies, production companies, radio stations, studios, and more will call for temporary help from time to time. sitcoms even hire temps to sit in their audiences to watch the show and provide feedback laughter for the actors to work with!

By temping in entertainment, you benefit by:
- Learning about a company or a different aspect of the business that you were unaware existed
- Getting to know an employer who is obviously short an employee and may be looking to permanently fill the position
- Getting paid to work in an office that has a fax machine that you can probably use to send your resume out should the opportunity arise, which will save you money and hassle if you don't own a fax machine at home.

Maternity Leave
Candy★ got her start in this business as a temp. Moving to California with a degree not related to film or television, she was open to any job she could find. She applied at a temp agency she found in the Yellow Pages. After typing tests and an interview, she was placed in several week-long positions. Shortly thereafter, Candy was placed

★ Not actual name

in a two-month job as an assistant to Mel Brooks, to fill in for a woman going on maternity leave. The woman quit her position as Mr. Brooks's assistant soon after her leave. Naturally, Candy was the most qualified candidate to replace her, and Candy's temp job turned into a lengthy full-time position working for a film legend. She grabbed the opportunity and launched herself into a career in entertainment. Now she's the technical manager at a large cable network.

Deferred Pay

Another unique job-finding opportunity is to work for free, or **deferred pay**. To "defer pay" is to defer your paychecks until after the project is sold and the company can better afford to pay you. Any project in this situation is likely to never make any money, so don't count on that paycheck finding you later. Just be happily surprised if it does.

Independent filmmakers across the globe are looking for free labor. By offering your services you will be helping out a future producer and/or director, and also learning your craft hands-on. Working on a low-budget (or no-budget) project is like an initiation into the business. Everyone does it at some point. Not only is it a great opportunity to network, but it can also be really fun. The key to working for free is that you are able to participate more and to put yourself in a higher position than you would normally have. For instance, you may be a P.A. on a large feature, but you can work as prop master in a low-budget Indie. The producer will be happy to have someone fill the position, and may be willing to hire a novice, using the saved money for big-name talent or equipment rental.

As you are learning a new position hands-on, you are also networking with people in the same situation. Get to know these inexperienced crew members. Someday they may be in a hiring position, and your key to getting the job you are striving for. Make sure you treat your non-paying job as if it were paying you richly. Give it the attention and concentration you would give to any job. As former producer Kim Blaise advises, "On any free job make it a point to get a paid job out of it." By working for free, someone owes you a favor. Work your new connection and do your best to find a paid position as your unpaid job comes to an end.

The Farm House

On *Pizza Wars* the crew worked for deferred pay. On this independent feature, people just out of school were working as art department coordinators, assistant directors, boom operators, and so on. Though I started as an office P.A., I was promoted to production coordinator halfway through the shoot, and was able to play an integral role in getting the film made. The commute from the city was far, and with long hours of work each day, we were a tired crew. The director offered to lend us her guest house, and shortly thereafter we found ourselves having a nightly slumber party. This feeling like a fraternity made for a. . . well. . . interesting experience.

After the film wrapped, we were all able to add our bigger and better job titles to our resumes. We walked away having learned or enhanced a skill set, and we all made contacts that we were able to use for future work. As for me, the producer recommended me to his friend for a paying job as a production coordinator on a feature film that had a slightly higher budget than this one. Many of my friends and co-workers from our small film have moved on to reach their goals. And I forever carry the memories of our time in the farmhouse.

Newspaper

Look in the Classified Section of the local newspaper. It is unlikely that you will ever find production positions in the Classified Section of a newspaper in any town. However, there are related positions that may pop up. Smaller towns may list production positions as opposed to larger cities that use industry networking to find their staffs. Conversely, looking in the Classified Section of a trade magazine is often a key resource for finding production work. Look in a local bookstore to find the trade magazines available to your industry. For instance, people in Los Angeles can choose from *The Hollywood Reporter* and *The Daily Variety*, whereas a person in New York may benefit more from *Shoot, Location,* or a local publication. These are just a few of the many publications that utilize their Classified Sections for production positions around the country.

Taking It to the Streets

Some people (especially those in New York City) tell me that they found their first jobs on foot. Either by contacting the local film commission, through the Yellow Pages, or from listings in *The Hollywood Reporter*, they hunted down films and production companies and applied for jobs in person. Have a generic resume (or a few geared toward the places you are visiting, assuming you've done some research and know who they are and what they do), and take a walk. Timing is everything. You just may be arriving at the right place at the right time.

The Information Highway

The Internet is becoming a source for job listings in the entertainment industry for regular full-time positions. Freelance positions are often filled before they are available for posting on the Internet. However, there are a few well-respected industry Web sites such as *www.mandy.com* and *www.filmpro.com,* which are updated frequently enough for this fast-paced business. (See the appendix for a listing of helpful Web sites.)

Other options for job hunting include newspaper Classified Sections, job hotlines from networks, film commissions, local industry magazines, etc.

Whatever means you use to find your contact, use your organizational skills to keep track of your pursuit and take notes that will bring you closer to reaching your goals. If you are not very organized by nature, learn to be! You will need organizational skills to work in most aspects of this industry.

Sending Your Resume

Now it's time to write the cover letter and to send your resume. This is assuming you had at least one successful phone call during which you were directed to send your resume to a specific person. Go over your generic resume and make any final touches that will direct it to a specific position at this company. For instance, if you are applying for a Walt Disney World movie of the week, having your summer job as a daycare counselor may grab their attention. It shows your interest in children and your ability to work with them, which is likely a good quality to have, especially if there are many child actors involved in the project. Use the suggestions from chapter 9 for guidance.

When hunting for a job opening, the key is to make the most of each phone call you place. Ask for the person who can help you; don't settle for just anyone who happens to answer the telephone. Take notes and assert yourself to get the information you need.

Remember that in this business, timing is everything. Be persistent and constantly continue your efforts to find places to send your resume. No doubt one of the places that you call will match your needs, and you will be granted an interview. It may take a while, so try not to be discouraged. A positive attitude and confidence will lead you in the right direction.

Are you ready? Don't fax in your resume just yet—you still need to write a cover letter!

CHAPTER 22

The Cover Letter—

Selling Your Skills

A cover letter needs to accompany your resume to the contact you made. As a person doing the hiring, I find it inappropriate when I am sent a resume without a cover letter. I have spoken to people who claim they don't read cover letters and find no value in them, but I disagree. The process of submitting your resume for review is a very precarious one. Any slip-up and you've lost your window of opportunity. What kind of impression are you making if you send in a resume with no cover letter? Not a professional one. A fax cover sheet does not suffice as a cover letter for a resume. Besides, the key to a good cover letter is that it allows you to expand on your talents and to enhance the information provided on your resume. It's an opportunity you have at the beginning of the process to introduce yourself and sell yourself to the employer.

A Hundred Resumes
Television director Eric Jewett says he first got his start in the business by sending out approximately a hundred resumes with cover letters to a hundred directors. Each letter was personalized and geared toward its recipient, telling the director, "You are my favorite director," and elaborating on how much he respected that director's work. Of the hundred letters, four responses came back stating that his resume would be kept on file for future reference. But one director responded with a phone call.

His assistant had just quit, and Eric's letter had perfect timing. Eric got his first job as a director's assistant from a resume sent with a gratuitous cover letter.

How to Start

Always address the cover letter to a real person. "To Whom It May Concern" is often a red flag to a prospective employer. If a letter is addressed to a specific person, that person is more likely to initially take interest in it, because it may be something important or personal. The addressee needs to find out what the letter is regarding. Make sure you do your homework and address your cover letter to someone who works at the company, spelling his or her name and title correctly. You've done all the work to get yourself a contact; this is the time when your initial conversation comes in handy.

Mistaken Identity

The envelope was your standard, business envelope. Neatly typed, it was addressed, curiously, to my friend who works for the competition. It was addressed to her name, but at my company's address. I opened it up to find a resume with a cover letter that explained the author's appreciation for our company and what we do. I would have believed her sincerity had she taken the time to find out exactly who she was sending the letter to and what it is that our company does. Instead of calling her for an interview, I let my friend at the other company know that she had some mail come our way.

There is not much credibility to a person's interest in a company if he or she can't even be bothered to get the name right.

Now it is your goal to keep the prospective employer reading the rest of the letter. It is a tough goal to accomplish. Once again, try to personalize. Remind your contact of your telephone conversation from today. By bringing up your conversation in the first sentence of your letter, the employer may be curious to read on for at least the rest of the paragraph. You have made this letter more significant than the others in the in-box by making it personal. You can use a simple sentence such as, "I enjoyed speaking with you today," or, "As we discussed in our telephone conversation today," and follow with a description of the conversation. You can also try to be more in-depth or detailed with a start like, "I really enjoyed our conversation about tropical rain forests today. Thank you for taking the time to speak with me on the telephone." Thanking this person for taking the time to speak with you is also a nice sentiment that will be appreciated.

The first paragraph should also state your reason for sending the letter and the resume. In this case, you are following up on your previous conversation in pursuit of employment. "I am following up on our conversation with a copy of my resume, as you suggested, for the opening in your department," or something along these lines will do the trick. It can be a few sentences or whatever you feel comfortable with, as long as the message is clear—you are looking for work. If the contact had told you that there were no openings, you can remind him or her in this paragraph that you are aware there are no openings at the moment but want to be kept in mind for the future. For example, "In our conversation this morning you informed me that *Prizzi's Honor* has no job openings at this time for a production assistant. However, I would like to meet with you for an informational interview and to introduce myself to you in person, at your convenience." Keep it short and to the point. Elaborating will only lose your audience, as these people are busy and in a hurry. Catch the reader's attention with a quick reminder of who you are and what your purpose is for sending the letter.

Your Story

The second paragraph is an opportunity to tell your contact something about yourself that you may not have covered in your conversation. You can use this opportunity to briefly elaborate on a topic about yourself and your qualifications that perhaps you only touched on over the telephone. This is also a perfect place to highlight a bullet point from your resume, with an explanation of how a particular experience relates to the job in question. See the sample cover letters listed in the appendix (pp. 186–188) for an example. You don't want to tell your life story here. This is your chance to brag about yourself and to show how vital you will be in the position you are aiming for. Remember, it is only a summary; you need to keep it short. For details, they will have to bring you in for an interview. You need to use this paragraph to make them *want* to have that interview. Entice them and stir their curiosity.

The End

The third and final paragraph is your summary. Remind the contact of why you are sending this letter. State your short-term goal. For instance, a simple "I would like to schedule an appointment to meet with you to further discuss my qualifications" can work. Leave a telephone number where you can be reached. This is a great chance to throw in one more personal note. You don't want to lose the reader while you're in the home stretch! Bring up your conversation about Brazil or wish him or her luck on the big project you discussed over the phone. It doesn't hurt to show that you were really listening and paying attention during the call by throwing in a reference.

It's a Small, Small World

After getting the proper information from a cold call I placed to the production office, I wrote a cover letter and faxed it with my resume to the production coordinator of *Party of Five*. In this letter, I had mentioned moving to Los Angeles from Chicago, which is what caught her eye. She called me immediately, very excited because she too was from Chicago. Over the telephone we hit it off. The next thing I knew, I was in the trailer on the Sony Studios lot in Culver City, waiting for my interview. There were no current openings, but she took me up on my request to meet in person for an informational interview. While in the office trailer, I learned a little bit about her position and about the fast pace of her office. I was able to meet other staff while I waited, and eventually had my five minutes to introduce myself to the coordinator. There was no immediate opening on the production itself, but one month later when they needed to hire a day-player to work on setting up the crew's Christmas party, I was one of the people she called. She kept me in mind because we had something in common and we clicked. The next season I was hired to be her assistant production coordinator on the show. A little commonality can go a long way.

There are many books available for standard letter-writing practices. The sample letters on the next pages will show you the standard formats. You always want to have your information at the top of the letter and a professional goodbye such as "Sincerely" at the end. Having your personal information at the top is crucial. If your letter somehow becomes separated from your resume, you will want the employer to have a way to contact you. Otherwise a busy executive will not try to hunt you down; he or she will simply toss your letter and find another one in the stack to call.

You also want to put the date at the top of the letter to keep track of how recent your resume is, and for prospective employers to know the age of a resume that they may be keeping on file for future reference. Once you proofread your letter, send it with your resume to the contact. The neater the package, the better it will be. This being said, you will benefit from typing the address onto the envelope. As on your resume, misspelling here is unacceptable. Most people will throw away a cover letter (and its resume) with a spelling error on it. The spell-check on your computer may not catch all of your mistakes. Proofread it thoroughly yourself. Simply put, if you weren't organized and detail-oriented enough to catch your typing mistake, what else will you let slip through the cracks while you're on the job?

If you want to be really organized, it wouldn't hurt to make a copy of the resume and letter for your records, especially if you've really changed this resume to gear it toward a specific company or position. You can refer to this copy to remember what you said when the contact calls you later for an interview. You can also use your copy to monitor which resumes and cover letters are getting you the most responses.

The Long Story, Short

When you submit your resume, remember to introduce it with a cover letter comprised of three areas of information: the header, which explains your letter's purpose; the middle, your opportunity to brag about yourself; and the end, your summary. At this point it would help to have a calendar. On your calendar, mark the week that your contact told you to call back. If you weren't given another date, then give it a few days for the resume to get there and for it to be read. Schedule a call-back into your plans. There is a strategy to be used for every move you make in your job hunt.

CHAPTER 23

The Follow-Up—What to

Do Next and How to Do It

The follow-up phone call is just as important as the resume and cover letter. Without following up, you will never even know if your letter was received. There is not much use in sitting around waiting for a phone call when the employer hasn't even received your phone number yet! This is one reason to follow up. The other is that by having sent your resume, the follow-up call is a perfect excuse to have to telephone your contact to make conversation again.

Planning the follow-up call can be very simple. Consider the seven days of a standard week, and how you feel about them when you are working. Generally speaking, you have Saturday and Sunday to either catch up on errands or to relax. Monday is generally a tough business day, one that people need to use to get back into the work groove that carries them through the week. It is not a good day to call in your cheery voice to ask for someone to consider you for work. It is likely that if you call on a Monday, your contact will either be swamped with work or just plain having a bad day. You don't want to be remembered as the person who interrupted his or her frantic day; you want to be remembered in a good light. I recommend not calling on a Monday.

Tuesday through Friday a random phone call like yours may be a welcome opportunity for a hard-working coordinator to take a break from the work he or she is doing. It may be a welcome stress reliever, in which case you are scoring bonus points for interrupting! However, if you are making a follow-up call on a Friday, you need to do it earlier in the day. You don't want to call to follow up only to find out that your contact left early for the weekend and now you have to wait another four days to call back.

As important as the day of the week may be, so is the time of day that you place the call. Calling early in the morning (before 9 AM) or late in the day (after 5 PM) will lead to greater opportunity for conversation. The person you are contacting is undoubtedly busy during the normal workday. By calling before the office phones start ringing and before the staff gets in, you will be calling before there are other distractions that will take attention away from you. The same may be true for calling in the evening. Using this strategy, the key will be finding the right time to call when the office is truly quiet, yet the person you are contacting is still there.

The point here is to think about your timing when you follow up with a phone call. Timing is everything in this business.

> **"Luck is a thing that happens when preparation meets opportunity."**
>
> **—Hugh O'Brian, actor**

Caught en Route

After graduation, once I was ready to seriously job hunt, I called my former boss from the internship I'd had on *Mo' Money*. I called to say hello and to touch base with him. I caught him in his car, on his way to his next feature, which was being shot in Indiana. We chatted for a while about school and about his next job. I mentioned that I had a friend in graduate school at the University of Notre Dame; perhaps I could visit her and pop in to see him while I was there. Like I said, timing is everything. He had been short-staffed in the locations department on this production, and the light bulb in his head went off. He suggested I bring clothes to stay for a week and maybe he could put me to work. My week turned into four months, and seven days after I had placed that call, I was holding the keys to Notre Dame's football stadium and greeting the caterers as they arrived to set up for another day's work.

The Follow-Up Call

Now you are dialing the number, but what do you say when someone answers? The office may be busy, but try to get through to the person to whom you addressed the letter. If you can't get that far, at least tell the receptionist or assistant that you are following up on a letter you sent to that person. He or she will likely tell you it was received and end the conversation. You can accept that answer or you can make yourself more memorable by trying to dig deeper for more information. Find out if the receptionist has any insight into future openings or into what your next step should be.

If you are able to reach your contact directly, start by stating that this is a follow-up call to your resume. Once you have your person on the phone, keeping him or her there to hear you out will be your task. You have your excuse, the reason for your call, to start off your conversation. Remember your goal. You are trying to get an interview. This conversation should add to any previous conversations you've had with this person. The key is to continue to make personal conversation and to find commonalties so this person will want to get to know you even better. Let him or her know that you would like to meet in person, even if just for a quick hello to introduce yourself. Let the conversation guide itself from here. If this is a bad time to call, ask about the possibilities of trying again in the future. Do whatever you can to establish a good relationship in this short time.

It is definitely important to take notes during the conversation. You may be surprised at how quickly you may forget elements of the conversation that could be key information in later meetings.

For starters, you are calling to follow up on the letter and resume that you sent. Was it received? Has your contact had a chance to look it over? If the employer tells you that he or she did look it over but there are no openings at the moment, is there something coming up in the future? Perhaps you can come in for an informational interview, to introduce yourself in person? Judge how busy this person is and how long you feel it is appropriate to continue the conversation without becoming annoying, as he or she needs to get on with the day. Again, make notes in the appropriate page of your notebook, recording anything specific that is mentioned, including a time and place to meet should you reach your goal of this call and get an interview. Make a note of the date and time of your conversation. If you are told to call back again another time, you will want to refer to the date of this call later. Mark a date in your calendar sometime in the future to call again. Try to estimate, based on your call, when the next call should take place. Persistence can often be the key to getting the job. How long to wait between calls depends on the situation. One sportscaster claims that he called his contact at a local station daily for weeks, and was eventually hired. Use your judgment and make a follow-up call plan.

Waiting in the Lobby

One future crewmember was not quite as prepared for her interview as she'd thought she was. She had scheduled her meeting with the prospective employer at the hotel where the crew was staying, where a temporary office was set up until a permanent one was arranged.

She arrived promptly, early actually, and waited patiently in the lobby. After waiting for over an hour, she realized that she had not repeated the plan back to the unit production manager over the telephone. Was she supposed to meet him in the lobby or in his suite? Sure enough, when she finally called his room, he had assumed that she was a no-show. He had expected her to call from the lobby upon arrival for the interview. Luckily for her, the UPM was in a good mood and a nice person. He hired her anyway.

Following up is important for being noticed and remembered. Plan your schedule and make time for follow-up telephone calls. Ask questions and take notes. You will see much greater results in your hunt this way.

Did you think that this process was a lot of work? Just wait, now it's time for your interview.

CHAPTER 24

The Interview—Making a

Lasting Impression

I t's exciting, isn't it? You hang up the phone having accomplished one of your goals and you've gotten yourself a job interview! Once the excitement wears off, you realize that now you have to prepare for the meeting that you worked so hard to get. For the most part, the interview process for a production position is significantly easier and more laid back than for a corporate position in another field. This is one of the easiest fields for which to interview, but it is still beneficial to be as ready as possible. From what to wear to what to say, there are a number of things to think about while preparing for the interview.

Research

Learning about the company that you want to work for is important not only for the interview, but also for the long run, as it helps to know who it is that you are about to spend most of your time and energy working with. By having an understanding about the background of the company and its basic structure, you will have more insight into the position and how you will fit into this particular production or office's structure. This is where the Internet can really come in handy during your job hunt. You can learn the basics about a company from their Web site. If you are looking to work on a specific program or film, you might find news articles written about it as it is developing, or perhaps you will find information about the person with whom you are about to meet. If it's an existing, on-air program series, make sure you watch a few episodes before your interview. You don't have that channel? Ask a friend to tape it. An interviewer may not quiz you or ask you questions to see what you know about the production, but your knowledge of the company will be noticed through regular conversation. One way to impress an employer is to let him or her see how knowledgeable you are about the company. This will demonstrate your resourcefulness, as well as your true desire to work there. Only a person with passion and dedication would put that much effort into getting to know the company that he or she is interested in, right? Knowing about the position you are interviewing for is equally, if not more, important. This meeting is to tell the employer that you are the person to do this job. Knowing as much as possible about the job in general will help your case. Prove your interest by doing your homework and using your knowledge while you are having conversations in your interview. Besides, this interview is also a tool for you personally. This is a chance for you to get to know your prospective employer and to assess whether or not this will be a good place for you to spend most of your waking hours. Remember, an interview is not only an effort to convince someone to hire you for a job, it is an opportunity for you to get to know the company and to ask questions as you decide if this is the place where you want to work.

Goals

Once again, it is time to take a look at your goals. This time you should prepare to answer questions about them. You may be asked about your long-term goals, as the interviewer is trying to determine what your potential is with this company. You may also be asked about your immediate plans. Do you want an entry-level position? Will you have any qualms about picking up the producer's dry-cleaning? Will you feel stifled by working behind the phones for months on end? Think about your goals and how you will answer those questions. The interviewer is looking to see how you will fit into the company's dynamic, and how you will help the company to accomplish its mission. Your answers will be important in helping the interviewer to assess your potential. Try to be honest and to be yourself. Just make sure that when you are answering questions about your goals that you answer within the context of how your goal or achievement will also help the company.

A good interviewer will allow time for you to ask your own questions. It is good to have questions planned just in case you are nervous and can't think of one off the cuff. But by taking in your surroundings as you arrive and listening carefully during the interview, you should be able to come up with some good questions regarding the position or the company itself. After all, you are trying to assess whether or not this is the place for you. There should be some questions that you have about your future workplace. A question as simple as "What would my work hours be like?" is enough to at least start a conversation. You can take this opportunity to ask more detailed questions about your duties in the position, or about your employer's background, or about the project's time frame and deadlines. Just have at least one question planned in case you aren't able to come up with one during the interview.

What to Wear

One of the nice things about working in production is that there is generally no real dress code, unless you work for a studio or on the business end of this creative industry. Being an artistic field, people tend to dress trendy or just plain comfortably since the hours are long and there is a lot of moving around. But the interview is where you are making your first impression. How you dress may be scrutinized just as much as your resume will be. Unless you are told otherwise, the standard business interview dress code should apply. Wearing a suit or a dress may be overkill for a production job interview, but it won't hurt you. If you are overdressed, it will be understandable, and the people that are meeting with you will appreciate your good intentions. On the other hand, by being underdressed you will give the impression that you are inconsiderate and that you are not going to be a good company representative because you do not take the company's attitude into consideration. For a freelance production position, slacks or a skirt and a nice shirt will suffice. This is a creative field you are entering. For production companies, unlike corporate studio environments, you can take risks and let your personality show through your wardrobe. Still, if you are normally very outlandish in your attire, a more conservative approach may better suit your goals here. The bottom line is to dress for a business meeting. After you've been hired you will be able to adapt to whatever dress code your office recommends. Asking about the dress code is an appropriate question to ask during an interview.

Props

When you arrive for the interview you should always bring a copy of your resume. For an entry-level position you will probably not be asked to show any form of artistic portfolio. However, if you are interviewing for a full-time position, you can always bring one with you just in case. Should your interviewer have the time, there may be an opportunity to show your true potential for a greater position later on down the road. Don't be crushed if he or she doesn't have time or the interest to see samples of your creative work. They are very busy people. The most important thing to bring with you is your resume. More often than not, an interviewer will have misplaced your resume or passed it on to others, and will want to refer to it during your meeting. By bringing a few copies with you, you can read along with the interviewer and also provide a copy for any other person that may be present.

Time

By the time you arrive at the interview, you will have hopefully learned something about the company through your research. There is still time to learn more as you are waiting for your meeting to begin. Arrive at least ten minutes early. By leaving yourself plenty of time to get there, you will alleviate any problems due to traffic or getting lost. During the waiting time before your interview, you have an opportunity to take in the surroundings and to learn about the company from the inside. Notice the layout of the office. Notice the atmosphere and the people you will be working with, should you succeed in gaining employment there. Watch the people at work and do your best to assess what it is that they are doing for the company.

When you meet a new person, try not to look like you're going to pass out from nervousness, and try to remember everyone's name. (If you want to bring a pad of paper to this meeting, you can jot down a few notes so that you won't forget the key information once you leave.) Having watched a few of the others in action, you will be able to better understand what might be expected of you while you are meeting with the interviewer.

Producer or Janitor?

It was my first interview—I was still in college. Dressed awkwardly (overdressed in high heels), I waited in the lobby of the production office of *Mo' Money* for my interview. A man came down the hallway and stopped by the front desk. He looked at me sitting there nervously with my briefcase and asked if he could help me. I explained that I was waiting for my interview and he sat casually at the edge of the table to chat with me, as if he had nothing better to do.

He introduced himself as Eric. I thought nothing of it. I was so nervous, just waiting for my big meeting. I thought he was part of the cleaning staff or some sort of outside vendor who just happened to be there. It was late and I couldn't imagine that any busy movie person would be sitting down to chat with me. Had I done my research and paid any attention at all, I would have realized that this was Eric Gold, the producer! Fortunately, he was very kind and laughed off any misunderstandings. Now I've learned to assume that everyone is an executive producer until I'm told otherwise. You never know who that person in the casual clothes may be. It pays to do your research.

Go for It!

Have a good time. Be yourself and remember that these people are just that—people. They have all been in interviews before and they understand that you are nervous. The more comfortable you are able to make yourself feel, the more comfortable the interviewer may feel in return. It's all about making an impression and winning the interviewer over.

Whether this is merely an informational interview or a meeting about a particular job, now is your time to shine. You are given the floor and asked to speak about yourself. Now is the time to fill in the details about the bullet points on your resume. These are your five minutes to elaborate about yourself, as you are not merely the name on that resume, but a skilled and wonderful person who is a shoe-in for this job, or any job that may become available later. Do your best sales pitch about how you see yourself fitting into this role in this company. Be honest; don't sell yourself as something that you're not. Employers will find out the truth soon enough and you'll lose your job, along with your place in the local production community. By being yourself you'll be more at ease and you'll relate better to the interviewer.

As you are wrapping up the conversation, make sure you find out the next step. Are they hiring for this position immediately? Are they interviewing other candidates as well? Should you call to check in soon? Will they be calling you? Find out what the next step is before you leave. Always think ahead, as this is a skill that will also come in handy on the job. When you wrote your cover letter, you followed up with a phone call. Now that you have had an interview, you need to know what the next steps are so that you can again follow up.

Try not to pigeonhole yourself. If the only job available is as an office P.A. but you were hoping to work on set, don't frown. The office job can lead you to a set job next time. Or, you may decide that you like working in the production office after all. This is only the interview; you haven't accepted a job offer yet. By showing displeasure, your negative body language will be a turn-off and you may lose your chance for this job and any others that may turn up at this company later.

Angry Interview

I had interviewed three people for the office P.A. position on *Return to Me*. There were two left to go. Never mind that I had a sky-high pile of work to do on my desk. I had called this person (I'll call him Peter*), because he sounded intelligent from the cover letter and resume I'd read, although he was just out of college. The interview went well; I really liked him. Unfortunately for him, I also really liked one other candidate who had more experience. At the end of my interview with Peter, I had told him that I was interviewing one more person, and that I would be calling him the next day with the final verdict. After much deliberation, I decided to go with the other candidate and reluctantly called Peter with the bad news. I made a mental note to call any friends who were in hiring positions to recommend Peter and I put his resume in my notebook for future reference. But he did not take the news well. He got very angry with me. He insisted that I had given him the job at the interview and that I was not only taking back my job offer, but that it was horrendous of me to wait until 6:30 PM to call him with this news. (Peter did not think that I had anything better to do all day than to call him.) He had quit his day job and thought for some reason that he was starting with me on Monday. I was astounded. How could anyone looking for a job (and having just graduated) take that tone with a prospective employer? I was appalled.

Needless to say, the first thing I did when I hung up the phone (actually, he had hung up on me mid-sentence) was to call my friends to tell them not to ever call him for work. He turned what could have been a very positive experience into a very negative one. A prime example of "what not to do" after an interview, Peter probably did not find a position on a film crew for a long while.

---

* Not actual name

We're Number 1!

After my interview with Don at World Cup 1994, I asked him what the next step would be. He paused for a minute to ponder where we would go from here. He had one more person to interview and then would be making his decision. Aha! He had a solution. "I'll page you with all 111111s if you get the job. If you don't get a page with all 111111s, you didn't get it." As strange as it sounds, it was kind of exciting, and he was so thrilled with his goofy idea. Needless to say I've never been so happy to hear my pager go off or to see all 111111s in my life.

Thank You

After the interview (you guessed it), you need to follow up. Unless you were told that you needed to come back the next day or that another step would be taken immediately, a thank you note is the most appropriate next step.

Some books will tell you that a standard, typed, formal letter for a thank you is proper protocol. I feel that it is up to the individual. This is your story and you are the author. You can type a formal letter, or perhaps you want to hand-write a thank you card. Whatever method you decide is most appropriate for your thank you note is fine. The fact is that the thank you note is yet another opportunity to remind the employer that you exist. It is a way for you to make another appearance and to make another plea for the job.

A thank you note should be simple. It should be a thank you to the interviewer who took time out of a busy day to meet with you, as well as a thank you for the opportunity to introduce yourself and to meet the interviewer in person. This note can be as simple as two lines, or as long as a full page that summarizes the key points of the interview. The important part of the thank you note is that you write one. Most people will not be expecting such a note, as many people in production company interviews fail to write them. From experience I have found that by sending a thank you note, you make yourself more memorable to a busy person who meets many applicants for your job. You want the employer to remember you, and to have you in mind when jobs become available.

The interview is the first impression you make with a prospective employer. Be courteous, dressed appropriately, and on time. Come early and study the office atmosphere before your appointment. Bring your resume and any questions you may have, as you are also trying to get to know the company and to learn about the position while the interviewer studies your qualifications.

Be your own salesperson, and sell yourself to the employer. With a positive attitude there is no stopping you!

SECTION III:
ON THE
JOB

CHAPTER 25

The Work Ethic—Keeping

the Job & Moving Up

Congratulations! If you've made it this far, you have accomplished a major goal for yourself—you've been hired!

Most likely you have obtained an entry-level position in production. Whether you are an office P.A., a runner, a set P.A., or someone's assistant, there are some general codes of conduct that you should live by. There are also specific unwritten rules to know as you integrate into the family of a production company. Once you know the basics, you will be ready for more aggressive measures to ensure your job security and a future in your career.

But First, the Rules

Mr. Big Film in Chicago gives a printout of these basic rules to office runners when they start at the company. These rules are global to the industry and apply to any runner or assistant (as well as many other positions in the business).

❶ *Listen carefully when you are asked to do something. If you do not understand any part of the request, just say so. Always be sure you understand exactly what information is needed and when. You will be respected for asking questions and getting clarification.*

❷ *Write down everything. You will be asked to do many tasks at once and by multiple people. It's easy to forget who asked you for what. When making calls or researching make sure you write down confirmation numbers, who you talked to and when, and the number you called. Get a small notebook and keep it with you throughout the job. Don't take notes on little pieces of paper that will get lost.*

By not writing down everything you will look suspicious. Your employers may wonder if you are going to be able to retain everything you are asked to do, and by not having a notebook and a pen at all times, you may just prove them right.

❸ *Follow through on anything you are asked to do. If a more important task is required of you that precludes another, make sure to let the person who is bumped know when he or she can expect completion. If you need help prioritizing tasks, just ask the production manager. You don't need to figure it out yourself.*

It will help you to find out when a task needs to be completed. There may be an urgency to a task (however small it is) that you don't know about. By having this information from the start, you will be able to better prioritize as other tasks are added to your list throughout the day.

❹ *Don't be late. Regarding call times and deadlines, don't just be on time. Be early.*

❺ *Don't be too chatty. Don't volunteer what features and famous people you have worked with. Always be polite, friendly, and helpful, but protocol warrants that you don't solicit conversations with agency people or clients. Also don't make personal phone calls on the job, especially on cell phones. Never work on a future job while on the current one. Don't be a kiss-ass to the VIPs. People see right through it.*

❻ *Get busy. Don't just hang around the set watching the action. Ask the production manager what can be done. Never sit down on the set unless you are in the production office working.*

If your situation allows, it is recommended that you do go to the set to watch the action after your job is done for the day and you are off the clock. Some of your best learning and networking opportunities will be found by watching the crew at work. Just make sure that you are out of the way and following the other rules of conduct listed here while you are there. This is, of course, only after you have done all that can be done in your work area, including offering to help others who are still in the office (and after you've done all that you can according to the next rule below).

❼ *Think ahead. What can you do now for tomorrow? Has the dinner reservation been made? Can you fill out any FedEx forms? What can you do that will save time later?*

❽ *Be neat. Always make sure there are enough garbage bags around the production office, crew area, video tape, production vehicles, etc. If there's not a receptacle, tape one to a table. Remember to empty them often and pitch old food lying around. Don't wait until they are stinky or overflowing.*

Depending on the company, there may be someone specifically in charge of garbage bags or clean-up such as craft service or the locations department. Then again, it may be *your* job. It's always good to be proactive and to offer the help to others if it is not originally your responsibility. If there is a person in charge of keeping the place clean, ask before you start taping bags to tables. People may be particular about this sort of thing if it effects their position, but they will most likely appreciate your offer and make a mental note of your enthusiasm to help.

❾ *The quickest route to not being a P.A. is to be a great one.*

Office Notes

If your new job is in an office as an assistant or a runner, there are a few basic tools that you need to master to be as reliable and outstanding as possible. What may seem like common sense is often unknown to the standard assistant during the first day on the job.

The Copy Machine

Yes, there are things you need to know about the copy machine to be a savior to your boss. Familiarize yourself with how it operates from top to bottom. Learn how to fix every type of paper jam and you will be a hero when your boss is rushed and needs your help. A hint, you should flip your fingers through the paper before adding it to the paper tray. The paper that has been sitting on shelves for months can stick together. If you run your fingers through it first, it will prevent many jams to come. This is probably the first rule of thumb that the copy machine fix-it person will teach you when you call for help. If you see the toner getting low or that someone left a jam in the machine, be proactive and solve the problem. Don't just walk away; instead use preventative measures to make your life easier so that you're not stuck fixing jams in the copy room when you can be learning about filmmaking somewhere else.

Typing

Lately I've discovered that recent graduates do not know how to put paper into a typewriter. I realize that in this day and age, computers are what we train on, not word processors. However, forms such as Insurance Certificates and SAG contracts may still require your typing skills to be used on a good old-fashioned typewriter. It is recommended that you spend a few minutes getting to know your office machinery right off the bat. Ask for help and you will most likely get it. Wasting three hours trying to figure it out when you have deadlines to meet will not go over well with your boss. If you see a typewriter in your office, I recommend you type yourself a letter for practice.

Computer

Are you a whiz on an IBM-compatible PC, but have never turned on a Mac? Again, learn the machinery in your office. If you are unfamiliar with a program, say so. You can always buy a how-to computer book, and you can learn by practicing in your off-time.

Telephones

As simple as it may sound, the telephones of your office workplace can be the trickiest part of your job to learn. Every office has its system, and you need to have that system mastered. You don't want to be the assistant that disconnected the head of the studio, do you? Learn every function of your phone, even if you don't see a need for every function right away. Transferring a call will happen more often than a conference call, but you never know when you'll be asked to do any arrangement of phone connecting. Start by using your home telephone number and call yourself and two friends on a conference call, for practice (just make sure you keep it brief and your boss knows you were teaching yourself the phones and not goofing off).

Use a carbon-copy memo pad for phone messages, and save the copies. If you are asked to use a plain-papered phone log, make copies of the message pad before you hand it to your boss. For every message you should take down a phone number, the person's full name, and the time of the call. If you don't catch the name right away, ask the person to repeat it. Still didn't catch it? Ask for proper spelling and the caller will do the work for you. Be sure to collect all of this pertinent information no matter how rushed the caller sounds. Your accuracy is important enough for the caller to wait a moment. Three months from now you will be looking for an important phone number and you'll be happy you saved your copy of the message from the last time he or she called. In the same vein, always keep your Rolodex updated. A good assistant is resourceful and always has the answers the boss needs.

Paging

When paging someone to call you, assess the situation before using "codes" of urgency on the page. Common practice among pager users is to press "911" following the phone number, to stress the urgency of the page. Be certain of a crisis before resorting to a 911 page. 911 tells people that their sick grandmother has died, or that their house is on fire. They don't want to get a 911 to hear that you paged them to ask when the script will be delivered. In my experience with a pager, I set up rules with my staff to page me with an "811" if they need an immediate response but it is not a personal tragedy. You may also want to have other codes that you set up with your boss, or perhaps you will decide to use a text pager where you can type in the dilemma verbally, rather than only leaving a return number.

On-Set Protocol

A set P.A. has an entirely different set of challenges to face than an office P.A., as office filing and photocopying will not be the focal points of the set P.A. position. Working on set, you will need to learn how to effectively do your job, yet stay out of the way of others so that they can do theirs. You will learn to work with actors and with directors, as well as extras and animals. Each will come with egos and temperaments to which you will have to adjust. As a set P.A., you will be exposed to situations that you never in your wildest dreams imagined you would encounter. No college course can prepare you for some of the crazy stuff you will be asked to do. Fasten your seatbelt and enjoy the ride!

To add to the rules from pages 155–157, here is a list of rules to follow on the set:

❶ Keep a notepad and pen in your pocket at all times. You do not want to be scrambling for paper when the director shouts out his coffee order.

❷ Have a small flashlight handy, either with you or nearby for after dark. This comes in handy for paperwork, or when an actress loses a contact lens and everyone is on their hands and knees looking for it.

What to Have in Your Fanny Pack

During training, producer Brook Holston tells her P.A.s that they should have the following tools at all times: pen, notepad, small flashlight (Mag light), calculator, and petty cash slips. You will find in your experiences that there are other props that come in handy as well. Lots of big pockets are a must for a set P.A.

❸ Dress appropriately. Are you filming in a steel mill, in a cave, on a roof, or in a field? Wear comfortable, waterproof shoes and a thick winter jacket when you need to. In the winter (if you will be around snow) wear gloves you can work in and boots you can run in. Whatever you wear, make sure you have a place to hold a pen and paper and your walkie-talkie. A belt works well for the radios, and you may want a necklace to hold the pen and/or a mini notepad.

Human Bowling

Kendall had on so many layers of clothing that when she had to run from one side of the house to the other, she tripped and fell down the stairs with no injury. Like a Weeble-Wobble doll, she sprang right back up and continued on to her destination, leaving a stunned crew doubled over from laughter. Clothes can come in very handy.

❹ Stay fit. You will be doing a lot of running, walking, and lifting. Being in good shape is helpful.

❺ At night, wear bright clothing. In low light you want to be seen, especially if working near traffic.

☛Note—Try to keep your hands free and available to take notes or coffee orders, or to maneuver around a crowded set. Wear a sturdy pant belt to hold your walkie-talkie, pager, and other accessories. Have deep pockets for flashlights and petty cash. The less you are holding in your hands, the easier it will be to assist others.

What a Dump

Working as a set P.A. on Nickelodeon's *Pete and Pete*, Kim found herself directing traffic. This is a common tale for locations assistants and for set P.A.s, but this time the set was a bit difficult. It was a garbage dump in New York. Kim was directing large garbage trucks and hoping they would see her and not run her over as she stopped them to redirect them away from the shoot.

Having nose plugs handy as a P.A. may also be a good idea!

Stay out of the actors' sight line during a scene. If you are on set and have the opportunity to watch a scene being filmed, stay out of direct eye contact with the actors in the scene. It will undoubtedly distract them and you will instantly become one of the more despised people on the crew by messing up the shot.

No autographs. Once you make it onto a production, you will see how celebrities are truly bombarded with autograph requests on a daily basis. Often, shows will hold all autograph requests so a star can sign them all at once. For instance, they may hold onto them for signing during a lunch break, at a publicity shoot, or perhaps schedule a set weekly time so the requests are a little more controlled. You too will find family and friends asking you to obtain autographs from your co-workers to bring home to them, and you too will want to find a system to manage these requests. Otherwise, the actors will see you coming their way and run for the hills. This is not how you want your image to be, is it? The bottom line is, actors are people too. So use the golden rule and treat them as equals and with respect. You will find that this mindset alone will get you far in this business. Go through personal assistants for celebrity autographs whenever possible, to keep your request separate from your relationship with the actor.

Don't have an attitude. Marcie Friedman, freelancer in both the art and location departments, says that some of the best advice she was ever given was, "Keep your opinion to yourself when you think you know better." Keep quiet until you really, really, (really) know what you are talking about. If you are just out of school, chances are that even though you think you know the answer, the experienced crew around you knows better. One producer agrees, "You will get much further if you are able to admit the things you don't know. . . . You will get more respect." "The people who listen and 'do' are the best people to work with," says producer Moira Michiels. She adds that experienced production people who have been working for years in the business don't want to hear a recent college graduate tell them what to do, or argue methodology. She says, "The key word is to listen." Similarly, questioning authority will not get you very far. When an experienced crewmember has been working in the business for fifteen years, having a fresh P.A. question his or her instructions does not go over well. Holston says, "When I give (him) the airport pickup schedule, that's it—no conversation."

The Chicken Analogy

Holston relates to her P.A.s that if someone tells you that Wednesday you must have twenty white chickens on the set, don't ask why. Your question is, "Male or female?" It is not for you to question why. She says, "If they ask you for two hundred purple balloons, don't ask, 'Why purple?' There is not enough time to answer." Most of the time if you are instructed to do something, there is a valid reason for it. Sometimes there isn't, but it's not for you to question authority. However, if you have a question that is important to how you perform the task, you should ask it. Use your judgment. In the balloon scenario, to ask, "Helium, or just a package of uninflated balloons?" is reasonable. Also, asking the urgency of the task is always a good idea. Are the balloons needed immediately? Are they a higher priority than getting the paint bucket the art director asked for? Ask the questions you need answered in order to do the job efficiently. When there is time and your boss isn't crazed, you should ask the "why" questions if you are curious and want to learn. As time goes on, you will learn to understand the "why" and you can give instructions to new P.A.s based on your knowledge, hoping that they get their tasks accomplished unquestioned.

Attitude is also important when working with other crewmembers, extras, and when addressing the public. As a set P.A. you, along with the locations department, are the people most often coming into contact with the general public. As mentioned in previous chapters, you are representing the company, and making a first impression on outsiders to the production. Your job is not only to carry out tasks as instructed, but also to carry out those tasks in an appropriate manner. So many P.A.s take their position for granted and let their heads fill with attitude on the job. The local film commission and the locations department work hard to see to it that productions do not do any damage to the neighborhoods, and that the community is happy at the end of the shoot. As a set P.A. who is constantly in contact with people on the street and with extras who are often living in the same community, your role is to ensure that the process goes smoothly for both the crew and the neighborhood. Understand that your job is an important one, but don't abuse it. You are a guest to the community when filming on location. Work with the public to answer their questions when they approach you, and help to leave their neighborhood cleaner than you found it.

Accept blame. People make mistakes. Passing the buck and using others as your scapegoats will make you look bad in the long run. Things happen and people make mistakes. A good person accepts the errors, learns from them, and moves on. Rather than worry about who should be blamed, confess and work on a solution to the problem. In the end, having a solution that works is all that matters. You will be well respected if you accept your mistakes and become a problem-solver.

Putting It Off For Later

On *Beneficiary*, Michael* had been hired as a P.A. via networking and recommendations from friends. Shooting nights in January, he and the rest of the crew were cold and tired. At wrap, the P.A.s were told to clean up boards that the art department had put up all over the building's exterior. This group of P.A.s decided to go home instead, thinking they could leave the mess until tomorrow. Needless to say, the UPM was not pleased by their decision when the crew arrived to a messy location the following day. Michael pulled her aside and fessed up to being the one to blame. His confession saved his job. The other P.A.s were eventually let go for various reasons, whereas Michael had gained respect by his admission, and remained on the crew for the rest of the show. The UPM actually thanked Michael for his honesty. As he continues on in his career, Michael speaks up when he is at fault and finds more and more jobs coming his way.

Smile; it will make you feel better and it will tell your co-workers that you are enjoying the job and are eager to please. Life is too short for frowning anyway.

Food with a Smile

On a shoot with a budget lower than a Roger Corman B-Movie, no one wanted the job of craft service. There was no money and the challenge was not worth the effort to those who were asked to do the job. That is, until the producer's dream employee was found. This person (I'll call him Mark*) wanted to work in the camera department and was willing to work in craft service for peanuts to get his foot in the door on a production. He had never done this job before, but did it with all of his might. He asked every crew person what their favorite snacks were, how they liked their coffee, and what type of cigarettes they smoked, always with a smile.

As the days went on the positive attitude was still there. In a situation where a jaded craft service person might have been aggravated and annoyed to be pandering to the director, Mark simply gushed with enthusiasm. He often told his co-workers how excited he was to be there and how much this opportunity meant to him.

At the end of the shoot, everyone on the crew agreed amongst themselves that Mark was going to be successful in his endeavors. No one had ever seen him work with a film camera, but they were confident that his positive attitude would carry him, and that he would realize his dream. The camera department approached Mark as the

---

★ Not actual name

show was wrapping and offered him a P.A. position in their department on the next project. Five years later, Mark is a well-respected camera operator. He was so memorable for his positive attitude and enthusiasm for the business that people remember him and continue to share his story.

As a P.A., you are the person people will come to for just about everything. From escorting actors to escorting animals, you just never know what you will be asked to do. Saying "okay" with a smile goes a long way. If you hem and haw or complain at all, you likely will dig your own grave at the company. Paying your dues is part of the process in this business. If you can make it through the tough times, you will reap the rewards later.

There will be many nights when you will find yourself reciting "I hate my job" over and over again, and asking yourself why you chose a job that is so underappreciated and tiring. But you'll make it through those times, and you will learn a lot from them. Just keep your chin up and do what you are asked with a smile.

Cows, Cows, and More Cows

On *The Boys Next Door*, Eric recalled a country scene being shot outside of Los Angeles. In the middle of the shoot, cows began to wander over to check out the action that was taking place on their turf. Once one cow meandered over, the others followed. Before he knew it, an entire herd was leaning over the fence to see the activity. Next they began to "moo." Quickly, the 2nd A.D. was sent to hop the barbed wire fence to shoo the cows away. With no hay or other ordinary animal incentives, he worked his magic by yelling "shoo" and flailing his arms up in the air.

Producer Moira Michiels recalls being on a plot of rural land for a Toyota SUV commercial shoot last year. You guessed it, cows walked up and yet another P.A. suddenly found himself trying to move them out of the camera's way.

We were filming in a rural suburb near the Illinois–Wisconsin border. Our location was a field on a farmer's acre. Kim was in the art department and had spent weeks creatively using her tiny budget. For our first day of filming, her department made fake cows out of foam board (don't ask). As the camera rolled and the action began, there was suddenly an unscripted movement on the field. The director yelled "cut!" and the A.D. called for the art department to "go save your cows." The local herd of real cows had taken an interest in their fake friends, and were making their way over to the set to check them out. Kim had not realized that an agricultural class in college would have been a handy class to take. She managed to learn a lesson on her first day of working on a film—how to effectively use hay to move a cow.

Kim's advice to future filmmakers is to not be afraid of anything. . . and to wear waterproof shoes. You never know when you will need to spend your day in a flooded, marsh-like field, where you are moving props, painting houses, or shooing cows away.

Using Walkie-Talkies

Set P.A.s, much more often than office assistants, need to learn how to master the radios, as everyone working in production will be asked to use a radio at some point. There is a protocol for walkie-talkies that is important to follow. On a large production, every department is assigned a specific channel on which to speak. Usually channel one is the designated film production channel. The production department (mostly the assistant directors and production assistants) uses this channel to communicate with each other throughout the shoot. Generally, there is a channel (usually channel two) that is an open channel for people to use for longer conversations. When speaking on a walkie-talkie, you are expected to keep your messages short and to the point. If you have a longer question or answer, or something that is of a private nature, common practice is to find the person you need on their designated channel, and immediately ask them to switch over to the open channel for that conversation.

For example, if Jim the key P.A. is on channel one and looking for Sarah, the 2nd A.D., to help with a tricky situation that has come up on set, he will find her on channel one and ask her to go to the open channel to discuss the matter in private:

Jim:	Sarah, come in.
Sarah:	Go for Sarah.
Jim:	Go to channel two.

Immediately they both switch to channel two and the conversation continues:

Jim:	On two (letting her know he has joined her on this channel)
Sarah:	Go for Sarah.
Jim:	Yeah Sarah, Johnny was stepping out of his trailer and he tripped over a cable. He scraped his eye on the lamppost and needs both the medic and makeup. He's swearing up a storm; looks like we'll be a few minutes late over here. Over.
Sarah:	Copy that Jim. Let him know that we'll be there right away and get him settled back into his trailer. Over.
Jim:	Copy that. Back to one.

With that said, Jim and Sarah each flip their walkie-talkies back to channel one and move on to their next tasks.

Walkie-Talkie Do's and Don'ts:

- Keep your walkie-talkie on your assigned channel unless you need to find someone on another channel or to talk to a person on the open channel. If you leave your channel, remember to switch back when you are done.

- Keep your conversation short and to the point. Move longer conversation (if at all necessary to have longer conversation) to the open channel.

- Do not speak on a walkie-talkie while the camera is rolling (while the scene is actually being filmed). Turn your radio volume down when the camera is rolling in case someone does speak during this time. Otherwise the chatter will be picked up on film and the scene will be disrupted. You don't want to be the person that ruins the perfect shot. Just remember to turn it back up as soon as the director yells "Cut."

- Let the person you are speaking to know that you heard their message by responding with "Copy" (radio jargon for "I heard that").

- Beware of what you say over a radio. You might think that your conversation on channel two is private, but chances are someone is being nosy and has joined you on channel two for a listen.

- Carry an extra battery and know where the charger is hiding. You never want to be without a functioning radio.

- Don't key your walkie. Make sure that you haven't pressed down the "talk" button into permanent "talk" position. You may accidentally key your radio while it's on your belt or in your pocket. By being constantly "on" a channel, you are preventing others from using this channel to communicate with one another. There is always someone accidentally keying their walkie-talkie and therefore there is always a frustrated crewmember trying to talk to his or her department but having first to find the culprit tying up the radio channel.

A Tough Day at the Office

It had been a long week, and a tough day in particular, when Kim found herself with a moment to stop and regroup. Working in the locations department on *The Package* was a rough job, at least that is what she was telling her co-worker on set when she accidentally keyed her walkie. As she continued on and on, lamenting about the rigors of her job to this sympathetic ear, the rest of the crew was working on a street scene. The cars were rigged with camera gear to get this difficult moving shot on a busy street. For some reason, production was at a standstill, as Kim continued to describe how hard she had been working. Suddenly, there was a tap on the window. It was the transportation captain. The director, A.D.s, and transportation department were trying to coordinate the cars for the scene but were unable to talk to each other because someone was monopolizing the radio channel. Kim was horrified to learn that her diatribe had gone over the airwaves to the entire crew and held up production. And all of the *other* hard workers had to stop what they were doing to hear about her tough day.

We know one location assistant who will be careful with her walkie-talkie in the future!

- Charge your battery and keep track of when you might get low and need a fresh one. You don't want to be stranded in a field down the road when your battery dies.
- Don't lose your walkie-talkie; turn it in at the end of the day.

The bottom line on equipment at work is not to let technology hold you back. Have your equipment mastered so that you can concentrate on your job. Part of becoming valuable to your employer is being the go-to person for any task, including office equipment. If you are the person that everyone goes to for handling tasks large and small, then you are on your way to more responsibilities and the next step up in your career path.

Mentally Preparing

Now on to the mental tasks. Stress management, multi-tasking, and interaction with others are all skills that are necessary for success in this business, as in any business.

Working in production means long hours at work and less sleep. Sleep deprivation added to the fast pace and stress involved in daily decisions makes for a difficult workplace. Keeping your sanity during critical moments is important to maturing in this business. By remaining calm and keeping your wits about you when confronted with stress of this magnitude, you will gain respect and you will be able to manage your job well. If you feel like something is overwhelming, take a deep breath and slow down before going any further. Talk to your boss or your co-workers about the problem and they can help you make your way through it. Production work is made up of massive teamwork. There are people who are only out for themselves, but in the long run you are a team and you should be able to rely on each other for support.

Mindy* had an assistant in her office on a commercial shoot whose resume was impressive. She had graduated from a prestigious film school and seemed to be intelligent. Unfortunately, what employers don't see on many resumes are hints of a person's personality. Mindy's new hire proved to have a low tolerance for stress and for the fast pace of commercial production work. This employee constantly cried and whined to the producers about how she was being treated. A good P.A. will not need their hand held all day. A good P.A. will think ahead and just "do" without argument. A good P.A. will not take quick or short answers personally because a good P.A. will be too busy to listen to wordy responses, and will understand that the people around him or her are too busy to elaborate when it's not necessary.

Multi-tasking

Production work has such a fast pace to it that it seems there are not enough hours in the day to accomplish all the work that needs to be done. This is why *multi-tasking*

★ Not actual name

is so important. Work needs to be done quickly and efficiently. Learning to handle multiple tasks will make you invaluable. It can be very challenging, but it must be done. Start by writing down everything you need to do. Write down even the small tasks such as organizing your desk or sorting the mail. Then prioritize these tasks. You can number them on your notepad if it helps. The next step is to then work on how to do some of them simultaneously. Perhaps you can solve a crisis over the telephone while typing a less important memo on your computer. You can proofread the memo after you've solved the crisis. Keep your notepad handy to add to your "to do" list as you go. As soon as you accomplish one task you will likely be given another. Just keep smiling and know that you can do anything you set your mind to.

Follow Through

Follow every task you are given through to the end. If you see that something is going wrong or having the task accomplished will not be possible, speak up. It is better to ask for help than to just fail. If you are asked to do something, see it through all of its stages. Call to check on the food order you placed, make sure the FedEx arrived at its final destination on time, check with the art department to make certain that they delivered the banner to the set like they told you they would. Simply asking for it and getting a reply does not mean it will get done. If you are given a task it is solely your responsibility, so you'd better make sure it gets done. No one will be checking up on you like a teacher asking for homework assignments. When someone is checking up on you, it's usually after he or she noticed that something wasn't done. Follow through.

Communication

Interaction with your co-workers and your boss can be very critical to your rise or fall within the company. If you say the wrong thing to the wrong person, you may not be forgiven. Similarly, if you say the right thing, you can have a mentor for life. Obviously you will learn a lot of this as you go. But use your judgment before you speak. If you are stressed and start raising your voice or talking down to someone, it will not go unnoticed. Take that deep breath and think about your answer. Or say "yes," walk away, and consider the task ahead of you. If it still seems unrealistic, go back to your boss with your concern and a possible solution. An assistant who constantly balks or over-explains him or herself before fulfilling an assignment will be overlooked for that promotion, whereas an assistant who answers "yes" and walks away to do the task (however small) will likely be appreciated as a go-getter and problem-solver down the road. Make your first impression a lasting one in the eyes of your co-workers.

Be Prepared

No matter which department you are working in, there will be key props necessary to do your job well. As mentioned, everyone should always have a pen and paper, but different departments will also have other needs. For instance, in the wardrobe department you will likely need a tape measure and stick pins, just as in the locations department you will need duct tape, rope, and/or nails to hang signage. Plan ahead for tomorrow and foresee what props you will need to get your job done. The more ready you are, the more reliable you will become, and the more respected you will be by your co-workers.

Frozen Tongues

They say your tongue will stick to a flagpole in freezing temperatures. That may be true, but just for your information, duct tape doesn't. Nope, duct tape slides right off frozen poles. Why do I know this? Because, as a location assistant, I had to hang directional signage all over town—no matter what the season. I felt like a postal worker—neither rain nor snow nor sleet could stop me. But duct tape was not my friend. I tried my hardest to get it to stick to the streetlights in South Bend, Indiana. Somehow I managed to rig signs to poles with rope and staples. Later I learned to hammer nails on foam board to rig my signs.

Come prepared and remember to wear waterproof gloves while you're out there in the snow!

Moving Up

Once you have grasped the technicalities of your job and learned how to do what you are paid to do, it is time to take advantage of your environment and to begin your climb to the next level. Most of this is done through observation and by being inquisitive. It also takes ambition and a very hard-working mentality.

If you are working in a production office, use your environment to gain access to information. If you are asked to fax a memo, read it as you are walking to the fax machine. Absorb the information that is available around you. When you are told to sort the mail, look at it to understand what type of mail your boss or other departments are receiving. Maybe you will learn something about these departments and what they do from their correspondence. When you are done for the day, or maybe during your lunch hour, take the opportunity to ask another department if you can watch or help in some way. Find creative ways to make yourself useful to others and they will notice. While you are helping them, you are also learning the trade. After you have helped them, you will find it much easier to ask questions of them and to network with them later when the opportunity arises.

If you are working as a set P.A., notice the other people on set and what they are doing. Inquire if something puzzles you about their duties. If you are asked to deliver correspondence to another department or to the production office, take a look at it (unless it's private or sealed). Being on set and accessible to every department, you have the opportunity to ask people in many different roles how you can be of use to them to make their jobs easier. You will undoubtedly be busy with your own duties, but in your down time you can make yourself useful to others.

A willingness to do anything and everything to get your start is the key to being successful and moving up. Laziness will cause your career to end abruptly. Unmotivated slackers can just skip this process and stick to watching movies at home. Working in this business is too competitive and entirely too fast-paced to be tolerant of lackadaisical attitudes.

☛Note—Save your call sheets and receipts. If you decide to join a union, they will want to see proof of your experience on union productions. Call sheets become as valuable as your tax forms, so save them for years to come, as you decide what direction you want to take in your career. If you spend money for your job, the company can't reimburse you without a receipt. Talk to an accountant about what purchases can be written off as job expenses, such as the special gloves you had to buy to work in the snow, or a flashlight for your pocket. Save your receipts.

Self-Promotion

As a director's assistant on a production, Eric's primary responsibilities were to locate the director's copy of the script and to fetch coffee. After he got the routine down, Eric started to look at other crewmembers on the set to find what piqued his interest. He decided that the A.D. work was interesting, and made a point of getting to know the A.D.s on the show while he was on set. He learned to lock up the set and to be of help to them whenever he could. By the end of the production, they had become friends and they took Eric under their wing. This friendship provided fifteen years of freelance employment for Eric, as they hired him wherever they found their next project.

A job assisting the director and fetching his or her coffee can lead to almost anywhere, if you let it.

Your first job (and any job thereafter) in production is your chance to show people what you're made of. Contribute to the team and do whatever you can to make the job happen better and more smoothly than it would without you. Take advantage of your surroundings. Use your position to your fullest advantage. Teamwork and passion will get you far.

Get to know the tools of your trade, whether it is a computer or simple hardware, and be as knowledgeable and eager to learn as you can be. Know your surroundings and be a resourceful problem-solver. Your efforts will be recognized and will lead you to higher levels. Be a master of multi-tasking. Also, be careful not to step on any toes and to listen before speaking. In so doing, you will succeed in reaching your goals.

For additional on-the-job tips, visit Web sites of state film commissions. Many have P.A. tips listed on their home pages. My favorite to-date is Texas' (www.governor. state.tx.us/film). See the appendix for other listings.

CHAPTER 26

The End of the Line—What To Do

When the Job Comes to an End

I t is a set filled with emotion. Some look tense, others worn and teary-eyed. The director calls out "It's a wrap," and this time he means it. On any other day, these words bring only a brief sigh of relief, followed by a busy shuffle as the crew prepares for another day's shoot. But today's wrap spawns an outpouring of emotion. Today was the last day of production. Some crew people are sad to be saying "goodbye" to the family they've acquired during this time. Others are worried about their steady paychecks that will cease shortly with no immediate future income in sight.

The entertainment business is unique in that many jobs only last as long as the project. Inevitably a film will be completed, a television series will be canceled, and a play will close. As one project comes to an end, somewhere another is just beginning. Unless you work full time for a production company or have a studio position, you will likely work as a freelancer moving from production to production. A feature film may guarantee you several months of work, whereas a commercial may only guarantee a few days. You must also take into account the occasional fallout with a crazy boss, or a major error on your part that causes you to lose your job prematurely. By nature this is not a stable business. It is most unstable for people like you, just starting out and first trying to establish yourself in the industry. With freelance work, one needs to be both mentally and physically prepared to move from job to job.

Family and Friends

While working long hours with your production crew every day, different bonds form. There are the usual companionships that form in a workplace, and then there are also the unusually strong bonds that are akin to family relationships. Most crew people work so many hours together that they see their co-workers more than they see their own friends and families. Spending this much time together gives an unusual opportunity to get to know people much more closely in a much shorter period of time. With bonds as strong as these, the notion of leaving a production or parting from this family can be saddening. But unlike a functional family bond, once the tie is severed it can be very easy to move on to the next crew family. Freelancers learn to disconnect and to start new bonds quickly as they move from job to job. Good job-hunters know that the key to finding future work is through networking, so these friendships are not completely severed at the end of a production. Film communities keep tabs on their members and are in constant communication. The key to longevity in a freelance career is making real friends and connecting to people who will respect you enough (and vice versa) to keep you in the loop and connected to the family of the local film community.

When your job comes to an end, try not to burn any bridges with your co-workers. It is important that you leave on a good note with as many people as possible. You never know where a good recommendation or a negative report will come from. If you are terminated from a job due to a personality conflict, try to salvage as much as you can from the experience. We'll cover more about this situation later in the chapter. Just because the nutcase production coordinator replaced you when her best and only friend moved to town does not mean that the rest of the crew won't support you as you look to move forward.

Chair Rental to the Rescue

As my job in the locations department of *Baby's Day Out* was coming to an end, I had no idea where my next job would be coming from. Every day for the past seven months I had been working long and hard to make movie magic in my department, and suddenly it occurred to me that I had no idea what the future would hold. One day I was on the phone with my local chair rental company, AAA Rentals, who out of the blue provided me with the solution. I had been bringing them a lot of business, and talking to them on a daily basis as they provided all of the chairs for our crew and extras to sit on during lunch every day. Unbeknownst to me, they had also begun working for World Cup Soccer to set up Chicago's Soldier Field for the international festivities. Everyone needs tables and chairs! They realized that my job in the locations department was coordinating many things, more than just furniture rental, and that similar skills would be needed in special event planning. They gave me their contact information at the World Cup offices and the rest was history. I never thought my next job would come from my contacts at a rental place. You just never know. I'm glad I had bonded with my contact there because it taught me a great lesson, and my career path took a completely unexpected turn.

Positive Attitude

Not knowing where your next paycheck is coming from can be very nerve-wracking. But if you're hard-working and easy to get along with, your next job will be just around the corner. Keep a positive attitude and it will come. The hard part is to not live your life as if it comes to a screeching halt between each job. On the contrary, you need to find a balance between not spending any money (staying cooped-up inside) and partying 'til the cows come home. Working in production will leave you with very little free time to catch up with friends, see a movie, or try new restaurants. At the end of a project you will likely need a day or two (or ten) to unwind and refresh yourself. Take advantage of your free time when it comes. You should watch your budget so you have something to fall back on if your down-time is longer than usual. Just make sure you have a little fun—you deserve it after all of that hard work.

Blow to the Ego

Being let go is not easy on anyone. Even people with tough exteriors feel the sting if they are terminated from a job. It's relatively easier to handle if the feeling is mutual and you aren't enjoying yourself anyway. Either way, it is a tough thing to go through. Everyone in this business experiences these emotions, whether they are let go, choose to quit, or for an instant wish they had chosen a different career. Being unappreciated, picked on, or feeling like you just can't seem to do anything right is a blow to one's self-esteem and ego. Should you encounter this life lesson, try to remind yourself to stay positive. I'm a believer in the notion that "everything happens for a reason, " even getting fired or being forced to quit. Each job you have contains value. You can learn from both the good experiences and the bad. Having to leave your job prematurely feels embarrassing, but try to learn from your mistakes and incorporate your knowledge into the next job. Maybe you didn't make any mistakes and your premature departure is based on a personality conflict with a co-worker. This happens more often than you'd think. Reflect on this experience; there is undoubtedly a lesson to be learned. Whether it is a lesson in better communication skills or in how to handle other people's egos, the lesson will be found if you work hard enough to gain from each experience.

The Ex

Driving the long commute to work every morning was getting to be more and more painful. Sarah* dreaded being in the production office. The crew had disliked the production coordinator but since the production coordinator was intimate with the screenwriter the only solution was to move her to a different department within the production. Sarah had filled the coordinator opening in that production office when it became available. But the original coordinator didn't leave quietly. As the shooting days came and went, she stayed involved and prohibited Sarah from doing her job.

---

* Not actual name

Sarah was miserable. Not to mention the fact that every time the producer came into the office, he would say hello to everyone but her. He never once looked her in the eye. It was awful. The production manager who had hired her was out with bronchitis so Sarah was left to fend for herself.

On the day that Sarah felt she couldn't take it anymore, she decided to quit. That same day, the production manager came back in from her sick bed and asked to speak with Sarah privately. They were letting her go. At first she was stunned. She was torn between being angry that she didn't get to be the one to quit, and sad that they agreed that she wasn't fitting in. The UPM asked her not to tell anyone the reason she was fired but Sarah feels it is worth repeating if it will help someone to better understand this business. The producer was uncomfortable with Sarah. She reminded him of his ex-girlfriend.

Sarah wasn't sure if it made her feel better or worse to hear this excuse, perhaps a little of both. She laughed and cried. But she learned early on that she knows in her heart when she is unhappy. If things don't seem to "click" it is probably best to end the torture early and to move on. Sarah found a much better job within weeks. Her new job propelled her career. Things happen for a reason and we learn from our experiences. Sarah takes her knowledge with her and improves her life's story with each new beginning.

Bad people get what's coming to them eventually. This feature-turned-made-for-television-movie bombed in the ratings.

The bottom line? The freelance life takes a special mentality. Working sporadically and under tense conditions can be scary. Make the best of your down-time and enjoy your life while you're looking for your next job. Give yourself a short break to the beach on a Tuesday (take your pager and cell phone so you can be reached), do laundry, cook yourself a gourmet meal. Just be practical and put money aside in case you hit a dry spell. A full-time job with a steady paycheck definitely has benefits to it, but so does freelancing. Remember to keep that positive attitude, and if you network with your fellow freelancers, the next job will come.

CHAPTER 27

The Next Job—Moving to

a New Level

Going from one job to the next can be easy or difficult, depending on your situation. If you are well-connected and/or likable, it may be easy to land a plum job through networking. For someone just starting out with few connections or a high-maintenance ego, it may be more challenging to find work. But you've done it once, so you can absolutely do it again.

Networking

There's that word again—networking. Start by approaching your co-workers from the job you are leaving. Ask them where they are going for their next gig. Do they have any leads that you can follow? Did you meet other crew people from different productions while you were working? Call them up and ask if they have any leads. Word of mouth is the best chance you have for finding another job quickly. Get contact information from these people if you can, and follow up on leads yourself. Leaving your next job up to someone else can be risky; that person may not be as reliable as you need him or her to be in order to secure your next source of income.

Notebook

Find that notebook you were working out of when you first found your current job. Make phone calls to the people who had sounded interested or who you connected well with. Take notes! Look at the dates of your last phone calls to these contacts and place follow-up calls as you did during your initial job search. Utilize your notebook by referring back to past conversations, and make notes about your new chats so that you can use this notebook again after your next job is completed.

If you have to, start with your notebook from square one. Get yourself some trade magazines and, using "The *Reporter* Method," look for any new productions that are out there. If you've been employed long enough, there will be entirely new listings of films and television shows in production across the globe for you to use in your new search. Go back to chapter 11 and let the hunting begin.

CHAPTER 28

The Reassessment—Taking

Another Look at Your Goals

Every once in a while it is important to look back to your goals from chapter 2 to remind yourself of your original plan and to see if that plan is still appropriate. (Sometimes it's easy to lose sight of the ultimate goal when you're wrapped up in the short-term.) As I discussed earlier, it is okay to change your mind or to add new goals to the list. It is up to you to do the work in order to keep your career on the right path.

Reflect

Looking back on your last job, think about what you liked. Whether it was a great job or a mentally draining one, pull out the good things that you enjoyed and write them down. Make a similar list of the bad things that you experienced on another page.

The task in front of you now is to determine from these lists where your next job venture should be. You need to decide whether to continue in this career direction or to veer off onto a new avenue. The trick to a happy career is to learn about your dislikes and to steer clear of them while you continue to narrow the list of the things that really make you content. Be as specific as possible. From photocopying scripts to attending production meetings, think about all aspects of your job and how you really feel about them.

Next, use the list of job options in chapters 6–16 to refresh your memory of what is out there. Don't forget any positions you discovered that are not listed in this book. Make notes about the jobs you saw others doing that grabbed your attention. Is it feasible for you to try a new route? Did you learn any job skills that you found intriguing? Did you get to know the people working in that other department? Can they possibly help you shift to their department?

You will probably need to hold the same production assistant position a few more times on different projects before you find your answers. That is okay. Some production assistants do their jobs forever and never make any moves through the chain of command. Most production assistants work for months or even years before moving up or into different departments. Everyone is different. You know yourself better than anyone else knows you. It is up to you to take the time to assess your feelings at the end of the day and to determine the next step to happiness.

Remember that the goals you set for yourself at the beginning of this process are changeable. No one will hold you to them if you change your mind. You can decide to be a still photographer even if you originally thought you wanted to direct. You can decide to join the wardrobe department when you had thought you wanted to be a camera operator. No one will respond negatively to you should you decide to go back to school for your Masters Degree in Recreation after you find your true calling. Anything is possible. It is up to you to listen to yourself and to steer yourself in the direction that will bring you the career that you desire the most.

Video assist operator Kevin Boyd says, "There are people in this business who find some sense of balance. . . " It is this sense of balance that leads to a lifestyle that can include all of your goals as you described them in chapter 1. The people who only concentrate on work and exclude a private life can quickly burn out. They will either quit at some point or will slide downhill into a bitter and lonely life. It is necessary to try to keep in mind what is important to you and what your personal goals are so that you can continue to have this balance in your life without losing yourself in the production work cycle.

Teacher

Kim wanted to be an editor. She took the job in the art department of *Pizza Wars* because. . . well, because there was an opening and it was an opportunity for her to get her foot in the door.

Shortly thereafter, Kim was working as a producer across the country on talk shows and videos, to name a few aspects of her work. Years later she is an elementary school teacher who is looking to edit during her time out of the classroom, as both a hobby and possibly to earn supplementary income. She listened to herself and sought out what made her most happy. Her new career as a teacher is fun and fulfilling. With her passion for film still lingering, she talks of incorporating editing into her life. Kudos to Kim for continuing her pursuit to stay happy yet challenged in her career.

My career went from features to corporate video production to special events to television to editorial houses. It seems like a lot of different avenues, but they are all related in a way. All of these choices were somehow connected to the job that came before them. I made choices in part due to timing and circumstance. But I also made choices by listening to my gut instinct. I assessed what worked for me, what didn't work, and what piqued my curiosity in each position I held.

One of the reasons that I moved to Atlanta for the Paralympics was because I had enjoyed the special event portion of my corporate job and wanted to pursue event planning on a larger scale. Later down the road, I temporarily quit my pursuit of production coordinating work because it was no longer making me happy. The people I was working under were crushing my spirit. I assessed the job I had been doing and realized there were specific duties I enjoyed and elements that were lacking. I put together some of the traits of my ideal job. They included:

- Scheduling. Whether in daily tasks or departmental meetings, I enjoyed knowing all that was going on in the production, and the challenge of making it all happen on time.
- Dependency. I liked people coming to me with their needs because I liked to feel needed and important.
- Camaraderie. Having co-workers and/or employers that I could talk to and get along with was something I needed. While working long hours, I wanted to be supported by my co-workers, not struggling with them.
- Crisis Management. I enjoyed putting out fires, being caught up in the moment, and finding solutions.
- Social Life. I liked having free time and a social life, and being able to enjoy myself and my friends and family.

These realizations correlated to a job that became available as a scheduler in a post-production facility. At first I had to take a step back in salary and prestige, as I had to start as the new kid on the block in an area of the industry that was new to me. But I was willing to make that sacrifice for the job I thought would make me the happiest. Besides, I know that I can always change the direction of my career path and return to television production if I want to. It's never too late to change your mind.

I followed my instinct and now I am at my happiest. Listen to yourself and to what truly makes you content. With creativity, you can apply many of your preferences and skills to unique positions.

CHAPTER 29

The Conclusion—

Positive Reinforcement

The business of entertainment production is unlike any mainstream business. Crew positions are temporary and people tend to work as freelancers moving from production to production. Production work is filled with uncertainty and adventure as every day, week, month, or year can lead you to a new setting and a new territory.

This industry can be difficult at times. It is occupied by people who are often fiery and stubborn, as each person must look out for his or her self-interests in order to make it to the next job. However, if you follow the advice below, you will be sure to succeed in the production business.

Celebrity

Movies and television programs may add to celebrity worship and the idea of glamour and high fashion in our society. But as a person working behind the scenes, you need to separate yourself from these notions. It is your job to produce entertainment, not to fawn over your co-workers. Gawking at celebrities is unacceptable in the workplace. Learn your trade and do it to the best of your abilities, leaving the idol worshipping to the everyday fans.

Resources

Whether you're just out of school or changing your career later in life, looking for a job in film or television production seems intimidating at first. It doesn't need to be. Use the resources around you to get started. Research your field. Read the trades, watch the credits, look in the classifieds, and ask around.

As a student, take advantage of your school curriculum and outside activities. Having an unrelated major will open up your possibilities later. Make mental notes of the subjects that pique your interests. Study subjects that will give you a well-rounded knowledge in addition to the courses necessary for your career or major.

Volunteer to work on the crew of the school's television station or get a shift as a D.J. on the college radio station. Participate in a sport or join a club—do whatever interests you. By being active you will enhance your skills, learn new subjects, and learn about responsibility, time management, and multi-tasking. You will learn new information related to your trade. Each extracurricular activity will help you to define your interests and will bring you one step closer to a job after you graduate.

For mid-career changers or non-students looking to break into the business, you should also take advantage of your surroundings. Join a local club or committee related to your field. Sign up to volunteer at a public access station. Be resourceful and find opportunities in your community to learn your craft hands-on.

By participating in activities related to your area of interest, you will also have the opportunity to network and to make friends in the business. Working together, you can help each other to achieve your career goals.

Intern

By having an internship you open a door to opportunities in your field. Not only are you networking and introducing yourself to employers, you are learning the business hands-on. Remember that as an intern, you are representing the company when you interact with the public. Whether you are answering phones or getting coffee, you are portraying an image to the outside world. Act professional and be as helpful as you can to your employers and the people you deal with.

Again, take advantage of your surroundings. Use your internships to learn about the entertainment business and the company you are working for. With every internship comes another opportunity to narrow down your likes and dislikes as you set your career goals.

Location

Take into consideration your personality and in what type of environment you will feel most comfortable living and working. Read about your job options and get to know the different markets available for pursuing these options. Keeping in mind moving costs and the processes involved in relocating, the world is open for you to choose where you want to work and live.

Tools

Use tools that are available to you for your job search. Whether it is contacting alumni, college career counselors, or local film commissions, get your name out there and continue to network within the production community of your area.

Use the Internet, trade magazines, newspapers, and job hotlines as job hunting tools. They can provide you with all of the information you need to get started in your phone calling and resume mailing.

Be Prepared

Once you are job hunting, remember that timing plays a critical role in the process. Continue to be aggressive in your search. Pairing your inquiries with your organized note taking, you will be certain to land that first job. Keep track of the contacts you make and the conversations you have for reference as you are networking and job searching.

Job Hunting

Cover letters, follow-up calls, and interviews are important for having a relationship with a prospective employer. Entertainment is all about networking and self-promotion to others. Make your letters and conversations as personal as you can. Familiarity is important to being remembered and considered when job opportunities arise.

On the Job

Once you are hired for a position, demonstrate a good work ethic and create an opportunity for yourself to grow. Think ahead, ask questions, be efficient, and follow through on the tasks you are asked to complete.

Learn the tools of your trade. If you are in an entry-level position, you need to master the office machinery or location procedures. Even if you don't want to make this position your permanent career choice, you need to prove to others that you are capable of mastering this job before they will consider you for another. Learn to use the copier, the typewriter/computer, and the walkie-talkies. Master the telephones. Don't let technology get in the way of your career path. Master the little things so that you can pay attention to the bigger ones.

Goals

Set your short and long-term goals, and keep them handy for a reference once in a while. Be open-minded and remember that every job you do is really another opportunity to assess what makes you happy (and/or unhappy) in a job, and gets you one step closer to finding the career that will make you the most satisfied.

Attitude

Keep a positive attitude and work with a smile. Don't tell others that you are unhappy or frustrated with your position. A smile is infectious; as you make others happy they will want to keep you around. However, there is a difference between a positive attitude and a cocky one. Keep your opinion to yourself until it is asked for. Use your judgment on whether or not it is appropriate to disagree with a co-worker or boss. Choose your battles wisely. Be considerate of your co-workers' backgrounds and experience. You may think that you know better, but since you are new, chances are that they have learned some tricks of the trade that you have yet to discover. Sometimes by keeping your opinion to yourself you will discover another way of doing things, or another perspective on an issue. Just think before you speak, and express yourself with a smile.

Every day on a production is different. One day you may spend six straight hours riding up and down an elevator, bringing actors to and from the set in an office building. The next day you are riding in a helicopter, seeing the sun rise over the skyline. Try not to feel down if you're having a bad day, or even week. Each day brings new surprises and challenges that may lead your career in a new direction. On your next job you just may find yourself happier than you've ever been!

Enjoy your different job locations, whether they are an old steel mill or high in the sky inside a helicopter. Look at the bright side and remember that most people don't have the chance to see the world from such a unique perspective. If you continue to look at your glass as half-full and do the best job that you can, you will find success. Remember that success is not all about trophies or your name in lights. It is about what makes you happy and fulfilled. The trophies may be a part of that fulfillment, but try to be open-minded and you will find your true calling.

Good luck!

P.S. To send feedback about how this book worked for you (please do!) and to submit any anecdotes you would like to share, please visit www.sandrasite.com.

SECTION IV:

OTHER RESOURCES

- Sample Cover Letters
- Internet Web Sites
- Periodical Resources
- Glossary
- US Film Commissions & Film Offices

SANDRA R. GORDON
5555 W. Main Street
Nowhere, Idaho 55555
555-555-5555

May 30, 2002

Ms. Jane Doe
WWWW Television
5555 N. St. Louis Avenue
Nowhere, Idaho 55555

Dear Ms. Doe:

Per our conversation today, I have attached my resume for your review. As we discussed briefly, I am interested in an entry-level position within your division of the network station at WWWW Television.

You will find that my background in entertainment covers a variety of areas ranging from international special events to feature film, television, and video production. Not described in detail is my current position as an intern at WPPX Radio. In my role as an intern I am able to utilize my organizational skills and to multitask on a daily basis. Being in charge of the annual company picnic, I have found my coordinating skills to be very useful in planning the entertainment, ordering and setting up equipment, and tracking the costs for the department. Additionally, I participate in filing the music selections for the morning drive show and answer the heavy volume of calls during the noon "Lunch Jam."

If there is any time available in your schedule to meet, I would love the opportunity to tell you more about my experience and passion for working in the entertainment business. I am especially interested in learning more about your new division at WWWW Television. Please call me at 555-555-5555 at your convenience. Thank you for your consideration. I look forward to speaking with you again soon.

Sincerely,

Sandra Gordon

SANDRA R. GORDON
5555 W. Main Street
Nowhere, Idaho 55555
555-555-5555

May 30, 2002

Mr. John Doe
Moby Meets Mayhem
XHB Studios
5555 N. Gower St.
Los Angeles, CA 99999

Dear Mr. Doe:

Susan in your office suggested that I submit my resume for your review.
I am interested in working as an office production assistant on *Moby
Meets Mayhem.*

My previous experiences as set production assistant on *Helping Santa* and
Rushing Home gave me the opportunity to work with both large and
small crews in various locations. I am hoping to now shift my skills to the
production office in an effort to continue learning the trade and to work
in yet another area of production.

I am interested in meeting with you personally to further explain my
qualifications. I understand you are not yet hiring for this position, but
I would like to meet with you for an informational interview and to
introduce myself in person if your schedule permits. Please call me at
555-555-5555 at your convenience. I look forward to speaking with
you soon.

Sincerely,

Sandra Gordon

SANDRA R. GORDON
5555 W. Main Street
Nowhere, Idaho 55555
555-555-5555

May 30, 2002

Ms. Kathy Lovell
Skiers
Hilltop Productions
5555 Madison Avenue
Santa Monica, CA 99999

Dear Kathy:

I enjoyed speaking with you yesterday afternoon. Thank you for your information about the *Skiers* series. As you suggested, I am sending you my resume for any openings.

As I mentioned in our conversation, I have been working as a runner at WRXR Television for six months and am looking to work on a television series. My duties at WRXR include data entry, pick-ups and deliveries to various stations around the Los Angeles area, and heavy telephones. I have a new car and am ready to run for you!

Please call me at your convenience to schedule an interview. I can be reached at 555-555-5555 or on my pager at 444-444-4444. Good luck with your meeting tomorrow. I look forward to hearing about it when you call.

Sincerely,

Sandra Gordon

INTERNET WEB SITES

☞ www.assistantdirectors.com
Lists services, production companies, publications, resources, equipment, special events, movies, workshops, news, crews, etc.

☞ www.careercraftsman.com
General job-hunting information

☞ www.cinemaspot.com
Industry guides and news

☞ www.Cinemedia.org

☞ www.filmmaker.com
Library of annotated film schools

☞ www.haleisner.com
Growing broadcast news community with message boards and up-to-date information, production-related programs and organizations, Emmy Award and L.A. area broadcast news

☞ www.hollywoodnet.com
Themed community

☞ www.ifilmpro.com
Development/job boards and listings

☞ www.L2g.com
Links to film industry Web sites

☞ www.Mandy.com
International film & television production directory. Sends out weekly job listings

☞ www.media-match.com
Subscription database and job board

☞ www.productionweekly.com
Subscription job listings

☞ www.showbizdigest.com
Links to all things film related

☞ www.thrillnet.com
Specializes in extreme sports yet also lists industry productions

☞ www.variety.com
Trade magazine with free classified ad listing

PERIODICAL RESOURCES & TRADE MAGAZINES

American Cinematographer
Academic trade journal

Box Office Magazine
Industry news

Bright Lights Journal
Pop culture and academics

Cineaste Magazine
The art and politics of the cinema

Cinema Journal
An academic journal

Film Comment
Published by the Film Society of Lincoln Center

Film Culture
Independent film industry news

Film Feature Forum
Articles from foreign film journals

Film and History
Journal of film and television studies

Film and Philosophy
Published by the Society of the Philosophic Study of the Contemporary Visual Arts

Filmmaker Magazine
Independent film industry news

fps
Animation news

The Hollywood Reporter
Daily entertainment trade magazine

Journal of Popular Film and Television
Examines commercial films and television from a socio-cultural perspective

Makeup Artist
For makeup artists in the production industry

Millimeter
Motion picture and television

Movieline
Consumer magazine for film enthusiasts

Moviemaker Magazine
The art and the business of making movies

Premiere Magazine
Consumer magazine devoted to film

Quarterly review of film and video
Critical and theoretical essays and reviews

RES
Digital format filmmaking and broadcast design

Scenario
Screenwriting

Starburst
Sci-fi entertainment

The Independent
Film and video monthly

Total Movie & Entertainment
Movies, music, and multimedia

Variety
Daily entertainment news trade magazine

GLOSSARY

background artists
Extras. Actors who have no on-camera lines and are seen in the background of the scene.

base camp
The staging area for the production department, hair/makeup, catering, and actors' trailers, as well as any other trucks and trailers from other departments that may be staged in the area for the shoot.

boom microphone
Microphone attached to long pole that is held over or under the frame of the shot for recording dialogue in a scene.

call sheet
The itinerary for the day's shoot. A detailed list of scene, location, and call time for each cast and crew member.

call time
The time of day that a crew (or an individual on the crew) is required to be at their location for the day's shoot.

camera log
Form filled out by camera department to keep track of film negative that is used during a shoot.

camera ready
Phrase used to explain that a person or set is dressed and ready to be filmed.

camera truck
Vehicle used on-location to house the camera department's equipment and the film for the shoot.

clapper
Nickname for the 2nd assistant camer-aperson who claps the stick on the slate, marking the synchronization point of the audio and film of a particular scene.

company move
Movement of the entire crew and all production vehicles to a new shooting location during a shooting day.

condor
Piece of machinery used to hoist a person or object higher than a ladder. Usually used to reach sides of buildings or to hold lighting equipment overhead for a large shot.

cost reports
Report generated by the accounting department to show expenditures against the budget to date.

"copy"
Response used over walkie-talkie radios to let the other person know that their transmission or message over the radio was heard by the receiver.

cover set
Backup location (plan "B") used in case of foul weather or an emergency situation necessitating a change of location.

crew lunch
Lunch break taken by the crew six hours after call time.

dailies
Film from yesterday's (or otherwise specified date's) shoot that has been processed. Generally, dailies will be transferred to video tape or projection equipment will be provided to screen the footage that has been shot to make sure that the shoot day in question was successful.

deferred pay
Term used to describe a situation in which a person agrees to waive their salary until a later time, usually after the film has been released and the production company has revenue for salaries.

dolly
Piece of equipment used to physically move a camera from one point to another while it is filming. This piece of equipment is operated by a grip.

extras holding area
Designated area for extras (background artists) to sit when not working.

first team
Nickname used to describe the lead actors in a film or television production.

gaffer
Head of the electric department.

heads
The front end of the film roll.

hot set
A set that is dressed and ready to be used on-camera, or a set that was used on-camera and must remain as-is to be used again.

location map

Map specifically designed by the locations department to guide the cast and crew to the location for a given shooting day. This map will generally be stapled to the call sheet for the day to which it pertains.

"locking up" the set

Term used by production department to control non-crew people from walking through (and talking near) a set or secure area during a shoot.

loop (verb)

Term used in post production. To re-record audio for an existing piece of film. Actors will watch their scene and re-record their lines into a microphone in a studio as necessary. Often done when outside noise has interfered with sound quality on a particular shoot.

pick-up shots

Shots from a scene or transition scenes that are added to a shooting schedule after a shoot. Usually used after it has been decided that another shot is needed to better tell the story, after the dailies have been seen by the director and/or editor.

production report

Form filled out by the 2nd assistant director that details everything that took place during the day's shoot. Listing the scene numbers that were shot, the actors involved and their in and out times, the in and out times for the entire crew, any special props or equipment that were used, the call time, the time the cameras actually began filming, and the time the camera was wrapped for the day, this form details everything anyone would ever need to know about one particular shooting day. This report also notes any union penalties incurred, and anything that went wrong or was unplanned for during the shoot.

purchase orders

Form used to track each expense throughout a production. Form is filled out by person making the purchase and copied to the accountant to keep track of expenses against the budget as they are incurred.

second meal

Term used to describe the meal following lunch, which can happen at any time of day, depending on the shooting hours of a shooting week.

second unit

Additional shooting crew brought on to the production to shoot pick-up shots or scenes not involving the lead cast, simultaneous to the regular shoot taking place.

set dressing

The objects and furniture used to make a set look like a specific room (interior decoration). Also the name of the department that arranges for and places the interior decor of a set.

set-up

Placement of a camera (and therefore all other necessary equipment) for an angle to shoot a scene. There may be several set-ups used for one scene being shot.

shooting schedule

Schedule created by the assistant director, detailing the daily schedule as planned for the duration of the shoot. This schedule includes scene numbers, actors or characters involved, props, special effects, special transportation needs, and any other needs from every department as they apply to each scene.

sticks

The clapping device used by the camera department to mark the beginning of a scene—when the camera and sound are rolling just before the scene begins.

tails

The end of a roll of film.

tech scout

A meeting with the director and department heads during pre-production, during which the group visits the shooting locations and discusses each department's needs along with the director's visions for the shoot for each location.

wrap

Term used when the shoot is over, meaning to put away equipment or to end work for the shooting day.

US FILM COMMISSIONS & FILM OFFICES

ALABAMA
Alabama Film Office
Brian Kurlander, Director
401 Adams Avenue
Montgomery, AL 36104
334-242-4195/ 334-242-2077 fax
www.alabamafilm.org

City of Mobile Film Office
Eva Golson, Director
164 St. Emanuel St.
Mobile, AL 36633
334-438-7100/ 334-438-7104 fax
golson@ci.mobile.al.us

ALASKA
Alaska Film Program
550 W. 7th Ave., Suite 1770
Anchorage, AK 99501
907-269-8114/ 907-269-8125 fax
www.alaskafilm.org
alaskafilm@dced.state.ak.us

ARIZONA
Arizona Film Commission
Linda Peterson Warren, Director
3800 N. Central Ave., Bldg. D
Phoenix, AZ 85102
602-280-1380/ 602-280-1384 fax
www.azcommerce.com
film@azcommerce.com

Cochise County Film Commission
Karla Jensen, Public Information
Officer
1415 W. Melody Lane, Bldg. B
Bisbee, AZ 85603
520-432-9454/ 520-432-9656 fax
www.cochisecounty.com
kjensen@co.cochise.az.us

Cottonwood Film Commission
Peter A. Sesow, Executive Director
1010 S. Main St.
Cottonwood, AZ 86326
928-634-7593/ 928-634-7594 fax
http://chamber.verderalley.com
cottonwoodchamber@sedona.net

Globe Miami Film Commission
Gerald Kohlbeck
1360 N. Broad St., U.S. 60
Globe, AZ 85501
928-425-4495/ 928-425-3410 fax
Gmchamber@cybertrails.com

Kingman Chamber of Commerce
Beverly J. Liles
P.O. Box 1150
Kingman, Arizona 86401
928-753-6253/928-753-1049 fax
www.kingmanchamber.org

Page-Lake Powell Film Commission
644 N. Navajo Drive
Page, AZ 86040
928-645-2741/ 928-645-3181 fax
chamber@pagelakepowellchamber.org

City of Phoenix Film Office
Luci Fontanilla
200 W. Washington, 10th Fl.
Phoenix, AZ 85003-1611
602-262-4850/ 602-534-2295 fax
lfontani@ci.phoenix.az.us

Prescott, Arizona Film Office
Greg Fister
Economic Development Officer
928-776-6204/ 928-771-5870 fax
gregfister@cityofprescott.net

Safford/Graham County Regional
Film Office
Sheldon Miller, Director
1111 Thatcher Blvd.
Safford, AZ 85546
928-428-2511/ 928-428-0744 fax
www.chamber.safford.az.org
chamber@safford.az.org

City of Scottsdale One Stop Shop
7447 E. Indian School Road
Scottsdale, AZ 85251
480-312-2500/ 480-312-7011 fax

Sedona Film Commission
Frank Miller
Sedona, AZ 86339
928-204-1123/ 928-204-1064 fax
info@sedonachamber.com

Tucson Film Office
Shelli Hall
P.O. Box 27210
Tucson, AZ 85726-7210
520-791-4000/ 520-791-5413 fax
www.filmtucson.com
shall1@ci.tucson.az.us

Wickenburg Film Commission
Julie Brooks
216 N. Frontier Street
Wickenburg, AZ 85390
928-684-5479/ 928-684-5470 fax
www.wickenburgchamber.com
www.outwickenburgway.com
jbrooks@w3az.net

Yuma Film Commission
Yvonne Taylor, President
850 W. 32nd St., Suite 6
Yuma, AZ 85364
928-341-1616/ 928-341-1685 fax

ARKANSAS
Arkansas Film Office
Joe Glass, Team Leader

1 Capitol Mall, Room 4B-505
Little Rock, AS 72201
501-682-7676/ 501-682-FILM fax

Hot Springs Film Office
Steve Arrison, Director
Hot Springs, AS 71902
501-321-2027/ 501-620-5008 fax
Sarrison@hotsprings.org

CALIFORNIA
Amador County Film Commission
Tom Blackman, Film Commissioner
106 Water Street
Jackson, CA 95642
209-223-2276/ 209-223-3406 fax
www.volcano.net
filmamador@volcano.net

Antelope Valley Film Office-Lancaster
Pauline East, Film Liason
44933 N. Fern Avenue
Lancaster, CA 93534
661-723-6090/ 661-723-5914 fax
www.avfilm.com
peast@cityoflancasterca.org

Baja California Film Commission
P.O. Box 2448
Chula Vista, CA 91912
526-634-6330/ 526-634-7157 fax
www.bajafilm.com
info@bajafilm.com

Berkeley CVB/Berkeley Film Office
Barbara Hillman, Executive Director
2015 Center St.
Berkeley, CA 94704-1204
510-549-7040/ 510-644-2052 fax
www.visitberkeley.com

Berkeley Film Office Convention &
Visitors Bureau
Barbara Hillman, Executive Director
2015 Center Street, 1st Floor
Berkeley, CA 94704-1204
800-847-4823
510-549-7040/ 510-644-2052 fax
www.berkelycvb.com
hillman1@ix.netcom.com

Beverly Hills
Robin Chancellor, Director of
Communications & Marketing
City of Beverly Hills
455 N. Rexford Drive
Beverly Hills, CA 90210-4817
310-285-2438/ 310-273-1096 fax
www.ci.beverly-hills.ca.us
rchancellor@ci.beverly-hills.ca.us

Big Bear Lake Film Office
Kresse Armour, Manager
P.O. Box 10000
Big Bear Lake, CA 92315

909-866-5831, ext. 109
909-866-6766 fax
www.citybigbearlake.com/film.html
bblfilm@aol.com

Chico Chamber of Commerce
Alice Patterson, Film Commissioner
300 Salem St.
Chico, CA 95928
800-852-8570/ 530-891-5556 ext. 309
530-891-5559/ 530-891-3613 fax
www.chicochamber.com
alice@chicochamber.com

Calaveras County Chamber of
Commerce
Phyllis Wright, Film Liaison
P.O. Box 1145, 1211 S. Main Street
Angels Camp, CA 95222
209-736-2580/ 209-736-2576 fax
www.calaveras.org
chamber@calaveras.org

or Claveras County Chamber of
Commerce
Lisa Reynolds, Film Liaison
P.O. Box 637
Angels Camp, CA 95222
209-736-0049/ 209-736-9124 fax
www.visitcalaveras.org
frogmail@calaveras.org

California Film Commission
Karen R. Constine, Director
7080 Hollywood Blvd., Suite 900
Hollywood, CA 90028
323-860-2960, ext. 135
323-860-2972 fax
www.film.ca.gov
filmca@commerce.ca.gov

Catalina Island Film Commission
Shirley Davy, Film Liason
125 Metropole Ave., Suite 103
Avalon, CA 90704-0217
310-510-7646/ 310-510-1646 fax

Contra Costa County Convention
& Visitors Bureau
Steve Shenton
Convention Sales Manager
1333 Willow Pass Road, Suite 204
Concord, CA 94520
925-685-1184/ 925-685-8190 fax
shenton@cccvb.com

El Dorado/Tahoe Film Commission
Kathleen Dodge, Film Commissioner
542 Main St.
Placerville, CA 95667
800-457-6279 toll free
530-626-4400/ 530-642-1624 fax
www.eldoradocounty.org
film@eldoradocounty.org/filmcom-
mission/

Fresno Film Commission
Kristina Krivochier
Film Commissioner
848 M. Street, 3rd Fl.
Fresno, CA 93721
559-233-0836/ 559-445-0122 fax

www.fresnocvb.org
tourfresno@aol.com

Humboldt County Film Commission
Barbara Bryant, Film Commissioner
1034 Second St.
Eureka, CA 95501-0541
707-444-6633/ 707-443-5115 fax
www.filmhumboldt.org
filmcom@filmhumboldt.org

Imperial County Film Commission
Executive Director
230 S. 5th St.
El Centro, CA 92243
760-337-4155/ 760-337-8235 fax
www.filmhere.com
filmhere@earthlink.net

Inland Empire Film Commission
Sheri Davis
301 E. Vanderbilt Way, Suite 100
San Bernadino, CA 92408
909-890-1090/ 909-890-1088 fax
www.filminlandempire.com
sdavis@ieep.com

Kern County Board of Trade
Barry Zoeller, Film Commissioner
P.O. Bin 1312
Bakersfield, CA 93302
800-500-KERN
661-861-2367/661-861-2017 fax
www.fillmkern.com/
kerninfo@co.kern.ca.us

Lake County Community
Development Services
Jeff Lucas, President
4615 Workright Circle
Lakeport, CA 95453
800-525-3743 toll free
707-262-1090/ 707-262-1092 fax
www.lakecounty.com
cds@pacific.net

Lassen County
McFerrin A. Whiteman, CAO
221 South Roop Street, Suite 4
Susanville, CA 96130
530-251-8333/530-257-4898 fax
coadmin@co.lassen.ca.us

Placer-Lake Tahoe Film Office
Beverly Lewis, Director
175 Fulweiler Ave
Auburn, CA 95603
Toll Free: 877-228-FILM
530-889-4091/ 530-889-4095 fax
blewis@placer.ca.gov
www.placer.ca.gov/films

Long Beach Office of Special Events
& Filming
Jo Ann Burns
Director of Special Events
1 World Trade Center
Long Beach CA 90831
562-570-5333/ 562-570-5335 fax
www.filmlongbeach.com
joburns@ci.long-beach.ca.us

Los Angeles Film Office
Cody Cluff, President
7083 Hollywood Blvd., 5th Fl.
Hollywood, CA 90028
323-957-1000/ 323-962-4966fax
www.eidc.com/info@eidc.com

Madera County Film Commission
Sabina Balabin, Film Commissioner
40637 Highway 41
Oakhurst, CA 93644
559-683-4636/ 559-683-5697 fax
www.yosemitefilm.com
ysvb.sierratel.com

Malibu City Film Commission
Kimberly Collins-Nilsson, Director
23555Civic Center Way
Malibu, CA 91360
805-495-7521/ 310-456-5799 fax
www.ci.malibu.ca.us
kim@sws-inc.com

Mammoth Film Locations
James R. Vanko, Director
P.O. Box 24, #1 Minaret Road
Mammoth Lakes, CA 93546
760-934-0628/760-934-0700 fax
www.mammoth-mtn.com/
jvanko@mammoth-mtn.com

Mendocino County Film Office
Stephanie Wood, Film Liaison
(FLICS) for Mendocino County
332 N. Main Street
Fort Bragg, CA 95437
707-961-6303/ 707-964-2056 fax
www.mendocinocoast.com
Stephanie@mendocinocoast.com

Merced County Conference &
Visitors Bureau
Karen Baker, Executive Director
710 W. 16th St.
Merced, CA 95340
209-384-2791/ 209-384-2793 fax
www.yosemite-gateway.org/
mercedvb@yosemite-gateway.org

Modesto Convention & Visitors Bureau
Sandie Silveria, Film Commissioner
P.O. Box 844
Modesto, CA 95353
800-266-4282 toll free
209-571-6480 ext. 112
209-571-6486 fax

Monterey County Film Commission
Executive Director
P.O. Box 111
Monterey, CA 93942-0111
831-646-0910/ 831-655-9250 fax
www.filmmonterey.com
filmmonterey@redshift.com

Oakland Film Office
Ami Zins, Film Coordinator
150 Frank H. Ogawa Plaza #8215
Oakland, CA 94612
510-238-4734/ 510-238-6149 fax
www.filmoakland.com
oakland@filmoakland.com

Orange County Film Commission
Janice Arrington, Film Commissioner
Fullerton, CA 92834-6850
714-278-7569/ 714-278-7521 fax
www.ocfilm.org
jarrington@ocfilm.org

Palmdale Film, Convention &
Visitors Bureau
38300 Sierra Highway
Palmdale, CA 93550-4798
661-267-5119/ 661-267-5122 fax
www.cityofpalmdale.org
blafata@cityofpalmdale.org

Pasadena Film Office
Ariel Penn, Film Liason
175 N. Garfield Avenue
Pasadena, CA 91109
626-744-3964/ 626-744-4785 fax
www.filmpasadena.com
apenn@ci.pasadena.ca.us

Redding/Shasta County Film
Commission
777 Auditorium Drive
Redding, CA 96001
530-225-4100/ 530-225-4354 fax
www.visitredding.org
info@visitredding.org

Ridgecrest Regional Film
Commission
Ray Arthur, Film Commissioner
139 Balsam Street
Ridgecrest, CA 93555
760-375-8202/ 760-375-9850 fax
www.filmdeserts.com
racvb@filmdeserts.com

Sacramento Film Commission
Lucy Steffens, Film Commissioner
1303 J Street, Suite 600
Sacramento, CA 95814
916-264-7777/ 916-264-7788 fax
www.sacramentocvb.org/film
lsteffens@cityofsacramento.org

San Diego Film Commission
Film Commissioner/CEO San
Diego Film Commission
1010 Second Ave., #1500
San Diego, CA 92101-4912
619-234-3456/ 619-234-4631 fax
www.sdfilm.com
info@sdfilm.com

San Francisco Film
& Video Arts Commission
1 Dr. Carlton B. Goodlett Place, #473
San Francisco, CA 94102
415-554-6241/ 415-554-6503 fax
www.ci.sf.ca.us/film
film@ci.sf.ca.us

San Joaquin/Stockton Chamber
of Commerce
Mary Pennini, Film Liason
445 W. Weber, #220
Stockton, CA 95203
209-547-2767/ 209-466-5271 fax

San Jose Film & Video Commission
125 South Market Street, #300
San Jose, CA 95113
408-792-4134/ 408-295-3937 fax
1-800-SAN-JOSE toll free
jokane@sanjose.org
www.sanjose.org/filmvideo
jokane@sanjose.org

San Luis Obispo County Film
Commission
Jonni Biaggini, Executive Director
1037 Mill St.
San Luis Obispo, CA 93401
805-541-8000/ 805-543-9498 fax
www.sanluisobispocounty.com/
slocvcb@slonet.org

San Mateo County Convention &
Visitors Bureau
Brena Bailey, Film Commissioner
111 Anza Blvd., Suite 410
Burlingame, CA 94401
800-288-4787 toll free
650-348-7600/ 650-348-7687 fax
www.smccvb.com
bbailey@smccvb.com

Santa Barbara Conference & Visitors
Bureau, and Film Commission
Martine White
County Film Commissioner
1601 Anacapa Street,
Santa Barbra, CA 93101-1909
805-966-9222 ext. 110
805-966-1728 fax
www.filmsantabarbara.com
SBCVB website:
www.santabarbaraCA.com
job listings website:
www.scamp805.com
martine@filmsantabarbara.com

Santa Clarita Valley Film Office
23920 Valencia Blvd., Suite 300
Santa Clarita, CA 91355
661-259-4787/ 661-259-8125 fax
www.santa-clarita.com/

Santa Cruz County Conference and
Visitors Council
Ranee Ruble
Publicity Director/Film Liason
831-425-1234, ext. 103
831-425-1260 fax
www.santacruzfilm.org
rruble@santacruzca.org

Siskiyou County Film Commission
Joanne Steele, Commissioner
508 Chestnut St.
Mt. Shasta, CA 96067
(mailing address: P.O. Box 1138, Mt.
Shasta, CA 96067)
530-926-3850/ 530-926-3680 fax
1-800-575-3456 toll free
www.filmsisq.org
info@visitsiskiyou.org

Sonoma County Film office
Catherine DePrima
Film Commissioner

401 D College Ave.
Santa Rosa, CA 95401
707-524-7347/ 707-524-7231 fax
www.sonomacountyfilm.com
edeprima@sonoma-county.org

South Pasadena
Joan Aguado, Film Liaison
1414 Mission Street
South Pasadena, CA 91030
626-403-7263/ 626-403-7215 fax
www.ci.south-pasadena.ca.us/
jaguado@ci.south-pasadena.ca.us

Trinity County Film Council
Dee Donaldson, Carol Eli
P.O. Box 1739
Weaverville, CA 96093
800-487-4648/ 530-623-5755 fax
nys@snowcrest.net

Tri-Valley Film & Video Commission
Film Commissioner
260 Main Street
Pleasanton, CA 94566
888-874-9253 toll free
925-846-8910/ 925-846-9502 fax
www.trivalleycvb.com
alison@trivalleycvb.com

Tulare County Film Commission
John Stevens, Film Liason
5961 S. Mooney Blvd.
Visalia, CA 93277
559-733-6291
559-730-2591 fax
www.co.tulare.ca.us
jstevens@co.tulare.ca.us

Tuolumne County Film Commission
Nanci Sikes, Interim Film
Commissioner
542 Stockton Road, P.O. Box 4020
Sonora, CA 95370
800-446-1333/ 209-533-0956 fax
Website: www.tcfilm.com
Email: tcfilm@mlode.com

Vallejo/Solano County Film Commission
Jim Reikowsky, Film Liason
495 Mare Island Way
Vallejo, CA 94590
707-642-3653/ 707-644-2206 fax
www.visitvallejo.com/film
film@visitvallejo.com

Ventura County Film Council
Dawn Barber
1601 Carmen Dr., Suite 215
Camarillo, CA 93010
805-384-1800 ext. 23
805-384-1805 fax
www.edc-vc.com
dawnbarber@edc-vc.com

West Hollywood Film Office
Terry House, Film Liason
8300 Santa Monica Blvd.
West Hollywood, CA 90069-4314
323-848-6489/ 323-848-6561 fax
www.weho.org/
wehofilm@weho.org

COLORADO

Boulder County Film Commission
Joy Kosenski, Film Commissioner
2440 Pearl St.
Boulder, CO 80302
303-442-1044/ 303-938-8837 fax
www.bouldercoloradousa.com
joy@bouldercvb.com

Clear Creek County Tourism Board
and Film Commission
Stephanie Donoho
P.O. Box 100
Idaho Springs, CO 80452
303-567-4660/ 303-567-0967 fax
www.clearcreekcounty.org

Colorado Film Commission
Stephanie Two Eagles
Program Manager
1625 Broadway, Suite 1700
Denver, CO 80202-4729
303-620-4500/ 303-620-4545
www.coloradofilm.org
coloradofilm@state.co.us

Colorado Springs Film Commission
Edwina foreman, Film Commissioner
515 S. Cascade Avenue
Colorado Springs, CO 80903
800-888-4748 ext. 131 toll free
719-645-7506 ext. 131
719-635-4968 fax
http://filmcoloradosprings.com
eforeman@filmcoloradosprings.com

Denver Mayor's Office of Art,
Culture & Film
Ronald F. Pinkard
Director of Film & Television
1380 Lawrence St., Suite 790
Denver, CO 80204
303-640-6941/ 303-640-6960 fax
www.denvergov.ord/artculturefilm
Rpinkard@ci.denver.co.us

Fremont/Custer County Film
Commission
403 Royal George Blvd.
Canon City, CO 81212
719-275-2331/ 719-275-2332
Chamber@canoncity.com

Southwest Colorado Film
Commission
Jane Zimmerman, Director
295-A Girard
Durango, CO 81301
970-247-9621/ 970-247-9513 fax
swctr@frontier.net

CONNECTICUT

Connecticut Film, Video &
Media Office
Guy Ortoleva, Managing Director
805 Brook St., Bldg. #4
Rocky Hill, CT 06067
800-392-2122/ 860-721-7088 fax
www.ctfilm.com
film@cerc.com

Danbury Film Office
Molly Curry
POB 406, Danbury, CT 06813
203-743-0546/ 203-790-6124 fax
hvtd@snet.net

Southern Connecticut Film Office
Phillip Hanson, Director
P.O. Box 89
470 Bank Street, c/o Mystic & More
New London, CT 06320
888-467-FILM/ 860-442-4257
phmystic@ctol.net

DELAWARE

Delaware Film Office
Cheryl P. Heiks
Film Office Coordinator
99 Kings Highway
Dover, DE 19901
302-739-4271 ext. 140
302-739-5749 fax
www.state.de.us/dedo
cpheiks@state.de.us

DISTRICT OF COLUMBIA

Washington D.C.–Office of Motion
Picture & T.V.
Crystal Palmer
410 8th St., NW 6th Fl.
Washington, D.C. 20004
202-727-6608/ 202-727-3787 fax
www.film.dc.gov
film.dc@dc.gov

FLORIDA

Bahamas Film & Television
Commission
19495 Biscayne Blvd., Suite 809
Aventura, FL 33180-2321
305-932-0051/ 305-931-4715 fax
www.bahamasfilm.com
aarcher@gobahamas.com

Broward Alliance Film/TV
Commission
Barbara Cordoves, Director
300 SE 2nd St., Suite 780
Fort lauderdale, FL 33301
954-627-0128
800-741-1420 toll free
www.browardalliance.org/film.html
ewentworth@browardalliance.org

Collier County Film Commission
Maggie McCarty, Film Commissioner
755 8th Ave. South
Naples, FL 34102
941-659-3456/ 941-213-3053 fax
collierfilm@aol.com

Governor's Office of Film &
Entertainment/State of Florida
Rebecca Dirden Mattingly
Film Commissioner
The Capitol
400 S. Monroe St., Ste. 2002
Tallahassee, FL 32399-0001
877-FLA-FILM (352-3456) toll free
850-410-4770 fax

www.filminflorida.com
mattingr@eog.state.fl.us

Florida Keys & Key West Film
Commission
Rita Brown, Film Liason
1201 White St., Suite 102
Key West, FL 33040-3328
305-293-1800/ 305-296-0788 fax
keysfilm@aol.com

Jacksonville Film Commission
Todd Roobin, Director
220 E. Bay St., 14th Fl.
Jacksonville, FL 32202
904-630-2522/ 904-630-2919
www.coj.net/film
troobin@coj.net

Metro Orlando Film &
Entertainment Commission
Katherine Ramsberger
Film Commissioner
301 E. Pine St., Suite 900
Orlando, Fl. 32801-2705
407-422-7159/407-841-9069 fax
www.filmorlando.com
info@filmorlando.com

Miami/Dade Mayor's Office of Film
& Entertainment
111 Northwest 1st St., Suite 2540
Miami, FL 33128
305-375-3288/305-375-3266 fax
www.filmiami.com
film@filmiami.org

Northwest Florida/Okaloosa Film
Commission
Wendy Griffin, Filming Liason
1540 Miracle Strip Parkway
Ft. Walton Beach, FL 32548
850-651-7644/ 850-651-7149 fax
wgriffin@co.okaloosa.fl.us

Palm Beach County Film &
Television Commission
Chuck Eldard, Film Commissioner
1555 Palm Beach Lakes Blvd., Ste 414
West Palm Beach, FL 33401
561-233-1000/ 561-683-6957 fax
celdard@pbfilm.com

Space Coast Film Commission
Bonnie King
8810 Astronaut Blvd.
Cape Canaveral, FL 32920
407-868-1126/ 407-868-1139 fax
www.film-space-coast.com
bkingfilm@aol.com

Tampa Bay Film Commission
Edie Emerald, Film Commissioner
400 N. Tampa St., Suite 2800
Tampa, FL 33602
813-223-1111/ 813-229-6616
www.visittampabay.com
eemerald@visittampabay.com

GEORGIA

Georgia Film, Video & Music Office
Greg Torre, Director
285 Peachtree Center Ave., Suite 1000
Atlanta, GA 30303
404-656-3591/ 404-656-3565 fax
www.filmgeorgia.org
film@georgia.org

Savannah Film Commission
Jay Self, Film Services Director
City of Savannah, P.O. Box 1027
Savannah, GA 31402
912-651-3696/ 912-238-0872 fax
jself@ci.savannah.ga.us
www.savannahfilm.org

HAWAII

Big Island Film Office
Marilyn Killeri, Film Commissioner
25 Aupuni St., Rm 219
Hilo, HI 96270
808-961-8366/ 808-935-1205 fax
www.filmbigisland.com
film@bigisland.com

Hawaii Film Office
Donne Dawson, Manager
808-586-2570/ 808-586-2572 fax
ddawson@dbedt.hawaii.gov

Honolulu Film Office City &
County of Honolulu
Walea L. Constantinau
Film Office Director
530 S. King St., Rm. 306
Honolulu, HI 96813
808-527-6108/ 808-527-6102 fax
www.filmhonolulu.com
info@filmhonolulu.com

Kauai Film Commission
Judy Drosd, Film Commissioner
4444 Rice St., Suite 200
Lihue, HI 96766
808-241-6390/ 808-241-6399 fax
www.filmkauai.com
info@filmkauai.com

Maui County Film Office
Amy Kastens, Film Commissioner
200 S. High St., 6th Fl.
Wailuku, Maui, HI 96793
808-270-7415/ 808-270-7995 fax
www.filmmaui.com
akastens@filmmaui.com

IDAHO

Idaho Film Bureau
Peg Owens, Film Specialist
700 W. State St.
Boise, Idaho 83720-0093
208-334-2470/ 208-334-2631 fax
www.filmidaho.com
powens@idoc.state.id.us

ILLINOIS

Chicago Film Office
Richard Moskal, Director
1 N. LaSalle St., Suite 2165
Chicago, IL 60602
312-744-6415/ 312-744-1378 fax
www.ci.chi.il.us

Illinois Film Office
Ron VerKuilen, Manager Director
100 W. Randolph St., 3rd Fl.
Chicago, IL 60601
312-814-3600/ 312-814-8874 fax
rverkuil@commerce.state.il.us

INDIANA

Indiana Film Commission
Jane Rulon
1 N. Capitol Ave., #700
Indianapolis, IN 46204-2288
317-232-8829/ 317-233-6887 fax
www.filmindiana.com
filminfo@commerce.state.in.us

IOWA

Cedar Rapids Area Film Commission
119 1st Ave. SE
Cedar Rapids, IA 52406-5339
319-398-5009 ext. 127
319-398-5089 fax
www.cedar-rapids.com/iowa/cvb
visitors@fyiowa.infi.net

Iowa Film Office/Developing Iowa's
Film Opportunities
Wendol Jarvis, Manager
200 E. Grand Avenue
Des Moines, IA 50309
515-242-4726/ 515-242-4809 fax
515-242-4757 – Action Line
www.state.ia.us/film
wendol.jarvis@ided.state.ia.us

KANSAS

Kansas Film Commission
Heather Ackerly, Assistant Director
1000 SW Jackson St., Suite 100
Topeka, KS 66612
785-296-4927/ 785-296-6988 fax
www.kansascommerce.com
danderson@kdoch.state.ks.us

Kansas III Film Commission
Lawrence CVB
734 Vermont
Lawrence, KS 66044
785-865-4411/ 785-865-4400 fax
director@visitlawrence.com

Greater Wichita Convention &
Visitors Bureau
100 S. Main, Suite 100
Wichita, KS 67202
316-265-2800/ 316-265-0162 fax

KENTUCKY

Kentucky Film Commission
Jim Toole, Director
500 Mero St.
2200 Capitol Plaza Tower
Frankfort, KY 40601
501-564-3456/ 501-564-7588 fax

www.kyfilmoffice.com
jim.toole@mail.state.ky.us

LOUISIANA

Louisiana Film Commission
Mark Smith, Director
P.O. Box 94185
Baton Rouge, LA 70804-9815
225-342-8150/ 225-342-5389 fax
www.lafilm.org
msmith@lded.state.la.us

New Orleans Film & Video
Commission
Kimberly Carbo, Executive Director
1515 Poydras St., Suite 1200
New Orleans, LA 70112
504-565-8104/ 504-565-8132 fax

Shreveport-Bossier Film Commission
Betty Jo LeBrun, Executive Director
Shreveport, LA 71166
318-222-9391/ 318-222-0056 fax
filmcom@shreveport-bossier.org

MAINE

Maine Film Office, Director
59 State Hinse Station
August, ME 04333-0059
207-624-9827/ 207-287-8070 fax
www.filminmaine.com
filmme2@mint.net

MARYLAND

Maryland Film Office
Michael B. Styer
217 E. Redwood St., 9th Fl.
Baltimore, MD 21202
410-767-6340/ 410-333-0044 fax
www.marylandfilm.org
mdfilm@state.md.us

MASSACHUSSETTS

Massachussetts Film Office
Robin Dawson, Director
10 Park Plaza, Suite 2310
Boston, MA 02116
617-973-8800/ 617-973-8810
www.mass.gov/film
film@state.ma.us

MICHIGAN

Michigan Film Office
Janet Lockwood, Director
717 W. Allegan - P.O. Box 30739
Lansing MI 48909
517-373-0638/ 517-241-2930 fax
1-800-477-3456 toll free
http://film.michigan.gov
jlockwood@mi.gov

MINNESOTA

Minneapolis Office of Cultural Affairs
Nicole Hinrichs-Bideau
Film & New Media Coordinator
302 City Hall
Minneapolis, MN 55415
612-673-2947/ 612-673-2933 fax
www.ci.minneapolis.mn.us
nicole.h-b@ci.minneapolis.mn.us

Minnesota Film & T.V. Board
Craig Rice, Executive Director
401 N. 3rd St., Suite 460
Minneapolis, MN 55401
612-333-0436 hotline
612-332-6493/ 612-332-3735 fax
www.mnfilm.org
info@mnfilm.org

MISSISSIPPI
Canton Film Office
Jo Ann Gordon, Executive Director
Canton, MS 39046
601-859-1307/ 601-859-0346 fax
cantontourism@ayrix.net

Mississippi Film Office
Ward Emling, Director
P.O. Box 849
Jackson, MS 39205
601-359-3297/ 601-359-5048 fax
wemling@mississippi.org

Natchez Film Commission
Laura Ann Godfrey
640 S. Canal St., Suite C
Natchez, MS 39120
601-446-6345/ 601-442-0814 fax
ncvb@bkbank.com

Tupelo Film Commission
Linda Butler
399 E. Main St.
Tupelo, MS 38802-0047
662-841-6521/ 662-841-6558 fax
www.tupelo.net
tour20@tsixroads.com

Vicksburg Film Commission
Al Elmore, Film Commissioner
P.O. Box 110
Vicksburg, MS 39181
601-636-9421/ 601-636-9475 fax
grouptour@vicksburgcvb.org

MISSOURI
Missouri Film Commission
Jerry Jones, Director
301 W. High Street, #720
Jefferson City, MO 65102
573-751-9050/ 573-522-1719 fax
www.showmemissouri.org/film
mofilm@mail.state.mo.us

Kansas City, Missouri Film Office
Tiffany Way, Film Projects Director
10 Petticoat Lane, Suite 250
Kansas City, MO 64106-2103
816-221-0636/ 816-221-0189 fax
www.kcfilm.com
fway@edckc.com

MONTANA
Montana Film Office
Sten Iversen, Director
301 S. Park Ave.
Helena, MT 59620
406-444-3762/ 406-444-4191 fax
www.montanafilm.com
montanafilm@visitmt.com

NEBRASKA
Nebraska Film Office
Laurie J. Richards, Film Officer
Dept. of Economic Development
Lincoln, NE 69509-4666
402-471-3680/ 402-471-3365 fax
www.filmnebraska.org
laurier@filmnebraska.org

Greater Omaha Film Commission
Julie Ginsberg/Kathy Sheppard
Managers
6800 Mercy Rd., Suite 202
Omaha, NE 68106-2627
402-444-7736/ 402-444-4511 fax
shootomaha@juno.com

NEVADA
Nevada Film Office-Las Vegas
Charlie Geocaris, Director
555 E. Washington, Suite 5400
Las Vegas, Nevada 89101-1078
702-486-2711/ 702-486-2712 fax
www.nevadafilm.com
lvnfo@bizopp.state.nv.us

Nevada Film Office-Reno/Tahoe
Robin Holabird, Deputy Director
108 Proctor Street
Carson City, NV 89701
800-336-1600/ 775-687-4450 fax
www.nevadafilm.com
rhbird@bizopp.state.nv.us

NEW HAMPSHIRE
New Hampshire Film & TV Office
172 Pembroke Rd.
Concord, NH 03302-1856
603-271-2665/ 603-271-6784 fax
www.filmnh.org
filmnh@dred.state.nh.us

NEW JERSEY
New Jersey Motion Picture &
Television Commission
Joseph Friedman, Executive Director
P.O. Box 47023, 153 Halsey Street
Newark, NJ 07101
973-648-6279/ 973-648-7350 fax
www.nj.com/njfilm
njfilm@nj.com

NEW MEXICO
Las Cruces Film Commission
Ted Scanlon
211 N. Water Street
Las Cruces, NM 88001
505-541-2444/ 505-541-2164 fax
cvb@lascruces.org

New Mexico Film Office
Nancy Everst, Director
1100 S. St. Frances Drive
Santa Fe, NM 87504-5003
800-545-9871/ 505-827-9799 fax
www.nmfilm.com

Santa Fe Film Office
Ken Loerzel
201 W. Marcy St.
Santa Fe, NM 87504
505-955-6213/ 505-955-6222 fax

www.santafe.org
kloerzel@ci.santa-fe.nm.us

Taos County Film Commission
Jonathan Slator, Film Commissioner
121 North Plaza
Taos, NM 87571
505-751-3646/ 505-751-3518 fax
www.filmtaos.com
taosfcom@laplaza.org

NEW YORK
Nassau County Office of
Cinema/TV Promotion
Debra Markowitz, Director
1550 Franklin Ave., #207
Mineola, NY 11501
516-571-3168/ 516-571-4161 fax
www.co.nassau.ny.us/tv/html
debfilm@aol.com

New York State Governor's Office for
Motion Picture & TV Development
Pat Swinney Kaufman
Deputy Commissioner & Director
633 3rd Ave, 33rd Fl.
New York, NY 10017
212-803-2330/ 212-803-2339 fax
nyfilm@empire.state.ny.us

New York City Mayor's Office of
Film, Theater & Broadcasting
Patricia Reed Scott, Commissioner
1697 Broadway, #602
New York, NY 10019
212-489-6710/ 212-307-6237 fax
www.nyc.gov/html/film.com
nycfilm@verizon.net

Rochester/Finger Lakes Film
& Video Office
June Foster, Director
T.C. Pellett, Assistant Director
45 East Ave, Suite 400
Rochester, NY 14604-2294
716-546-5490/ 716-232-4822 fax
www.filmrochester.org
jfoster@visitrochester.com

Saratoga County Film Commission
Linda Toohey, Executive Vice President
28 Clinton St.
Saratoga Springs, NY 12866
518-584-3255/ 518-587-0318 fax
www.saratoga.org
info@saratoga.org

Yonkers Mayor's Office for Film &
Television Development
Danielle Francini
40 S. Broadway/City Hall
Yonkers, NY 10701
914-377-6083/ 914-377-6048 fax
Danielle.francini@cityofyonkers.com

NORTH CAROLINA

Charlotte Region Film Office
Marcie Oberndorf-Kelso, Director
1001 Morehead Square Dr., Ste. 200
Charlotte, NC 28203
800-554-4373/ 704-347-8981 fax
www.charlotteusa.com
mkelso@charlotteregion.com

Durham Film Commission
Carolyn Carney, Film Commissioner
101 E. Morgan St.
Durham, NC 27701
919-680-8313/ 919-683-9555 fax
www.durham-nc.com
carolyn@durham-cvb.com

North Carolina Film Commission
Bill Arnold, Director
4317 Mail Service Center
Raleigh, NC 27699-4317
919-733-9900/ 919-715-0151 fax
www.ncfilm.com
barnold@nccommerce.com

North Carolinas Northeast Partnership
Vann Rogerson, Film Commissioner
119 W. Water St.
Edenton, NC 27932
252-482-4333/ 252-482-3366 fax
www.nc.northeast.com
film@ncnortheast.com

Piedmont Triad Film Commission
Rebecca Clark, Director
7614 Business Park Dr.
Greensboro, NC 27409
336-393-0001/ 336-668-3749 fax
www.piedmontfilm.com
info@piedmontfilm.com

Western North Carolina Film
Commission
Mary Nell Webb, Film Commissioner
3 General Aviation Drive
Fletcher, NC 28732
www.awnc.org
film@awnc.org

Wilmington Regional Film
Commission, Inc.
Johnny Griffin, Director
1223 North 23rd St.
Wilmington, NC 28405
910-343-3456/ 910-343-3457 fax
www.wilmington-film.com
commish@wilmington-film.com

NORTH DAKOTA

North Dakota Film Commission
Allan Stenehjem, Director
James Pursley, Information
400 E. Broadway, P.O. Box 2057
Bismark, ND 58502-2057
800-328-2871/ 701-328-4878 fax
www.ndtourism.com
jprusley@state.nd.us

OHIO

Greater Cincinnati & Northern
Kentucky Film Commission
Kristen Erwin, Director

602 Main St., Suite 712
Cincinnati, OH 45202
513-784-1744/ 513-768-8963 fax
www.film-cincinnati.org
kje@film-cincinnati.org

Greater Cleveland Film Commission
Christopher Carmody, President
50 Public Square, Suite 825
Cleveland, OH 44113
216-623-3910/ 216-623-0876 fax
www.clevelandfilm.com
info@clevelandfilm.com

Ohio Film Commission
Steve Cover
State Film Commissioner
P.O. Box 1001
Columbus, OH 43216-1001
614-466-2284/ 614-466-6744 fax
www.ohiofilm.com
scover@odod.state.oh.us

OKLAHOMA

Oklahoma Film Commission
Dino Lalli, Director
15 N. Robinson, #802
Oklahoma City, OK 73102
800-766-3456/ 405-522-0656 fax
www.oklahomafilm.org
Dlalli@oklahomafilm.org

OREGON

Oregon Film & Video Office
121 SW Salmon St., Suite 1205
Portland, OR 97204
503-986-0212 job hotline
503-229-5832/ 503-229-6869 fax
www.oregonfilm.org
shoot@oregonfilm.org

PENNSYLVANIA

Pennsylvania Film Office
Brian Kreider, Director
Commonwealth Keystone Bldg.
400 North Street, 4th Floor
Harrisburg, PA 17120
717-783-3456/ 717-787-0687 fax
www.filminpa.com
ra-film@state.pa.us

Greater Philadelphia Film Office
Sharon Pinkenson, Executive Director
100 S. Broad St., Suite 600
Philadelphia, PA 19110
215-686-2668/ 215-686-3659 fax
www.film.org
mail@film.org

Pittsburgh Film Office
Dawn Keezer, Director
Conestoga Bldg.
Pittsburgh, PA 15222
412-261-2744/ 412-471-7317 fax
www.pghfilm.org
info@pghfilm.org

RHODE ISLAND

Providence Film Commission/
Mayor's Office of Film & Video Arts
Eric B. Olin, Executive Director
400 Westminster St., 6th Fl.

Providence, RI 02903
401-273-3456/ 401-351-9533 fax
www.providenceri.com/film
provfilm@providenceri.com

SOUTH CAROLINA

South Carolina Film Office
Mary Morgan Kerlagon, Director
1201 Main St., Suite 1750
Columbia, SC 29201
803-737-0490/ 803-737-3104 fax
www.scfilmoffice.com
mmorgan@teamsc.com

SOUTH DAKOTA

South Dakota Film Commission
Chris Hull, Director
711 E. Wells Ave.
Pierre, SD 57501-3369
605-773-3301/ 605-773-3256 fax
www.filmsd.com
chris.hull@state.sd.us

TENNESSEE

East Tennessee Film Commission
Mona May, Executive Director
601 W. Summitt Hill Dr., Suite 100
Knoxville, TN 37902
865-632-8762/ 865-524-3863 fax
www.etnfilm.com
etfc@kacp.com

Memphis & Shelby County Film &
Television Commission
Linn Sitler, Film Commissioner
Beale St. Landing/245 Wagner Pl., #4
Memphis, TN 38103-3815
901-527-8300/ 901-527-8326 fax
www.memphisfilm.com
filmcom1@ix.netcom.com

Nashville Mayor's Office of Film
Jennifer Andrews, Film Coordinator
222 3rd Ave. North, Suite 475
Nashville, TN 37201-1301
615-862-4700/ 615-862-6025 fax
www.filmnashville.com
jennifer.andrews@mayor.nashville.org

Tennessee Film, Entertainment
& Music Commission
Pat Ledford-Johnson
Executive Director
312 8th Ave. North, 9th Fl.
Nashville, TN 37243
615-741-3456/ 615-741-5554 fax
www.filmtennessee.com
julie.kerby@state.tn.us

TEXAS

Austin Film Office
Gary Bond, Director
201 E. 2nd St.
Austin, TX 78701
512-583-7229/ 512-583-7281 fax
www.austintexas.org
gbond@austintexas.org

Dallas/Fort Worth Regional Film
Commission
Roger Burke, Executive Director
504 Business Parkway
Richardson, TX 75081
972-234-5697/ 972-680-9995 fax
www.dfwfilm.com
movies@dfwfilm.org

El Paso Film Commission
Susie Gaines, Film Commissioner
1 Civic Center Plaza
El Paso, TX 79901
915-534-0698/ 915-534-0686 fax
www.elpasocvb.com
elpasofilm@hotmail.com

Houston Film Commission
Rick Ferguson
901 Bagby, Suite 100
Houston, TX 77002
713-227-3100/ 713-227-6336 fax
www.houstonguide.com
rferguson@ghcvb.org

San Antonio Film Commission
Leighton Chapman, Director
203 S. St. Mary's
San Antonio, TX 78298
210-207-6700/ 210-207-6843 fax
www.sanantoniovisit.com
filmsa@sanantoniocvb.com

South Padre Island CVB Film
Commission
Erica I. Pena
7355 Padre Blvd.
South Padre Island, TX 78597
956-761-3005
erica@sopadre.com

Texas Film Commission
P.O. Box 13246
Austin, TX 78711
512-463-9200/ 512-463-4114 fax
www.governor.state.tx.us/film
film@governor.state.tx.us

UTAH
Central Utah Film Commission
Marilyn Toone, Director
100 E. Center Street, Suite 3200
Provo, UT 84606
801-370-8392/ 801-370-8105 fax
www.utahvalley.org/film
ucadm.marilyn@state.ut.us

Kanab/Kane County Film
Commission
Donna Casebolt, Film Commissioner
78 S. 100 E
Kanab, UT 84741
435-644-5033/ 435-644-5923 fax

Northern Utah Film Commission
Maridene A. Hancock, Director
160 N. Main
Logan, UT 84321
435-752-2161/ 435-753-5825 fax
www.bridgerland.com

Park City Film Commission
Lynn Williams, Director
1910 Prospector Avenue
Park City, UT 84060
435-649-6100/ 435-649-4132 fax
www.parkcityfilm.com
lynnw@parkcityinfo.com

Utah Film Commission
Leigh Vonder Esch
Excecutive Director
American Plaza 3
Salt Lake City, UT 84101
801-741-4540/ 801-741-4549 fax
www.film.utah.org
lvondere@amplaza.state.ut.us

VERMONT
Vermont Film Commission
Lorrane Turgeon, Film Commissioner
10 Baldwin St.
Montpelier, VT 05601-0129
802-828-3618/ 802-828-2221 fax
www.filmvermont.com
vtfilmcom@dca.state.vt.us

VIRGINIA
Central Virginia Film Office
Kenneth W. Roy, Executive Director
15 W. Bank St.
Petersburg, VA 23803
804-733-2403/ 804 863-0837 fax
www.cvfo.org
cvfo@cvfo.org

Metro Richmond CVB & Film Office
Kendal Thompson
Film Commissioner
550 E. Marshall St.
Richmond, VA 23219
804-782-2777/ 804-780-2577 fax
www.richmondva.org

City of Virginia Beach Special Events
& Film Office
2101 Parks Ave., Suite 502
Virginia Beach, VA 23451
757-437-4800/ 757-437-4737 fax
www.vbgov.com

Virginia Film Office
Rita McClenny, Director
901 E. Byrd St.
Richmond, VA 23219-4048
800-854-6233/ 804-371-8177 fax
www.filmvirginia.org
vafilm@virginia.org

WASHINGTON
City of Seattle Mayor's Film
& Video Office
Donna James, Director
700 5th Ave.
Seattle, WA 98104
206-684-5030/ 206-684-0379 fax
www.cityofseattle.net/filmoffice

Washington State Film Office
Suzy Kellett
2001 6th Ave., Suite 2600
Seattle, WA 98121
206-956-3200/ 206-956-3205 fax

www.wafilm.wa.gov
wafilm@cted.wa.gov

WEST VIRGINIA
West Virginia Film Office
Mark McNabb
State Capitol Bldg. 6, Rm. 525
Charleston, WV 25305-0311
304-558-2234/ 304-558-1189 fax

WISCONSIN
The Greater Milwaukee Convention
& Visitors Bureau
Vanessa Welter, Director of Public
Relations & Communications
101 W. Wisconsin Avenue
Milwaukee, WI 53203-2501
414-273-4253/ 414-273-5596 fax
1-800-231-0903 toll free
www.officialmilwaukee.com
vwelter@milwaukee.org

Wisconsin Film Office
201 W. Washington Ave., 2nd Fl.
Madison, WI 53703-7976
608-267-6703/ 608-266-3403 fax
1-800-FILM-WIS (345-6947) toll free
www.filmwisconsin.org
wisconsin@filmwisconsin.org

WYOMING
Casper Area Film Commission
Kelly Eastes, Director
538 SW Wyoming Blvd.
Mills, WY 82644
307-235-9325/ 307-235-9611 fax
www.filmincasper.com
kellye@trib.com

Wyoming Film Office
Michell Phelan, Manager
214 W. 15th Street
Cheyenne, WY 82002
307-777-3400/ 307-777-2838 fax
www.wyomingfilm.org
info@wyomingfilm.org